God
the Father
Almighty

Other Titles by Millard J. Erickson

Christian Theology

Concise Dictionary of Christian Theology

Contemporary Options in Eschatology: A Study of the Millennium

Does It Matter How I Live? Applying Biblical Beliefs to Your Daily Life

Does It Matter If God Exists? Understanding Who God Is and What He Does for Us

Does It Matter Than I'm Saved? What the Bible Teaches About Salvation

Does It Matter What I Believe? What the Bible Teaches and Why We Should Believe It

The Evangelical Left: Encountering Postconservative Evangelical Theology

The Evangelical Mind and Heart: Perspectives on Theological and Practical Issues

Evangelical Interpretation: Perspectives on Hermeneutical Issues

God in Three Persons: A Contemporary Interpretation of the Trinity

How Shall They Be Saved? The Destiny of Those Who Do Not Hear of Jesus

Introducing Christian Doctrine

The New Evangelical Theology

Old Wine in New Wineskins: Doctrinal Preaching in a Changing World (with James Heflin)

Postmodernizing the Faith: Evangelical Responses to the Challenge of Postmodernism

Readings in Christian Theology: Vol. 1, The Living God

Readings in Christian Theology: Vol. 2, Man's Need and God's Gift

Readings In Christian Theology: Vol. 3, The New Life

Relativism in Contemporary Christian Ethics

Where is Theology Going? Issues and Perspectives on the Future of Theology

The Word Became Flesh: A Contemporary Incarnational Christology

God
the Father
Almighty

*A Contemporary Exploration
of the Divine Attributes*

Millard J. Erickson

Baker Books

A Division of Baker Book House Co
Grand Rapids, Michigan 49516

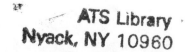

Published by Baker Books
a division of Baker Book House Company
P.O. Box 6287, Grand Rapids, MI 49516–6287

Printed in the United States of America

Library of Congress Cataloging-in-Publication Data

Erickson, Millard J.
    God the Father Almighty : a contemporary exploration of the divine attributes / Millard J. Erickson.
        p.   cm.
    Includes bibliographical references and indexes.
    ISBN 0-8010-1154-X (hardcover)
    1. God—Attributes. I. Title.
BT130.E75   1998
231′.4—dc21   98-10376

For information about academic books, resources for Christian leaders, and all new releases available from Baker Book House, visit our web site:
                              http://www.bakerbooks.com

To Carl F. H. Henry,
Dean of Twentieth-Century
American Evangelical
Theologians

Contents

Preface   *9*

Part 1: Introduction

   1.   The Importance of the Doctrine of God Today   *13*

Part 2: Challenges to the Traditional Understanding of God

   2.   Pluralism   *31*
   3.   Process Thought   *49*
   4.   Free Will Theism   *67*

Part 3: The Attributes of God

   5.   God and Change   *95*
   6.   God and Eternity   *114*
   7.   God and Outside Influences   *141*
   8.   God's Power   *165*
   9.   God's Knowledge   *184*
  10.   God's Being and Simplicity   *210*
  11.   God's Goodness   *233*
  12.   God's Immanence and Transcendence   *256*

Part 4: Conclusion

  13.   The Practical Implications of the Doctrine of God   *281*

Scripture Index   *295*
Subject Index   *297*

Preface

In the final decade of the twentieth century, the doctrine of God has re-emerged as a focus of theological discussion and debate. Much of this discussion centers on the attributes of God, in particular, the natural attributes, such as eternity, omniscience, and impassibility. A number of factors have contributed to changing the entire intellectual context within which these attributes are discussed.

For the most part, the issues on which controversy centers are not primarily exegetical in nature. Rather, they are largely philosophical, and much of the discussion is being carried on by philosophers. The increasing number of Christian philosophers active in major academic centers has produced a real bourgeoning of interest in philosophy of religion. To a larger extent than any of my earlier writings, this book therefore utilizes the resources of philosophical reflection. Most of the philosophical work being done, however, is from the perspective of modern (as contrasted with postmodern) thought. There are two points at which I have reservations about it. Modern thought is rooted in the idea of an objective rationality. Some of us have long held and postmodernism has now made explicit the insight that all thought proceeds from certain presuppositions. This realization should cause us to hold our conclusions with a certain degree of probability rather than absolute certainty. Sometimes the philosophical discussions proceed by refuting every argument for the opposing position and claiming all the relevant considerations support one's own. Second, there is not always adequate recognition and utilization of the fact that if God is indeed infinite, and we are finite, there are some points at which he will differ from us (even if some of those are only in degree), and some points at which we cannot expect fully to comprehend him. While the idea of mystery (or even of paradox) has often been invoked prematurely in theological thinking, it seems important to recognize this fact. I also have endeavored to make sure that it is the Christian God about whom we are speaking, by attending as fully as possible to the biblical revelation.

In the course of writing my earlier general survey of theology, *Christian Theology*, I discovered numerous topics on which I wanted to write

9

more extensively. This is one of those topics. At the same time, each of the chapters, or even topics within chapters, could well be developed into an entire book. The brevity of treatment herein cannot begin to match that of such single-attribute books.[1]

Some of the proposals made herein are tentative and exploratory. I am hopeful that continued study and reflection pon these matters will prove fruitful. An example of this is found in the attempt to introduce the concepts of transcendence and immanence into the discussion of God's eternity. Here the stalemate between atemporalists and temporalists suggests that attempting a new paradigm might be desirable.

I am indebted to students who have studied these subjects with me. These include the students in my doctrine of God elective at Southwestern Baptist Theological Seminary in the fall semester of 1995, at Western Seminary, Portland, in the fall semester of 1996, and at the George W. Truett Theological Seminary, Baylor University, in the January term, 1997. The ten students in my Ph.D. seminar in Contemporary Philosophical Problems at Southwestern in the fall of 1995 also added much to my thinking. Other informal conversations with colleagues and students, especially the members of the Dead Theologians Society at Southwestern, have helped sharpen my thinking. Mr. Bradley Green, a doctoral student at Baylor, was a member of the seminar at Southwestern and serves as my teaching assistant at Truett. His research and discussions with me have enlarged my understanding. I am grateful to the presidents who made the faculty appointments that created these opportunities for exploration of theological topics: Dr. Kenneth Hemphill of Southwestern Seminary, Dr. Ronald Hawkins of Western Seminary, and Dr. Robert Sloan Jr. of Baylor University.

Much of the material in this volume may seem to some to be abstract, dry, and spiritually irrelevant. All the chapters should be read in the light of the final chapter on the practical implications of the doctrine, and even in connection with another work I have written, *Does It Matter If God Exists?*[2] For in the final analysis, more important than what we know about God will be whether we really know, love, and serve him.

---

1. E.g., Paul Helm, *Eternal God: A Study of God without Time* (Oxford: Clarendon, 1988); William Hasker, *God, Time, and Knowledge* (Ithaca, N.Y.: Cornell University Press, 1989); Richard E. Creel, *Divine Impassibility: An Essay in Philosophical Theology* (Cambridge: Cambridge University Press, 1986); Jonathan Kvanvig, *The Possibility of an All-Knowing God* (New York: St. Martin's, 1986).

2. Millard J. Erickson, *Does It Matter If God Exists? Understanding Who God Is and What He Does for Us* (Grand Rapids: Baker, 1996).

Part 1

Introduction

1

The Importance of the Doctrine of God Today

At the beginning of the twentieth century, the Scottish theologian James Orr pointed out that various doctrines have received special attention at different points in the history of the church.[1] In part, this was because different cultural, practical, and ecclesial influences made that particular doctrine of prime importance at that time. Thus, in the fourth and fifth centuries, the focus was successively on the Trinity, the person of Christ, and the integrity or sinfulness of human nature. In the eleventh and twelfth centuries, major attention was given to the doctrine of atonement, and in the sixteenth century, to the doctrines of the church and salvation. In the twentieth century, the doctrines of eschatology, revelation and Scripture, and the Holy Spirit have been especially prominent. And today the doctrine of God is of great importance. There are a number of reasons for this, some of which are not restricted to our time, but speak of the importance of the doctrine of God for the church at all times. Some, of course, have special pertinence to the time in which we live.

Foundational Character of the Doctrine of God

One of these considerations is the fact that the doctrine of God is, in many ways, the first and most basic element of Christian belief. In that respect Christianity shares much with other world religions, for what makes each of these a religion is its conception of God, the fact that it maintains that there is some superhuman or supernatural reality, in

1. James Orr, *The Progress of Dogma* (Grand Rapids: Eerdmans, n.d.), pp. 21–22.

this case, a person. If one does not believe in a God, and in the case of Christianity, the Christian God, then the other topics of belief are generally not present either.

That the early Christians recognized this is seen by virtue of the place they gave to their understanding of God. The Apostles' Creed, one of the most ancient Christian confessions of faith, begins with the statement, "I believe in God the Father Almighty, maker of heaven and earth." This is the most basic of doctrines, without which the others crumble. It might, of course, be argued that the doctrine of revelation is more basic, since it supplies us with the authority and basis for our belief, and we draw all our other understandings from it. Yet even revelation assumes God, since it is the revelation of God and by God. Without God, there would be no revelation, no one to do the revealing.

This is what separates religious faith from all nonreligious views. It is the most basic issue of worldviews. This unites Christianity with a number of other religions, in some ways. On the other hand, it distinguishes it from naturalism and even materialism. It responds to the question, Is there anything other than this observable system of nature?

God the Framework for the Rest of Theology

The doctrine of God is also most basic, because it serves as the framework for the rest of theology. Indeed, the generic term "theology" means the study or the science of God. It is often defined in some fashion as "the study of the person and work of God and of his relationship to the creation." This is a major factor in what is sometimes referred to as the organic character of theology.[2] The position taken on one doctrine greatly affects our conclusions about other doctrines as well. This effect can be seen by observing an organism, such as a human being. The functioning of one organ affects that of other organs. So, if one's kidneys are not functioning properly, for example, the heart is eventually strained. In fact, different systems or aspects of the person are affected. That we are psychosomatic unities can be seen by observing what happens to our emotions when we are tired or ill. Parallels can even be seen in mechanical realms, where the correct functioning of the brake system of a car affects its steering efficiency, which is why antilock brakes were invented. In the *Apollo 13* crisis, as one system failed or went awry, others were affected. Even in teams of humans, this interconnectedness is essential. If a football team's offense has little success, the defense

2. The term is used here, not in the common sense of "relating to, or derived from, a living organism," but rather of "having systematic coordination of parts." It is part of what is meant by *systematic* theology.

will eventually also lose its effectiveness as a result of being on the field too long.

This organic character of theology is particularly true of the doctrine of God, which serves as the starting point or presupposition for the Christian's understanding of the other realities. It may be possible in some of the behavioral sciences to study humans independently of other creatures, or even, to some extent, of other persons. That cannot be the case in theology, however. It is not possible to define the human apart from God, for the basic and most important truth about human beings is that they have been made by God, in his own image and likeness. Any attempt to discuss humanity apart from this reference is not theology at all, but simply psychology or anthropology. Similarly, one cannot develop a theological understanding of the human predicament and what must be done to rectify it apart from consideration of God, for the most basic fact about humanity is that it is separated from and in rebellion against its Creator. All other human problems are secondary to this fact and, in a sense, derived from it. This is true of the church as well. If one attempts to develop a doctrine of the church apart from God as the reference point, what results is not theology, but sociology of religion or something similar. In short, one cannot have theology, even any of its parts, without first considering the nature of God and what he does. Thus, there is no such thing as changing the understanding of God without, sooner or later, also changing the doctrines of humanity, sin, and salvation. The extent of God's holiness and justice affects the seriousness of the human situation, the radicalism of the solution needed, and even the type of mediator needed to resolve the problem.

This organicism of theology can be seen in the effect of a shift in the doctrine of God on the doctrine of salvation. One of the tendencies in recent years is to emphasize the passibility of God. God definitely has emotions, and is not unaffected by the plight of humans. He is frequently depicted, in fact, as suffering with them.

If this is so, however, then there are implications for both eschatology and salvation. For this means that it brings pain to God to know that there are persons who are lost, who will, in other words, be eternally separated from him. In some versions of this doctrine, these individuals are sent to hell, a place of endless and intense suffering and anguish. If this is the case, however, and if God knows their condition, does this not mean that God will, at the very least, be eternally grieving and perhaps even eternally suffer through his sympathetic identification with his creatures? But this would seem to make God an inferior or at least a less than supremely blissful being.

Those who have recognized this problem have struggled to give some answer. Richard Creel, for example, holds to a rather traditional view of impassibility, but contends that to fail to do so would lead one toward a view of God in which his suffering simply increases.[3] It is interesting to note that a theologian like Clark Pinnock, who holds that God is not impassible,[4] has also made some adjustments in his doctrine of salvation and personal eschatology. So, for example, he has argued for a "wider hope" on the basis of the idea of implicit faith, whereby, through God's general revelation, a person without special revelation is able to exercise sufficient faith to be saved.[5] He also believes that the Bible teaches that there is an opportunity to hear and believe the gospel after death for those who have not heard it during their lifetimes.[6] Finally, he holds that those who do not accept the offer of salvation even after such opportunities will be annihilated, so that no one suffers everlastingly.[7] Is not some such expedient as these, or perhaps even universalism, a necessity in light of the understanding of passibility?

Influence of the Doctrine of God on the Practical Christian Life

The study of the doctrine of God is of great importance because the conclusions reached here greatly influence our understanding and practice of the Christian life. God is basic to our whole theology, and theology, held either consciously or implicitly, does eventually affect our behavior as Christians. Basic to the conduct of the Christian life is the question "Who is God?" or "What is God like?"

The way this happens is seen in J. B. Phillips' little book, *Your God Is Too Small*. He shows how we form various pictures of the nature of God, based at least in part on taking only part of the biblical picture of God and amplifying it. One is God as the resident police officer, a severe, demanding God who delights in catching his people in violations of the law and finding them guilty.[8] Another picture, common in our time and in some ways the opposite of this view, is God as the heavenly grandfather. This God is permissive, indulgent, always willing to look the other

3. Richard E. Creel, *Divine Impassibility: An Essay in Philosophical Theology* (Cambridge: Cambridge University Press, 1986), p. 125.

4. Clark H. Pinnock, "Systematic Theology," in *The Openness of God: A Biblical Challenge to the Traditional Understanding of God* (Downers Grove: InterVarsity, 1994), p. 119.

5. "The Finality of Jesus Christ in a World of Religions," in *Christian Faith and Practice in the Modern World: Theology from an Evangelical Point of View*, ed. Mark A. Noll and David F. Wells (Grand Rapids: Eerdmans, 1988), pp. 152–68.

6. *A Wideness in God's Mercy: The Finality of Jesus Christ in a World of Religions* (Grand Rapids: Zondervan, 1992), pp. 168–72.

7. "The Destruction of the Finally Impenitent," *Criswell Theological Review* 4.2 (Spring 1990): 243–59.

8. J. B. Phillips, *Your God Is Too Small* (New York: Macmillan, 1961), pp. 15–18.

way, to smile when human beings misbehave, not really being too strict a disciplinarian.

These conceptions of God, if understood and responded to consistently, produce different types of religious experience. These may not function on the conscious level, but they do affect our attitudes and actions. The person or the congregation who see God as the heavenly police officer will frequently be people whose Christian lives are characterized by fear and by judgment, directed both toward themselves and others. There may be a considerable legalism, of measuring spirituality by conformity to the teachings of Scripture, and even a tendency toward Phariseeism, of thinking of oneself as superior to others who do not follow these teachings as closely. On the other hand, a church or individual Christian who thinks of God on the model of the celestial grandfather may turn out to be rather casual about spirituality, and not too sensitive to sin since God does not hold it against us.

Currently there is considerable emphasis on Christian lifestyle. Indeed, there is more talk and concern about this than there is about specific Christian beliefs. "Don't tell me what to believe, just show me how to live" would summarize this view for many. Yet attempting to deal with lifestyle issues, apart from doctrinal questions, will ultimately fail. There is both a general and a specific reason for this. The general reason is that attitudes and actions cannot be sustained indefinitely, apart from some underlying basis of belief. Part of human nature, part of the image of God in which we were created, is rationality, and what is true will eventually have its impact on how we feel and live. One characteristic of the present time is its irrationalism, its tendency to experience and to believe independently of factual considerations. Yet this cannot, in the long run, be maintained. For example, when a close loved one dies, denial of the reality of death is a common reaction, especially at a particular stage of the process. Eventually, however, this cannot be maintained, at least if the person is to remain sane (or in touch with reality, as is sometimes said). Indeed, the very concept of sanity suggests that society is built on the idea of some sort of objectivity of truth. Those who recognize these truths are sane; those who do not are insane. Sooner or later, the fact that the missing one never appears, cannot be communicated with, and so on, becomes overwhelming. Optimism about the progress of the person in his or her struggle with the disease that resulted in death cannot be maintained after one has been to the funeral. The practice of displaying the body (or the "remains," as frequently referred to now) is intended to serve this purpose of bringing about acceptance of the reality of the person's death. So our theology will sooner or later be affected by the facts we accept, and our lifestyle will have to be adjusted accordingly.

There is, however, a reverse flow as well. Our lifestyle can also affect our theology. The reason is that if we are committed to a given lifestyle and unwilling to alter that, then we will find a way to rationalize our theology so that it fits with how we want to live. I once served as interim pastor of an evangelical inner-city church. Just about four blocks from our church building was a church comprised of persons who practiced an "alternative lifestyle" with respect to sexual practice. One day as I drove past this church building, I thought about their beliefs and practices. With respect to the usual doctrines of the Christian faith, these people held an orthodox set of beliefs based on a conservative conception and interpretation of the Bible. Yet when one approaches the Bible with that sort of understanding, one finds that it speaks rather clearly in opposition to the type of sexual ethics these people considered acceptable for Christians. Only by contrived and convoluted interpretations would one be able to justify such practices by Scripture. I asked myself, "How can this be, that such interpretations would be accepted?" and realized the answer was probably that having determined that they were going to practice what they did, they had come to Scripture and rationalized that practice by what they found there. Rather than conforming their lifestyle to their theology, they had adjusted their theology to fit their lifestyle.

This effect on our lifestyle can be seen quite clearly with respect to our understanding of God's knowledge and providence. Does God know everything? If not, is there any meaningful sense in which we can pray for him to guide us in our planning, choosing, and acting with respect to that future? Further, is God really able to control all that occurs, or are there limitations on what he can do? If so, perhaps it is possible for me or another human being actually to frustrate God and his purposes. To take this a step further, is the outcome of the struggle with evil assured? Will God definitely be victorious over evil, or is it possible that he will never gain victory over it? If so, my hope for the future and my own choice of values may be affected. And what about my freedom and consequent responsibility? To what extent am I really the sole determiner of my actions? These are questions that have a very definite bearing on my actions, and they stem directly from the beliefs I hold regarding God, his nature, and his actions.

This Doctrine an Intersection of Theology with Other Disciplines

Another major reason why the doctrine of God is important is also inherent in the nature of the doctrine, but is perhaps more acute in our present time than at some points in the past. It is because this doctrine forms a point of intersection of theology with some other disciplines.

Philosophy

The first is obviously philosophy. Traditionally, philosophy was concerned with God. Western philosophy, in the form of the Pre-Socratic Greek thinkers, began asking metaphysical questions, such as "What is ultimately real?" Sooner or later that way of questioning was bound to lead to the idea that there was a supreme being, or god, who had planned and created all that is. So, some sort of supernaturalism and even theism was a major answer given by philosophers. As such, this could be a challenge or alternative to the Christian biblical answer, a support for it, or a modifier of the tradition.

Eventually, however, the theistic tradition in philosophy began to fade. One major objection came from Immanuel Kant's critical philosophy. Kant was concerned to understand the several varieties of cognitive experience, and wrote three massive *Critiques*, dealing respectively with the domains of epistemology or theoretical knowledge, ethics, and aesthetics. The first of these, *The Critique of Pure Reason*, had the greatest direct effect on Christian theology. Kant argued that all genuine knowledge must have two components. There must be the content, supplied entirely by sense perception, and there must be form or structure, supplied by the knowing mechanism of the person's mind. Without both components, there cannot be genuine knowledge. "Percepts without concepts are blind, but concepts without percepts are empty" became the rallying cry of those who adopted this epistemology. If it were somehow possible to have sense perception without having the structuring effect of such categories as quantity and cause, for example, there would not be true knowledge, but simply a blur of confusion, as bits of sense data pour in.[9] Conversely, when we try to apply our concepts of causation, for example, to the ideas that go beyond our experience, we run into difficulty. This comes in the form of antinomies, or mutually possible alternatives. So for example, the ideas that the world has a point of beginning in time and that it has no beginning are equally plausible. This is similarly true of the ideas that there is freedom and that all things are caused.[10]

The impact of this approach to epistemology on theology or the philosophy of religion was obvious and severe. For these disciplines claim to deal with a transcendent object, God, lying beyond human experi-

9. Immanuel Kant, *The Critique of Pure Reason* (Garden City, N.Y.: Doubleday, 1961), I, second division, book I.
10. Ibid., I, second division, book II, chap. II.

ence. Consequently, although we may have ideas about such a purported object, these ideas can have no real content. The existence of God and his nonexistence are equally plausible. As a result, we can say nothing about him.

If, then, religion is not a matter of the pure or speculative reason, what is it? Here Kant suggested an alternative to the traditional position. There are two other domains of human experience besides the theoretical: the ethical and the aesthetic. Kant proposed that religion be understood as a question of the ethical.[11] Albrecht Ritschl picked up this idea and elaborated on it, contending that religion is a question of value-judgments rather than truth-judgments.[12] Friedrich Schleiermacher followed yet a different path, relating his understanding of religion to the third of Kant's domains and making it a matter of feeling.[13]

This general hostility to metaphysics and with it to theology was accentuated in the twentieth century. Logical positivists were concerned not so much with the question of truth in a direct fashion, but with the issue of meaning. In what sense is language meaningful? In their analysis of the use of language, they concluded that there are only two cognitively meaningful types of propositions: a priori analytic and a posteriori synthetic. The former are mathematical-type sentences, in which the predicate is contained implicitly within the subject. They do not, therefore, inform us of anything that is not already present in the subject. The latter are scientific-type sentences, in which the predicate adds something to that which is present in the subject. The meaning of such sentences is the set of sense data that would serve to verify or falsify the proposition. All other claimed assertions, even if they take the grammatical form of assertions, do not really express anything. They are simply emotive in nature, giving vent to the subjective state of the person making them. Lacking sensory data that would count for or against their truth, they are literally non-sense, and therefore, meaningless statements. And here, unfortunately, are to be found theology's propositions about God.[14]

The other challenge to the language of theology came from the school of thought known as pragmatism. Pragmatism was impatient with speculative discussions of abstract issues of truth. In the judgment of

11. Immanuel Kant, *The Critique of Practical Reason*, trans. and ed. Lewis White Beck (Chicago: University of Chicago Press, 1949).

12. Albrecht Ritschl, *The Christian Doctrine of Justification and Reconciliation: The Positive Development of the Doctrine* (Edinburgh: T. & T. Clark, 1902).

13. Friedrich Schleiermacher, *On Religion: Speeches to Its Cultured Despisers* (New York: Harper & Brothers, 1958).

14. Frederick Ferré, *Language, Logic and God* (New York: Harper & Row, 1961), pp. 18–41.

the pragmatists, these frequently could not be resolved, and had no real bearing on the practical dimensions of life. Truth was defined functionally, as that which works or produces the desired results.[15] The objection to theology here was not so much to the traditional issues of truth or meaning, but to the relevance or meaningfulness of the concepts.

For a number of years philosophers considered theology an impossible or illegitimate discipline. After languishing for some time, however, the doctrine of God has recently come in for renewed interest and attention by philosophers. One factor in this increased interest has been the surge of Christian philosophers into the field. The rapid growth of the Society of Christian Philosophers and the increasing presence of evangelical Christians within philosophy departments of major universities are evidence of this phenomenon.

At the same time, there has been increased interest on the part of philosophers in general in what are perceived as neglected areas of philosophy. The more radical views of logical positivism had foundered on the fact that the verification principle (the idea that the meaning of a proposition is the sense data that would verify or falsify it) was, on its own criterion, meaningless. So this strongly prescriptive approach to questions of meaning gave way to more descriptive varieties of linguistic analysis. Here, however, there was still some skepticism about the validity of theology's language. The more recent philosophical discussion, however, has felt that normative questions were being neglected in favor of these purely descriptive types of philosophy. So epistemology has been especially explored. The question became not simply what type of language is being used here or how is it being used, but whether it is true and, in fact, how we discover truth. Metaphysical questions are also being explored again. Because of this long period of neglect, a backlog of questions of epistemology and metaphysics has been created, which has stimulated increased attention. This return to traditional fields of philosophy has been accompanied by a return to discussion of some of the traditional subjects of those fields, such as God. Because philosophy is once again concerned with this matter, it has the potential either to aid and strengthen theology, or to controvert it.

This increased openness to discussion of matters of theological interest has been evident in the resurgence of the discipline of philosophical theology. Once regarded as of interest only to Thomists, this field has generated a considerable literature of its own.[16] Such philosophers as

---

15. William James, "Pragmatism's Conception of Truth," in *Pragmatism: And Four Essays from the Meaning of Truth* (New York: Meridian, 1955), pp. 131–53.

16. Thomas V. Morris, *Our Idea of God: An Introduction to Philosophical Theology* (Downers Grove: InterVarsity, 1991), pp. 15–26.

Alvin Plantinga, William Alston, Thomas Morris, Richard Swinburne, Richard Creel, Charles Hartshorne, Nelson Pike, P. T. Geach, Norman Kretzmann, Nicholas Wolterstorff, Peter van Inwagen, George Mavrodes, Eleanor Stump, Keith Ward, and Paul Helm have contributed much to the discussions. Many of these thinkers are quite orthodox theologically and greatly interested in the types of questions that attach to the traditional doctrine of God.

This flourishing of philosophical theology has provided considerable resources for understanding the doctrine of God. The reason for this importance is that exegetical or biblical theology seems unable to contribute much more to new insights into these issues regarding the nature of God. Some of the attributes are quite clearly asserted in Scripture, such as the omnipotence of God, the fact that he can do all things. The difficulty comes, however, when we ask the further question, "What does this really mean?" For the biblical statements frequently do not address some of the questions that are asked at this level. There simply is not sufficiently detailed data to help us in this search. It is at this point that philosophical theology goes to work, posing additional questions that help refine and define the doctrine further. Thus, the entire enterprise is enriched by philosophy's contributions.

Anthropology

Philosophy is the traditional conversation partner with theology regarding the doctrine of God, but it is by no means the only one currently. In particular, anthropology has lately given increasing attention to the subject. The study of comparative religions, with their differing conceptions of the ultimate power, reveals some interesting facts and raises some significant questions. What are the common features of these different religions' views of God, and what are the notable differences? This in turn raises the question of the nature of religion. Is it some sort of human a priori, an experience based on an intrinsic quality or capacity of the human being? Are the various religions in some way basically the same in terms of the distinctively religious factors?

A further question raised by anthropology is, Is religion's form a function of the circumstances, the culture, and so on, in which it takes root? Is it transplantable, the way a tree is? Some trees, for example, if taken from one climate and moved to a more northerly one, perish, being unable to adapt to the colder climate, while others seem able to adapt quite well. But when a religion is transplanted from one culture to another, for example, Islam from Africa or the Middle East to North America, does it take on the coloration of that particular culture, or does it change the culture?

This question bears specifically on the idea of God. Are there distinctly Western and Eastern ideas of God, which reflect the mentality and the culture of that area and people? John Hick, for example, asserts that there are distinctly Eastern and Western frames of mind. These color the conception of the object of the religious experience. So the Eastern understanding of God is more pantheistic in nature, considering God pervasive and present everywhere, but not especially personal in nature. The Western way of apprehending the same reality is theism, or the idea of a personal God, who is at least in part transcendent. Hick contends that these are simply different ways of understanding and describing the same reality. If this is the case, then some adjustment in our understanding of God will have to be made. Either we must say that we cannot determine precisely what God is like, or that the conception itself is not really important: what matters is the experience obtained in connection with it. Perhaps, as an extreme, we will have to say that the understanding of God is purely subjective.

Sociology

A final discipline whose interest in God intersects that of theology is sociology. This may sound strange at first, because sociology has usually concerned itself with the manifestation of religion in social groups rather than its specific beliefs, but increasingly of late sociological considerations have borne on the doctrinal considerations people hold as well. This can be seen quite vividly in the case of feminist theology, for example. Essentially, the argument of some feminists is that traditional male terminology for God has had unfortunate sociological effects for women. Specifically, their contention is that such traditional language has contributed to patriarchialism, wherein men were given exalted status, and used this to oppress women. Further, leadership in the church has been affected by this view of God. Since God is male, his servants must be also. Consequently, priests and ministers are to be male, and women are excluded from positions of leadership.[17] So, assert the radical feminists, the traditional idea of God as Father, conflicting with the welfare of women, must be rejected in favor of an alternative view, such as goddess religion. Here more conventional theology, coming from the direction of exegetical and historical studies, shares a common object but a very different understanding of that object from that displayed by feminist theology, which derives its content from sociology.

---

17. E.g., Rosemary Radford Ruether, *To Change the World: Essays in Cultural Criticism* (New York: Crossroad, 1981), p. 46.

Religious Pluralism of Popular Culture

There are other reasons currently for the special importance of the doctrine of God and of thorough and careful discussion of it. One of these is that the Christian God is no longer a unique option for belief in today's world. We have noted that belief in a supernatural being or power is the most fundamental dividing factor among worldviews, separating theism from various kinds of naturalism. For Westerners, it has seemed natural to assume that Christianity, with its strongly theistic view of reality, was the only real alternative to naturalism. This, as a matter of empirical fact, was for most persons the choice. In recent decades, however, this has changed.

In the United States, increasing numbers of immigrants are bringing other religions with them, and these religions are also gaining increasing numbers of converts. For example, the growth of Islam among young African American males is significant. Americans who do not wish to be secular or naturalistic or irreligious now have other options besides Christianity.

Some of these alternatives are quite close to the Christian view of God, but nonetheless also display significant differences. Judaism does not base its view of God on something different than that employed by Christianity, but it lacks or at least does not consult the full Christian revelation. Islam is also a strongly theistic worldview, but its view of God is almost fatalistic.

Other non-Christian religions have views of God quite different from the Christian God. Hinduism and some varieties of Buddhism, for example, are more pantheistic, their view of God being less personal than is the Christian perspective on God. These tend to find God more within oneself and nature than as an external person. Here the option is radically different than Christianity, but it is still an alternative to naturalism. In fact, these religions stress that they represent spirituality, albeit quite a different spirituality than most Christians have associated with that word.

There is also the increasing appeal of nontraditional or noninstitutional religions, particularly "New Age" religion. Because its advocates do not form organizations, it differs from most religions, more nearly resembling, in some ways, a philosophy than a religion. Although claiming to be something new, this is actually a contemporary form of a very old type of worldview, pantheism. Here again, as in Eastern religions, God is thought of as within us and everything else, and we are to think of ourselves as "channels" of his activity. The appeal of this view to young people is that it is different from conventional religions in which they may have been raised or to which they have been exposed.

These religions, in various forms, will continue to exert an influence on our own understandings. American culture, through the legal and ideological systems that have undergirded our educational systems, tended to be influenced by Christian conceptions. This could be seen, for example, in the Ten Commandments hanging on classroom walls and the Lord's Prayer being recited. Similarly, the kinds of distinctions among forms of homicide in the Mosaic law found their way into the legal system and became part of people's ways of thinking. As our culture absorbs more content from religions other than the Judeo-Christian tradition, these values will also become part of that culture and will begin to influence Christians, gradually seeping into their thinking. Consequently, we can begin to expect growing confusion on the part of Christians as they attempt to understand what God is like.

The Shift toward Anthropocentrism

A further, very influential reason for the current importance of the doctrine of God is because of the shift that is progressively occurring toward a human-centered Christian practice, in several areas.

Evangelism

The first of these is evangelism, where we can note an increasing tendency to make appeals on the basis of meeting human needs. The discussion with the non-Christian is begun on the level of the examination of felt needs. The nature of the offer of salvation, or the appeal to accept Jesus Christ, is on the basis of his ability to satisfy these human needs, as experienced by the person.

To be sure, evangelism has always proceeded on some such basis as this, with the contention that Christ would meet the deepest needs of the individual, such as forgiveness, direction of life, and so on. Those were more distinctly "spiritual" needs concerning the person's relationship to God. Here, however, this is not necessarily the case, as physical health, provision of material needs, and solution of personal, social, and family problems become the focus of attention. The more anthropocentric approach differs from the more traditional view in two other ways. For one thing, this approach assumes the correctness of the person's judgment of his or her real needs. The older approach frequently contended that even in such matters the human is mistaken, and God's judgment in these things must overrule. The other difference is that many persons do not necessarily consider proper alignment with God's will, obedience to him, and glorification of him part of human need. Consequently, persons may enter the church on the basis of what they perceive to be the answer to their sense of weakness and their need of

God's help, and then discover that they are expected to serve this Christ and obey his commands. The result may then be disillusionment and resentment.

Worship

This same tendency may also be found, to an increasing extent, in Christian worship. We see a movement from worship as adoration to worship as celebration. While the shift may seem small and insignificant, the implications are really quite far-reaching. It may seem paradoxical to suggest that this is a more anthropocentric approach, since much of the music is directed to praise of God, but the actual focus of the activity is in many cases a reveling in the enjoyment of what God is, stressing the emotions involved. One seminary student who led the singing in a chapel service urged other students to "come and have fun before the Lord, which is what worship is."

Even the selection of those aspects of God on which to concentrate is revealing. The major emphasis is on the qualities of God that are reassuring, rather than disturbing, to his worshipers. Primarily, it is power of God, his mighty works, his loftiness, and so on, which are sung about. His holiness, his wrath, his judgment, and the like, are stressed much less. Consequently, expressions of guilt, repentance, remorse, and confession are largely absent. Since the psalms are heavily utilized, one would expect to find songs expressing repentance, such as Psalm 51, in the repertoire of songs. A search for them, however, is disappointing. God's natural attributes are emphasized more than his moral attributes, and when his moral attributes are examined, it is his love, mercy, compassion, and similarly comforting qualities, rather than more austere dimensions of his nature, which come into prominence.[18]

Pastoral Care

In pastoral care, a similar development can be noted. The question the pastoral counselor concentrates on is not necessarily, "What does God want this person to be?" Rather, it is more nearly the question, "What does this person think or wish to be?" Again, human rather than divine concerns set the agenda and the framework for what transpires. One way of putting this development is the observation that whereas the earlier program of care focused on holiness, this approach is more oriented to human wholeness.

18. See, for example, the choruses in *Maranatha! Music Praise Chorus Book* (Costa Mesa, Calif.: Maranatha! Music, 1983).

Administration

A final area of ministry is from the standpoint of leadership or administration. It is a question of the goal of the ministry. At one time, the aim was building the kingdom of God. That meant evangelizing the lost, building up believers in the faith, and overcoming societal evils. Increasingly of late, however, the goal is building the church. By this is meant the local church, the institutional church. The model of the pastor becomes less and less a matter of the spiritual teacher and healer, and more the chief executive, whose task is to build up the congregation, which usually means enlarging it numerically.

This is usually related to several factors. One is the personality of the pastor, which often becomes the center of the ministry, message, and appeal of the congregation. Personal charisma, or the ability to attract other persons, is a cardinal qualification for being the pastor of such a church. Further, this type of church is often characterized by "techno-ministry." The very best marketing methods are employed. Seminars are held by successful pastors of such churches for the benefit of other pastors, who come to learn how to make their own churches successful in similar fashion. The implication is that if properly planned and executed, results can be virtually programmed or guaranteed. One cannot help but wonder what the place of God in all this is, if the results are somehow directly correlated with human plans and efforts.

Theological Method

There also is an indication of a shift toward anthropocentricity in theological method. One of these will be the subject of major examination in this book, namely, free will theism or the "openness of God" school of thought. For those theologians, it is conflict of human free will and divine sovereignty and foreknowledge that leads to the redefinition of the doctrine of God that they are proposing.

Another indication of this shift in methodological orientation is found in the work of the evangelical revisionist, Stanley Grenz. He insists that the essence of evangelicalism is to be found, not in a particular doctrinal position, but in a specific type of spirituality.[19] Further, the very conception of the nature of theology is to be revised. Earlier evangelicalism had tended to define theology as the extraction, interpretation, systematization, and application of the teachings of the Bible, Grenz defines it as reflection on the faith of the Christian community. In so doing, however, there is a shift of orientation. Instead of compiling

19. Stanley J. Grenz, *Revisioning Evangelical Theology: A Fresh Agenda for the 21st Century* (Downers Grove: InterVarsity, 1993), pp. 30–35.

a list of what God has purportedly said, the focus is on what Christian believers believe.[20]

In light of the foregoing considerations, it is of great importance that we ask anew and with persistence, "What is God really like?" In the following pages we first examine at some length several current conceptions of God that challenge the traditional doctrine, to identify as clearly as possible the important issues that need to be discussed. We then seek to inquire more deeply into each of these issues, seeking to come to some satisfactory and responsible contemporary formulation of each.

---

20. Ibid., p. 85.

Part **2**

Challenges to the Traditional Understanding of God

2

Pluralism

A movement of growing influence within American religion and theology in recent years is pluralism. This is especially evident in the presence of a variety of religions within American culture and in the reactions to this presence. Pluralism is the idea that no one religion is exclusively true, to the exclusion of the others, but that there is truth in *each* religion.

John Hick has for many years been an outspoken advocate of this approach. Hick was raised as a nominal Christian, but during his university days was converted to a rather conservative variety of Christianity which regards Christianity alone as the true religion and all other religions as distortions of religious truth. Consequently, Christians are to engage in evangelization of these other religious persons, seeking to convert them to Christian belief. Gradually, however, Hick became disillusioned with this form of evangelical Christianity, and concluded that all religious persons are actually worshiping the same reality, although in different ways. In large part, this was a result of his contact with devout representatives of other religions in the United Kingdom.[1] While Hick's early theological writings dealt with specific doctrinal tenets and came from a conservative orientation, his later writing has especially focused on the matters of non-normative or nonexclusive religion. We shall use his writings as the basic source of the scheme we wish to develop regarding the view of God, supplemented at points by the thought of other pluralistic theologians. This will require treating several facets of his thought as background to and basic to Hick's view of God.

1. John Hick, *God Has Many Names* (Philadelphia: Westminster, 1982), pp. 12–18.

The Nature of Religion

As a philosopher of religion, Hick is aware of the various attempts to interpret the nature of religious language, many of which maintain that religious language has no cognitive referent. There is the phenomenon of a wide variety of religions, all of which claim that they have genuine knowledge of God and that he is as they have described him. One explanation, offered in different forms by Ludwig Feuerbach and Sigmund Freud, is that this represents human projection of hopes and fears. There is no objective referent for such language. Rather than God having created humans in his own image, they have created him in theirs. That is why the gods of different religions differ, because the cultures of the persons who have constructed them vary and these variations are reflected in their conceptions of deity. Hick firmly rejects this hypothesis as an overall theory, while acknowledging the element of truth that may be present in it.[2] He does not intend here to prove, but to assume the religious interpretation of these phenomena. He has provided the argument elsewhere.[3]

This phenomenon is indeed interesting. Unlike the later Wittgenstein and some Neo-Wittgensteinians like D. Z. Phillips, he is not going to argue that religious language is an autonomous language game, which cannot and need not be justified by any other, more general types of argument or language. This approach secures for religious discourse an immunity from criticism, but at the expense of any sort of positive argument for its truth or its meaning. Rather, Hick accepts the claim of religious people that they have genuine knowledge of God, but then asks in what sense this can be the case.

Hick's understanding of religious faith as cognition relies on a distinction between cognition in presence and cognition as absence. This is equivalent to the distinction between acquaintance and belief about. We cognize things in their presence, which we ordinarily call perception, and also cognize things in their absence, which should be termed "believing things about." Hick finds it extraordinary that Christian religious literature, such as the Bible, hymns, and so on, uniformly presuppose cognition by acquaintance, whereas theology ordinarily assumes that our knowledge of God is only cognition in absence. This latter approach, then, is correlated with faith as the acceptance of religious propositions, rather than a direct personal relationship.[4] Hick proposes

2. Ibid., p. 42.
3. *Arguments for the Existence of God* (London: Herder & Herder, 1971), and with Arthur McGill, *The Many-Faced Argument* (New York: Macmillan, 1967).
4. *God and the Universe of Faiths* (London: Macmillan, 1973), pp. 37–38.

to understand religious faith as genuine cognition, but to treat it as more closely related to perception than to believing propositions.

He recognizes the objection that will be raised, that religious faith cannot be sense perception, any more than God himself is a physical object. Although the Christian tradition has spoken of something known as the ultimate beatific vision, he is not referring to that, but to the believer's awareness of God in this present life. Nor is he thinking of a belief in the truth of the absent God. He wants to affirm, not that religious cognition *is* sense perception, but that it is more like sense perception than it is like believing propositions.[5]

This understanding of religious cognition is developed through Hick's idea of "experiencing-as." This is actually developed from Wittgenstein's idea of "seeing-as." Wittgenstein pointed to various types of puzzles and ambiguous diagrams. Some of these are the cube, which can be seen as a cube viewed from either above or from below; the duck-rabbit, which may be perceived as either a drawing of one or of the other; or the goblet-faces, which can be seen as either the outline of a goblet or vase, or as two faces looking into each other's eyes. In each of these cases, there are two different meanings that are made up by the same set of lines. Beyond this are the more complex sort of instances, when, for example, one sees what seems to be merely a random group of lines or of dots, and then comes to see that they form a face or some other figure. Hick summarizes by defining this as *seeing-as:* "We speak of seeing-as when that which is objectively there, in the sense of that which affects the retina, can be consciously perceived in two different ways as having two different characters or natures of meanings of significances; and very often, in these two-dimensional instances, we find that the mind switches back and forth between the alternative ways of seeing-as."[6]

Hick then proceeds to convert this idea of seeing-as to the idea of experiencing-as. Basically, this is the same type of phenomenon, applied to the other senses than sight. He illustrates this with sound, taste, and smell. Normally, of course, these senses do not function in isolation from one another, but as a single complex means of perception. By "experiencing-as" then, he means the end product of this complex perception in consciousness.[7] A further step is the move from perceiving these patterns, even complex ones, in puzzles and diagrams, to actual experiencing-as in life, in which one sees the tuft of grass as a rabbit or the shadows in the corner as someone standing there. All of this then forms

5. Ibid., p. 38.
6. Ibid., p. 39.
7. Ibid., p. 40.

an analogy with "two contrasting ways of experiencing the events of our lives and of human history, on the one hand as purely natural events and on the other as mediating the presence and activity of God." These two contrasting ways of experiencing the same physical environment and what happens within it are the religious and the atheistic experiences: "But in its actual concrete character in their respective 'streams of consciousness' it has for each a different nature and quality, a different meaning and significance; for one does and the other does not experience life as a continual interaction with the transcendent God."[8]

Does not such an analogy work to the disadvantage of the religious argument, however? Does it not reveal the rather subjective character of religious knowledge-claims as contrasted with sense perception's objectivity? Hick is very much aware of such an objection, and responds to it. One response would, of course, be the arguments for the existence of God, which, as we noted above, he has presented elsewhere. Beyond that, however, his argument here is to claim that *all* experiencing, not just religious experiencing, is experiencing-as. We have terms for ordinary experiencing-as, namely, "recognizing" or "identifying." Because these activities are so familiar to us, they are often not seen as what they are. For example, recognizing an object as a fork is ordinarily done so easily that we do not realize we have done so. If, however, the fork were of a sufficiently unusual design, we might have to acknowledge that some recognition was involved. Or, to take a somewhat different case, a Stone Age savage would not be able to recognize it as a fork at all. The reason is that he does not have the concept of fork, and thus cannot identify this shiny object as being such. The conclusion of the discussion is: "But simply as a physical object of a certain size and shape an artefact does not bear its meaning stamped upon it. To recognize or identify is to be experiencing-as in terms of a concept; and our concepts are social products having their life within a particular linguistic environment."[9]

The point Hick is making is that all experiencing is actually experiencing-as, whether of natural objects or artefacts. So, religious cognition, while it deals with situations of much greater complexity and broader generality, is not generically different in its epistemological character from ordinary secular perceiving. Beyond this, however, he wants to point out that experiencing-as occurs at various levels of awareness. So, for example, we may see something moving in the sky as a bird; then as a hawk; next as a hawk in search of prey; and, finally,

8. Ibid.
9. Ibid., pp. 41–42.

as a hawk about to swoop down on something on the far side of that low hump of ground. These are successively higher-level recognitions. Each presupposes and goes beyond the previous one.[10]

There is a correlate to this experiencing-as, which Hick calls "significance." He defines this by means of the idea of an appropriate response: "to recognise what is before us as an *x* involves being in a dispositional state to act in relation to it in a certain distinctive way or range of ways."[11] Thus, recognizing an object as a fork involves being in a different dispositional state than does recognizing it as a fountain pen, for instance.

The next step is to move from considering isolated objects as units of significance to larger and more complex units, which Hick terms "situations." A situation is composed of objects, but it is not merely a collection of objects; it is "a group of objects which, when attended to as a group, has its own distinctive significance over and above the individual significances of its constituent members. That is to say, the situation evokes its own appropriate dispositional response."[12]

As in the case of objects, so with respect to situations there can be different levels of significance. There is of course natural or physical significance, where one sees the interconnectedness of a large number of elements, and forms an interpretation of the physical whole. Beyond that, however, there is the ethical significance. For example, on the purely natural or physical level, one may observe an auto accident, in which someone has been injured and is now lying in the street, bleeding. Here one would see the wounds and the flowing blood, and hear the moaning and expressions of pain. On the ethical level, however, one would realize something needs to be done to help this person, and the need of doing that oneself. That is ethical significance, which presupposes the natural level, but goes beyond it. To be a moral, as contrasted with an amoral, being, is to experience this sense of obligation in connection with such a situation.[13] Yet another level of significance is the aesthetic, which sometimes presupposes the physical significance, but sometimes, as in much music and in abstract art, seems not to. Sometimes it has a practical-dispositional aspect, affecting attitudes, but sometimes it does not, being purely contemplative. One would expect that this level, if it is truly another level, would ordinarily also presuppose the ethical, but Hick does not address that, perhaps because his

---

10. Ibid., p. 45.
11. Ibid.
12. Ibid.
13. John Hick, *Problems of Religious Pluralism* (New York: St. Martin's, 1985), pp. 21–22.

treatment of aesthetic meaning is very brief and, in his earlier work, he does not mention this level at all.[14]

The level of religious significance is the most important to Hick and to our consideration of his thought. This is an awareness of the presence of the transcendent. While it goes beyond the ethical significance, the relationship to it is not simply that of building on it, as is the case of the ethical in relationship to the physical or natural. Sometimes it does, and sometimes it does not, build on the ethical. At times, as in connection with the beauty of nature, or simply contemplation apart from any specific environmental context, one is aware of God, but without any sense of moral obligation. Usually, however, this awareness leads one back to some sense of obligation to other human beings.[15]

There are different kinds of response to or interpretation of a situation deemed to have religious significance. One is the second-order formal sense of interpretation, like that of a historian interpreting the data; a lawyer, the evidence; a detective, the clues; or a metaphysician, the universe. On this level there are religious interpretations as well, which are theologies and philosophies of religion. Like Wittgenstein, Hick regards these second-order activities as much less important than the first-order religious experiencing of life and the accompanying attitudes of trust and acceptance and acts of worship and service.[16] This is simply to be conscious of being in the presence of God. Interpreting in this sense is largely an unconscious process, and involves "being in a dispositional state to behave in ways appropriate to the perceived meaning of our situation."[17]

It should by now be apparent that, for Hick, religion is especially a particular type of experience. Since all experience is actually *interpreted* experience, this is not different from other experiences. It is not necessarily a direct encounter with the transcendent, independent of any sort of physical context, but it is a particular type of experience or interpretation of even natural or physical circumstances. It is experiencing-as, which includes the awareness of the transcendent.

This brings us to the larger epistemology or theory of knowledge. Hick observes what is apparent to anyone who has examined the religions of our world: there are wide variations in the second-order interpretations, or doctrines of God or the ultimate, in these religions. It is in part this variety of understandings that has led him to the epistemology he espouses.

14. Ibid., p. 22.
15. *God and the Universe of Faiths*, p. 47.
16. *Problems of Religious Pluralism*, pp. 23–24.
17. Ibid., p. 24.

Hick sees his view as similar to and even drawing on the epistemology of Immanuel Kant. There are many interpretations of Kant's notoriously difficult *Critique of Pure Reason*, and the interpretation utilized here might be controversial in professional philosophical circles. The point, however, is not whether this is the correct interpretation of Kant, but that it is the interpretation with which Hick is working. What follows will be a broad and rough characterization of that Kantian epistemology.

Kant was endeavoring to trace a course midway between rationalism and empiricism in epistemology. Rationalists such as Descartes, Leibniz, and Spinoza contended that knowledge was gained through a process of rational reflection. This was a deductive approach, in which, if one began with a truth, it was possible simply by deductive logic to arrive at additional truth. Sense experience was not necessarily required, and could actually be deceptive. Frequently rationalists believed that humans hold certain innate truths, and the tests of truth were, in Descartes' terms, clear and distinct ideas.

Empiricists such as Locke, Berkeley, and Hume, by contrast, contended that there are no such things as innate ideas. The mind is a tabula rasa, a blank tablet, which contains nothing until written on by sense experience. All truth comes to us through sensory experience, and complex ideas are built up of combinations of simple ideas.

Kant saw elements of truth in both views. He therefore propounded a theory in which both experiential and rational factors were essential. All knowledge of a theoretical (as contrasted with practical) nature must have its content supplied by sensory data. For this sensory data to become knowledge, however, it must be processed through certain rational categories of the human understanding, such as cause, substance, and so on. This means that we never really know the thing in itself, or the noumena. All we know is the thing as it appears to us, or the phenomena. This should not be thought of as some sort of disadvantage, however, for if we somehow could come in direct contact with the noumenal world, it would be simply a mass of unorganized bits of sense data, not unlike what William James would later refer to as "the bloomin' buzzin' world."

While departing from this Kantian view in several respects, Hick uses its basic structure, in terms of the distinction between noumena and phenomena. In fact, he goes further back into the history of philosophy, to pick up on Aquinas's statement: "The thing known is in the knower according to the mode of the knower."[18] Although enunciated by philosophers, the principle has also been confirmed and developed

---

18. Thomas Aquinas, *Summa Theologica*, II/II, Q. 1, art. 2. Quoted by Hick in *God Has Many Names*, pp. 24, 48–49.

in modern psychology, sociology of knowledge, and philosophy of science.[19] Hick of course recognizes that his treatment of religion is much different from that of Kant, for whom there could be no rational or theoretical knowledge of God, but God is introduced as a postulate of the practical reason, required for ethics. Rather, Hick is taking a fundamental insight and a structural model from Kant's thought and using it in a sphere, the epistemology of religion, which Kant treated quite differently. He can do this because his conception of experience is broader than Kant's. Thus, Hick's thought is an analogy to Kant's thought, not an actual application of it.[20]

Hick contends that we experience that transcendent reality, but that we do so through a certain interpretational apparatus. This is not some innate structure, but rather "the continuum of historical factors which have produced our different religious cultures. It is the variations of the human cultural situation that concretize the notion of deity as specific images of God."[21] Thus, the conceptions of God are not really derived from the experience. Rather, these images "inform man's actual religious experience, so that it is an experience specifically of the God of Israel, or of Allah, or of the Father of our Lord Jesus Christ, or of Vishnu or Shiva."[22]

Of course, various interpretations of the variety of forms of religious belief and practice could be given. One would be that there are several different Gods, and each of these traditions is experiencing a different one. That, however, conflicts with the belief of each tradition that its God is the creator of the whole world. Another interpretation would be that there is one God, and that one religion correctly apprehends that one God. That religion is therefore true, and all the other religions are false. This view is often found within conservative Christianity, as well as in other religions. The difficulty here, however, is that even within Christianity, there are rather widely varying specific conceptions of God, as for example, of a stern judge and predestining power, on the one hand, and as a gracious, loving heavenly Father, on the other. Different Christian groups and even individuals seem to be worshiping the Christian God under diverse images.[23] There are large differences between Southern Baptist and Northern Episcopalians in the United States, and the same can be said of the differences between Zen Buddhism and Amida Buddhism in Japan. Thus, we almost need to speak, not of Chris-

19. *Problems of Religious Pluralism*, p. 92.
20. *God Has Many Names*, pp. 103–4.
21. Ibid., p. 105.
22. Ibid., pp. 105–6.
23. Ibid., p. 66.

tianity and Buddhism, for example, but of Christianities and Buddhisms. If one is to say that one religion, for example, Christianity, is true, one must then ask, *which* Christianity?[24]

There is a third possibility, which Hick believes to be the best option: "that there is but one God, who is maker and Lord of all; that in his infinite fullness and richness of being he exceeds all our human attempts to grasp him in thought; and that the devout in the various great world religions are in fact worshiping that one God, but through different, overlapping concepts or mental icons of him."[25]

On what does Hick base his acceptance of this third alternative interpretation? He gives a number of reasons. First, and one of the most prominent, is the similarity of the worship experience of several different religions. Hick examines several samples of religious songs from a variety of religions, and shows how they reflect basically the same pattern of experience.[26] Indeed, if devotees of one of those religions were to read the songs without knowing their source, they could easily mistake the song as a composition of a member of their own religion. Hick's conclusion is "that phenomenologically (or in other words, to human observation) the same kind of thing is taking place in them as in a Christian church."[27]

A second reason for this interpretation is the fact that each religion has produced its own saints. There is no significant discernible difference between the quality of piety of one religion and another. "Ptolemaic Christianity," as Hick terms it, "does not easily square with the evidences of salvation within other faiths in this present life—the evidence of saints, prophets, martyrs and mystics who have been intensely aware of the divine presence and whose lives have demonstrated the reality of their devotion."[28] Thus, on pragmatic considerations, there is no real basis for grading one ahead of the other, or for concluding that a truly supernatural force is involved in one but not in the others.

Third, religious belief is highly correlated with place of birth. In the great majority of cases, perhaps 98 or 99 percent, the religion one holds and practices depends on where he or she was born.[29] This is an easily verifiable fact. It is, however, a fact of which any credible religious faith must be capable of making sense.[30] How can we say, in light of such

24. *Problems of Religious Pluralism*, p. 30.
25. Ibid., pp. 66–67.
26. Ibid., pp. 62–66.
27. Ibid., p. 63.
28. Hick, *God and the Universe of Faiths*, p. 130.
29. *God Has Many Names*, p. 61; Hick, *God and the Universe of Faiths*, pp. 100, 132.
30. Hick, *God Has Many Names*, p. 61.

data, that one view is objectively true and the others, in various degrees, are false?[31] Being a Christian, Muslim, or Hindu is thus really no different from being born an American, Arab, or Indian.

Fourth is the relative lack of missionary success of the Christian religion. For what is apparent, as we study the growth of world religions, is that the success being experienced by Christian missionaries is generally "downward," that is, toward the relatively primitive religions, rather than "sideways," into territories dominated by the other world religions.[32] Most of Christianity's converts are coming from less sophisticated religions, which are primarily animistic and polytheistic.

There also is an amazing parallel in the histories of the religions. There is what Karl Jaspers has referred to as the "axial period" in the history of the human race, from approximately 800 to 200 B.C During this time, significant leaders arose through whom humans' awareness of the divine was greatly enhanced and developed. In China, Confucius and the writer(s) of the *Tao Te Ching* lived; in India, Gautama the Buddha and Mahavira the founder of Jainism lived and taught and the Upanishads and the *Bhagavad-Gita* were produced. In Persia, Zoroaster did his work, and in Israel, the great prophets, Jeremiah, Isaiah, Hosea, and others lived. In Greece, Pythagoras, Socrates, Plato, and Aristotle promulgated their teachings. To restrict this golden age to these particular centuries is to regard Christianity and Islam as major new developments within the Semitic monotheism that had produced the Hebrew prophets.[33] Although Hick really does not say so explicitly, he implies that this simultaneity of development is evidence that the same force was involved.

The Actual Understanding of God

The picture of God that Hick develops is of a single God who is variously conceived by the different religions in different doctrinal forms. He refers to this object of religious worship as "the Eternal One." This term does not bias the hearer toward one or another of the various religious traditions. Hick makes certain assumptions about this One, in keeping with the common ground of the several great religions. This One is infinite. Further, this One, in the fullness of what it is, is "beyond the scope of human thought and language and experience; and yet that it impinges upon mankind and is encountered and conceptualized and expressed and responded to in the limited ways which are possible to

31. Hick, *God and the Universe of Faiths*, p. 100.
32. Ibid., p. 138.
33. *God Has Many Names*, pp. 45–46.

our finite human nature."[34] At times he also refers to this transcendent reality as "the Real."[35]

When this assumption is applied to the actual history of humanity, interesting results emerge. It appears that humans have always had some sense of the religious, dating back as far as history can take us, and for at least the past half million years or more, there is evidence of religious practices. Archaeology supplies us with some of this information, particularly of religious symbolism in connection with death and sacred places. Observation in the nineteenth century of then-surviving "primitive" tribes also shows signs of religious practices. In these early stages of religious history the conception of the Eternal One was in images strongly resembling humans in many ways. This was the age of natural religion, or what Hick calls the "prerevelational" stage of religious history.[36] Then came the great axial period, referred to earlier.

If, however, this is the same reality impressing itself on the human consciousness in all these religions, why is there such a great difference? Hick notes that there are two major types of understandings of the Eternal One. These are the understanding of the One as personal, found in the great theistic religions, and the understanding of the One as nonpersonal, or the Absolute, found in the nontheistic or transtheistic religions.[37] When we look more closely at the specific varieties of belief in God within the two types, we find considerable variation. It is at this point that Hick introduces his analogy to Kantian epistemology.

Hick holds that the Eternal One has created finite personal beings in the presence of God, so that in being conscious of what is other than themselves, they are unavoidably conscious of God. To be personal beings, they must be genuinely free, capable of cognitive freedom and responsibility, and thus able to respond to God freely. The Eternal One has created the universe with its own laws and as religiously ambiguous. It can be experienced either religiously or nonreligiously. Humans have the capacity, the freedom, to control their own cognitive mode. Thus, the Eternal One is known in accordance with the mode of the knower.[38]

But what about the many variations in this understanding? Hick's answer is direct and clear: "Because, I would suggest, religious faith is not an isolated aspect of our lives but is closely bound up with human

34. Ibid., p. 42.
35. *Problems of Religious Pluralism*, p. 98.
36. *God Has Many Names*, pp. 43–45.
37. Ibid., p. 52.
38. Ibid., pp. 50–51.

culture and human history, which are in turn bound up with basic geographical, climatic, and economic circumstances."[39] These other factors give the particular form to the understanding of God. Hick quotes with approval the work of Trevor Ling, who contends that in nomadic, pastoral, herd-keeping cultures, the male principle tends to predominate in the religious understanding, whereas among primarily agricultural peoples, the female principle is dominant. These different cultural factors provide the concrete form of the awareness of the Eternal One.[40]

This understanding of God means that we cannot make any specific understanding of him as found in any one religion normative. These variations are but the culturally conditioned and culturally contributed form. We can only hold to those features of God that are found in common in all religious responses. This, however, yields a rather general understanding of God, for the variety of beliefs on particular facets of the divine nature is very great indeed.

Relationship to Other Doctrines

Because Christian theology is organic, the conclusions in one area of doctrine strongly affect those in other areas. Thus, the move toward greater generality is also found in other doctrines traditionally held by Christians.

Revelation

Revelation, for example, must be defined in such a way that it allows for the variety of responses found in the different religions. Hick recognizes that the very term "revelation" is better suited to a theistic view than that of the Eternal One as the Absolute. He is careful to define revelation in such a way that it does not involve "divinely disclosed propositions or miraculous interventions in the course of human history." This would tend to favor the claims of the religion within which these occur, being quite particular in nature. Rather, revelation should be understood as "the circumambient presence and prevenient pressure of the divine Reality."[41]

The Person of Christ

The same is true for the understanding of Christ. The traditional approach was to understand the incarnation as a literal metaphysical

---

39. Ibid., p. 51.
40. Ibid., pp. 51–52.
41. *Problems of Religious Pluralism*, pp. 97–98.

truth. Jesus, on this basis, was the unique incarnation of God, the one instance in which God was metaphysically united with a human being. If this is the case, however, then Christianity must be seen as superior to other religions. Hick takes the incarnation as metaphorical, or, as he prefers, mythological. We can speak of God as incarnated in Jesus in the same way in which we can speak of the spirit of defiance of the British people against Nazi Germany in 1940 as incarnated in Winston Churchill. Jesus was "so vividly conscious of God as the loving heavenly Father, and so startlingly open to God and so fully his servant and instrument, that the divine love was expressed, and in that sense incarnated, in his life."[42] Nor is this unique to Jesus. Hick favors the degree Christology of Donald Baillie, or the inspiration Christology of Geoffrey Lampe. The understanding of the presence and activity of God in Jesus is to be likened to the paradox of grace in the believer. But if this is the case, then the activity of God in Jesus was not qualitatively unique. And this raises the question of whether it was unique quantitatively, because of its being total and absolute. Here, however, Hick insists, we must settle the question on historical grounds, and in light of modern scholarly study of the New Testament, it is questionable whether we have enough historical data to make such a judgment. Lampe's suggestion that the incarnation of God be seen, not simply within the life of Jesus, but rather within the whole history of Christianity also fails, not because we have too little, but rather, too much, historical data.[43] The point, however, is that on either Baillie's or Lampe's Christologies, we can have an understanding of God's presence and working in Jesus' life that is not incompatible with a basic pluralism.

Salvation

In exclusive or absolutistic views of Christianity, salvation consists of a changed status in the individual's relationship to God. One who is guilty, because of one's own sin and that of Adam, becomes just or righteous by virtue of the death of Christ and the believer's participation in that death through faith in Jesus Christ. This being the case, salvation is restricted to those within the Christian community. Hick defines salvation more generally, however, as "the actual transformation of human life from self-centredness to Reality-centredness." This being the case, it is not restricted to the boundaries of any one religion.[44]

42. *God Has Many Names*, p. 58.
43. *Problems of Religious Pluralism*, p. 65.
44. Ibid., pp. 31–32.

Evaluating World Religions

With the diversity of religious beliefs and practices, is it not perhaps possible to evaluate them in terms of better or worse? Even if we grant that they are all human responses to the same pressure of the transcendent on human lives, may not some respond to this more adequately than others? It is commonplace for advocates of various religions to evaluate other religions. Indeed, frequently they evaluate the views and practices of other adherents of their own religions. How, then, shall we proceed?

Hick discusses this at some length in a chapter entitled "On Grading Religions." He notes that this is frequently done from within one religious tradition, using as criteria its own beliefs and practices. This approach cannot be followed, however, because of the two factors mentioned earlier: (1) most people are what they are because of the place and culture into which they were born; and (2) religions, once matured, have little success in converting persons from other major religions.[45] When we endeavor to evaluate, not the founders and principal teachers of world religions, but the totality of such religions, two possibilities emerge: rational or pragmatic. But there is a certain inappropriateness to testing a religion's beliefs rationally, because when examined, they are seen not to be rational constructs, but encounters with reality, powerful root experiences. Thus, the grading must be done on pragmatic grounds: "Is this complex of religious experience, belief and behaviour soteriologically effective? Does it make possible transformation of human existence from self-centredness to Reality-centredness?"[46]

Here again, however, efforts at evaluation prove unavailing. The teachings of the various religions propose ideal fruit that are largely comparable.[47] But what about the actual results produced by these religions? Here we find that each of the religions has produced beneficial results, but each has also failed to change some unfortunate situations, and in some cases, has actually contributed to human misery. Although Christians often claim that their religion has had a salutary effect on society other religions have not, that does not actually prove to be the case when concrete historical facts are examined.[48] Hick summarizes his evidence as follows: "But amidst all this untraceable detail the broad conclusion stands that, whilst we can assess religious phenomena, we cannot assess and grade religious traditions as totalities. We can, I suggest, only acknowledge, and indeed rejoice in the fact, that the Real, the Ul-

45. Ibid., pp. 70–72.
46. Ibid., p. 80.
47. Ibid., pp. 81–83.
48. Ibid., pp. 84–86.

timate, the Divine is known and responded to within each of these vast historical complexes, so that within each of them the gradual transformation of human existence from self-centredness to Reality-centredness is taking place."[49]

Analysis

Drawing out the major points of this view, we may note the following:

1. Religious epistemology is primarily concerned with experience, although in a broader sense than mere sensory experience. It is the total "experiencing-as" not merely of specific facts but of total situations, which is the basis for forming any sort of religious teachings.

2. Revelation, if it is appropriate to speak of such, is never taken in a pure or literal form and identified with some existing religious document. It is always mediated and interpreted in human experience.

3. We do not know the Supreme Reality, or God, in a direct fashion. All we know is the phenomenal, or the experience of that reality, as mediated through the total culture of which we are a part. The culture into which we are born has a very strong influence on our religious beliefs and practices, so that there is almost a 100 percent correlation between place of birth and religious alignment.

4. We cannot accept at face value the specific understandings of God in any of the world religions. There is one reality who (which) is pressing itself on all peoples. Only such elements of belief as are held in common by the several religions may be considered fully true.

5. The specific doctrines of each religion are not to be regarded as literally true, but as myths. Mythological truth means that the symbols involved in the myth have a powerful effect on the lives of those who accept them.

6. The conceptions of God found in the major religions vary greatly, but can be classified into two major groups or types: God as personal, or deity; and God as impersonal, or the Absolute.

7. There is considerable agnosticism about the details of the ultimate reality. From the Christian standpoint, only those "attributes" can be held that are common to the other great religions' conceptions of the ultimate reality.

Evaluation

Certainly, such a radical reconstruction of theology cannot be ignored. It echoes some widely held views in American and European so-

49. Ibid., p. 87.

ciety, and directly challenges much of what Christianity has traditionally held. There are some significant strengths to this approach, but also
some major problems.

Positive

1. Hick has recognized the genuine sincerity and piety of adherents
of many differing religions. He has attempted to take into account the
value of the best within those religious movements.

2. Hick recognizes that there has been conflict, even warfare, over religious beliefs and affiliations over many years of world history, and
even to the present time. To some extent, this has been the result of believing that one's own religion possessed the entire truth and nothing
but truth. Pluralism, if adopted, would logically lead to great acceptance and even appreciation for those of differing faiths.

3. Hick has recognized the effect that culture and other factors, even
geography and climate, have on the shaping of religious belief.

4. Hick has pointed out that religious experience is a powerful shaper
of doctrines, and frequently is a more potent factor in religious motivation than is intellectual belief.

5. This view fits well with the contemporary elevation of emotion
over intellect as the locus of religion.

Negative

The major problems are considerably more significant than the
strengths of this pluralistic view of God.

1. Hick has classified the various conceptions of deity into two major
types, personal and impersonal, believed to be different responses to
contact with the same basic entity or reality. The ideas of God as personal deity and of the ultimate Reality as impersonal absolute are, however, rather sharply different conceptions. It is questionable whether
they can be considered species of a common genus, or whether they are
not so radically different in nature that they must be treated as different
worldviews, alongside naturalism or materialism. For the most part,
most devotees of one type or the other would tend to regard their view
as not assimilable to the other view. This is particularly true of those
who believe in a personal deity.

2. The assimilation of all religions to one another requires a general-
izing of the beliefs of each in such a way as to become, in some cases, a
real oversimplification. Thus is seen especially in the understanding of
salvation. The shift from self-centeredness to centering on the Real or
the Eternal One, for example, has very different manifestation and
meaning, depending on the nature of the Real to which this relationship
is believed to obtain. In Christianity, for example, this is believed to in-

volve the forgiveness of sins, the declaration of a new, right standing with God through the atoning work of Jesus Christ. In Buddhism, however, this is believed to be a matter of achieving certain correct understandings and attitudes that put one at peace with the whole of reality. In Hinduism, it is a matter of being mystically united with the larger reality of which one really is a part. These are quite different understandings, as well as quite different experiences. To make them basically the same type of doctrine and experience would seem to require such a distortion as to be a less than adequate theory of the religions involved.

3. There is no real account of what might be termed revelation in this school of thought. Hick claims that the ultimate reality is exerting pressure on or contact with all persons, and that this becomes apprehended through the "experiencing-as" process. Yet there is no real explication of how this is done. One would expect some sort of theory of revelation, some explanation of the fashion in which the Eternal One does this. That is sorely missing in this view.

4. The motivation for some sort of social ethic is also largely bypassed in this theory. It is apparent that Hick aims to eliminate any sort of prejudice and ill-treatment of others by removing the conception that one religion is completely true, others are false, and therefore everyone must be converted to the one true religion. Just how the positive part is motivated is much less clear, however. Some religions urge love of one's fellow humans on the basis that we have all derived our existence from the same single reality. Others argue that these persons are creatures of the same God, made in his same image, and for whom he has provided redemption. None of these theories really is advocated by Hick, seemingly leaving a social ethic rather free-floating.

5. There is no explanation for the fact that virtually all religions regard their view of reality as the true one, or at least more correct than all the others. To be sure, this could be an erroneous conception, an error made by all religions. But if that is the case, then we have lost the one criterion that seems to be used in drawing inferences about God and other religious beliefs, namely, that they are held in common by the several religious traditions. Presumably, on this basis, they must all be wrong in thinking of their own religion in exclusivistic terms.

6. This, however, poses the further possibility that all these religions are also wrong in their belief in the ultimate reality. Perhaps they are not really laying hold on anything beyond themselves. It is questionable whether Hick has established the existence of this Real or the Eternal One. At least part of what each religion believes in is provided by projection, but perhaps it is entirely so.

7. In abstracting from the experience of the One two different types of conception, the personal and the impersonal, Hick argues that these

are not two different realities, or that the Real is of such nature that personal and impersonal both apply.[50] Yet why hold that there is one Real to which all are responding, rather than two or more? Hick says that the latter possibility cannot be ruled out a priori, but contends that these would not then be ultimate in nature. The reasons for not holding such are the difficulties of relating a multiplicity of such realities to the different geographical regions in which they are believed in and worshiped. This, however, hardly suffices as a reply. Perhaps we simply must say that there are multiple realities, or at least two different kinds of reality.[51]

---

50. *A Christian Theology of Religion: The Rainbow of Faiths* (Louisville: Westminster/John Knox, 1995), p. 61.

51. Ibid., pp. 69–71.

3

Process Thought

In process thought we see an attempt to build a genuine natural theology. John Cobb contends that even those theologies that explicitly repudiate natural theology actually have assumptions or have developed implications that should be recognized as belonging to the realm of natural theology. They simply do not recognize this fact or consciously address the issues involved. Those who are doing natural theology are doing so within a distinctively Christian theological context. Cobb also notes that many of the problems with which theologians are wrestling "arise out of assumptions formed for them by more or less consciously accepted ideas of a philosophical sort."[1] In light of this fact, he believes it is essential that such assumptions be addressed by critical and self-conscious reflection on them. This can be done only by dealing with the task of natural theology directly.[2] In short, he would contend that it is both necessary and possible to engage in this type of endeavor.

Process Metaphysics

The Necessity of Metaphysics

Even the breakdown of the great rational synthesis of the modern period does not deter process theologians from their metaphysical task. David Ray Griffin has been a leader in the examination of postmodernism, even editing a series of landmark volumes studying the phenomenon. He contends that there are several types of postmodern theology,

1. John Cobb, *A Christian Natural Theology Based on the Thought of Alfred North Whitehead* (Philadelphia: Westminster, 1965).
2. Ibid., pp. 11–13.

one of which he terms constructive postmodernism. This theology attempts to construct a valid metaphysic, employing different categories than those used in traditional or classical metaphysics. Griffin believes that, deconstructionists notwithstanding, this is possible and mandatory. Even where theoretically or verbally there is denial that there are any shared values or truths, nonetheless in practice there remains a common shared content. Some of these commonsense notions that prevent complete relativism are the convictions of personal freedom, the necessary distinction between better and worse, the existence of an outer world, and something of a correspondence theory of truth. It is not possible to dismiss all "inherited notions" as culturally conditioned. Some must be seen as "hard-core commonsense notions" presupposed by all cultures. Griffin asserts that "until someone can think consistently without presupposing these ideas, we have every reason to assume that these notions are universally presupposed. . . . By taking the hard-core common sense notions as the ultimate criteria, we can move toward a world view in which the inconsistency as well as inadequacy to the facts of experience can be progressively overcome."[3] On the basis of these hard-core commonsense notions, he intends to construct his natural theology.

Metaphysics and the Restoration of Meaning

It is the effort to construct an understanding of reality, specifically of God, which motivates the work of the process theologians. In the judgment of thinkers such as John Cobb, for large segments of the current population the Christian message does not seem to be a viable option because the categories in which that message has traditionally been conveyed have ceased to have any real meaning. This is more than just the perennial problem of translating the concepts of theology into everyday language and thought. The difficulty lies especially with the concept of God. Cobb says, "For much of the culture that is growing up about us and within us, 'God' has become an empty sound."[4] This problem is not simply one for Christians trying to communicate with the intelligentsia. It is also problematic for the suburban pastor trying to deal with youth and leaders in his church. Yet the problem is even more intense and serious: "Perhaps most of all it has become the problem of the perceptive minister in dealing with himself and his own understanding of his ministry."[5] Earlier, Charles Hartshorne had stated a similar concern: "The question considered in these lectures was not, Does the God

3. David Ray Griffin, "Postmodern Theology and A/Theology," in *Varieties of Postmodern Theology*, ed. David Ray Griffin (Albany: State University of New York Press, 1989), p. 31.
4. Cobb, *Christian Natural Theology*, p. 13.
5. Ibid.

of religion exist? but rather, What can most reasonably be meant by the religious term 'God'?"[6]

In Cobb's judgment, the loss of meaning came not from the content of faith, but from "that cosmology which has destroyed the horizons within which early Christian, medieval, and early modern man understood his existence."[7] If meaning is to be restored to the term "God," there must be consideration of these destructive forces, as well as continuation of the proclamation and the theology that rests on its meaningfulness. Thus, whereas process theology appears to the orthodox to be a serious threat to belief in God, at least as they understand it, in reality the process theologians see their contribution as a properly apologetic one, enabling contemporary humans to understand and believe in God in the midst of a radically changed cultural situation.

Process theology attempts to build a genuine metaphysic by rejecting two major twentieth-century trends, one in philosophy and one in theology. On the one hand, analytical philosophy thought metaphysics to be unattainable. On the other hand, theology of a generally neo-orthodox vein contended that the use of any sort of philosophical conceptuality is improper, since it imposes foreign categories upon what should be basically a biblical enterprise, and so distorts the theology. Yet, in the judgment of process theologians, both objecting alternatives contain hidden metaphysical views of their own. It is not to the grand metaphysical schemes of the past that the process theologians plan to return, however. It is a more modest metaphysic, in a new mode, which begins with concrete human experience and seeks simply to form a suitable and useful "vision of reality."[8]

Actual Occasions and Experience

In one sense, this can be said to be an experience-based theology, although it would perhaps be too narrow to term it an empirical theology. It encompasses the whole of human experience. One part involves an analysis of the concrete human experience of consciousness as a clue to the nature of the entirety of reality. To understand this, we must first understand the process view of human experience. While it has been common to think of this as a continuous flow, it should rather be thought of as a successive sequence of discrete and indivisible units, which Whitehead calls "actual occasions" or "occasions of experience."[9] These suc-

6. Charles Hartshorne, *The Divine Relativity: A Social Conception of God* (New Haven, Conn.: Yale University Press, 1964), p. v.

7. Cobb, *Christian Natural Theology*, p. 15.

8. Norman Pittenger, "Process Thought as a Conceptuality for Reinterpreting Christian Faith," *Encounter* 44.2 (Spring 1983): 110.

9. Alfred North Whitehead, *Process and Reality: An Essay in Cosmology* (New York: Harper & Row, 1960), pp. 33, 113.

ceed each other with a rapidity that escapes conscious attention, so that no single conscious occasion can be examined per se. We can, however, observe the characteristics of the entire flow and assume that the quality of the whole is also that of the individual occasion.[10] The one exception is change. An individual occasion does not exhibit change, which is a mark of the difference between one such occasion and the preceding one.[11] The characteristics of actual occasions will give us, then, the clue to the nature of reality in general.

In some ways Whitehead's treatment resembles that of Husserl's phenomenology. It also bears resemblance to Immanuel Kant's *Critique of Pure Reason*. Whitehead examines the nature of a concrete sensory experience. One major component is the sense data entering one's consciousness. Whitehead terms this the "physical pole" of the actual occasion.[12] Beyond that, however, there must be another element. For a sense experience to be more than just white, red, and brown blotches, for it to be experienced as a house, for example, requires something additional. Somehow the mind of the person takes the manifold sense data, forms them into the idea of an entity, and projects it back into that sensory location from which the sense data came. Therefore, to what the senses contribute is what the subject of the experience contributes to that experience. This may be termed the mental pole.[13] Part of what is brought to the experience is the content of numerous past experiences. There are also what Whitehead terms "eternal objects."[14] These are forms, qualities, and relations, abstracted from any concrete instance of them. They are pure possibilities for realization, apart from any specific occasion of such realization. In many ways, these resemble Plato's Forms or Ideas. Such eternal objects, independent of any concrete instance of them, Whitehead terms "conceptual prehensions," just as physical prehensions constitute the physical pole of the actual occasion.[15] An actual occasion is the combination of certain of these eternal objects, constituting the mental pole, and the physical pole of a physical prehension. It is important to understand that, for Whitehead, the eternal objects are not actual entities as are actual occasions. Rather, they are merely potentialities.

Actual Occasions and Modern Science

There is another factor in this analysis of experience or entity, however. There is some purpose the experiencer has in all of this, some goal

10. Cobb, *A Christian Natural Theology*, p. 29.
11. *Process and Reality*, pp. 52, 92.
12. Ibid., p. 49.
13. Ibid., p. 165.
14. Ibid., pp. 69–70.
15. Ibid., pp. 35, 49.

that is valued and sought. Whitehead refers to this as "subjective aim," and believes that it is present in every actual occasion.[16] It is natural for us to think of these events or occasions or experiences as those of human beings, with whom we can identify. In such cases, they are what in one sense we would call conscious experiences. It is important, however, in seeking to understand Whitehead's thought, to bear in mind that occasions or experiences are not limited simply to humans. These human experiences are a clue to the nature of the whole of reality. In experience in general we find such a pattern as well.

Here is a second aspect of the argument for this general metaphysical view. The first is that this description fits well with the nature of the human experience of the actual occasion. The second, however, is that this understanding of an actual entity also provides a good explanation of the nature of scientific data. An even prior question is that of the traditional body-mind or body-soul or material-immaterial relationship. There are three possible solutions to this puzzle. One is that matter is to be understood as an appearance to the mind. That was the position of subjective idealists, such as George Berkeley, who held that there really are no external physical objects, only our impressions or mental experiences of them. Such a view, Cobb contends, is philosophically plausible but common sense and the science of the seventeenth, eighteenth, and nineteenth centuries ignored it. The second approach is to say that matter alone is real, and that mind is but a product or emergence from it. Mind, in other words, is epiphenomenal. This, however, has proven unacceptable as well, for mental experience still seems to exist and to be important to us as humans. This leaves the third alternative: to subsume both aspects of reality under some more comprehensive unity. Cobb says: "This might mean that some kind of reality underlies our subjective mental states as well as that which seems objective to them; it might mean that all reality participates in both mentality and materiality without being either. This attempt to find a single type of reality explanatory of both what we call mind and what we call matter has taken many forms. Whitehead's philosophy is one of them."[17]

Cobb believes that developments in the physical sciences in the twentieth century have contributed to this third understanding, especially to the cogency of Whitehead's form of it. As long as atoms were thought of as the ultimate stuff of the universe, the concept of matter seemed appropriate, and the second view noted above seemed especially persuasive. Atoms seemed to be very small lumps of solid material, having def-

16. Ibid., pp. 37, 130.
17. Cobb, *Christian Natural Theology*, pp. 24–25.

inite location and moving continuously through space. Mechanical models could be used for understanding them.[18]

When, however, the understanding of atoms began to change, problems arose for a view like this. Atoms were discovered not to be the ultimate components of reality, but composed of electrons, protons, and "empty space." At first the attempt was made to understand these as simply smaller material particles, but while they at times behaved like this, at other times their behavior fit better with the conception of them as waves. This same duality of phenomena had also been noted of light. Further, however, these supposed ultimate entities of the world seemed to be able to move from one point to another without passing through intervening space. Also it became clear that electrons and protons are not things, capable of carrying electrical charges, but are themselves electric charges. As Cobb puts it, "It seemed that something happens now here, then there, with definite connection between one event and the next, but without continuous movement between them. Things happen in bursts or jerks rather than in an even flow."[19] As an analogy of this understanding of reality, he offers the conception of a motion picture, in which there seems to be continuous movement, but in reality there is merely a succession of discontinuous still pictures.

These new discoveries of twentieth-century physics proved puzzling to scientists and even more so to philosophers. Many scientists gave up the idea that the human mind can frame any notion regarding the nature of things, at least to form images or pictures of it. Theories were advanced that were quite counterintuitive, but which succeeded in explaining and predicting the results of experiences. In Cobb's judgment, many philosophers gave up the attempt to answer the questions philosophy had traditionally sought to answer, turning their attention instead to language analysis. Others, however, "refused to acknowledge the ultimate unintelligibility of the universe." They sought to construct new models by which to understand it in light of these puzzling characteristics. If the older metaphysics had been tied to Newtonian and earlier physics, this was an attempt to construct a metaphysics genuinely compatible with Einsteinian physics.[20]

Actual Occasions and "Freedom"

We have noted that each actual occasion, in terms of human experience, includes both a physical pole and a mental pole, both a physical prehension and a conceptual prehension, plus some sense of fulfilling

18. Ibid., p. 25.
19. Ibid., p. 26.
20. Ibid.

the subjective aim. Although the past provides a real determination, that is not absolute. There is still a degree of what we could call "freedom." The same is true on the subatomic level, where there appears to be an element of the spontaneous, the random, which has been identified in terms of Heisenberg's principle of indeterminacy. According to Whitehead, there is some degree of self-determination in all occasions. Sometimes this freedom is employed simply to reenact the past, but at other times a greater degree of the unpredictable is involved. While, therefore, it is not possible to predict the action of any given electron, there is a certain predictability to the action of groups of these.[21]

What we often refer to as entities, namely, objects and persons, are not so in Whitehead's philosophy. Entities are not things but occurrences. What about the apparent continuity of certain series of actual occasions, or the statistical predictability of groups of electrons or persons? What is the basis of the connection or continuity of series of actual occasions? Here Whitehead introduces the concept of "societies of actual occasions." We are not really conscious of individual or actual occasions, but of entities that are groupings of occasions. Any group of occasions tied together by any real interconnectedness at all is called a nexus.[22] When we find a collection of occasions that have a high degree of connection and persistence, we may speak of a society of occasions.[23] An example would be a molecule, which we may identify as having a certain set of characteristics over a long period of time. While on Whitehead's view these are simply molecular happenings or occasions, we must still account for the fact of a special connection between such occasions. We may identify this connected sequence as an "enduring object," which is a society of actual occasions that are temporally contiguous and successive.[24] Cobb describes this situation: "In such a society no two occasions exist at the same time, but at each moment one such occasion occurs, prehending all the preceding occasions in the society, reenacting the defining characteristic of the society, and mediating this pattern to its successors."[25]

The Doctrine of God

The doctrine of God follows from this metaphysic by virtue of God being part of the whole of reality and subject to its conditions. The pro-

21. Ibid., p. 39.
22. *Adventures of Ideas* (New York: Macmillan, 1933), p. 258.
23. Ibid., p. 261.
24. Ibid., pp. 51–52.
25. Cobb, *Christian Natural Theology*, p. 41.

cess doctrine of God will be a thoroughly philosophical theology. The approach is quite different in some ways, however, from the usual approach of philosophers of religion. They often advanced arguments for the existence of God, correlated with their own type of philosophy, frequently that of Thomism. Cobb and Griffin contend that process theologians have not utilized arguments for God's existence, as those are usually understood. Rather, they have developed a philosophical framework within which God's existence made good sense and was even required. They observe that Whitehead's principle of concretion was required to explain the "ordered novelty and novel order" in the world, but confess that "his reasons for affirming God are convincing within the context of his total analysis, but they lose their force if formulated outside his own system of thought."[26]

Rejection of Classical Theism

We observed earlier that process theologians do not see themselves as undermining belief in God, but, on the contrary, making it genuinely possible. Nonetheless, process philosophy has presented a strong challenge to the traditional or classical Christian view of God. This can be seen both in the specific theology, process theology, which it has spawned, and in the impact made on various classical elements of the doctrine of God by its challenge to those elements. That this is indeed the case can be seen in the summary by David Griffin and John Cobb of views of God or aspects of his nature that process theology rejects.[27]

1. God as cosmic moralist. This may take varying forms, all of which are unacceptable to the process theist. The worst variety is the picture of God as a divine lawgiver and judge, who has set forth a collection of moral rules arbitrarily defined by him. He keeps a record of human beings' conformity or nonconformity to these rules, and rewards and punishes people accordingly. A more enlightened version is a god whose most fundamental concern is the fostering of moral attitudes.

2. God as unchanging and passionless absolute. This concept of God as completely unchanging, unaffected by anything external to himself and without any passion or emotion, derives from Greek thought. It has, however, played a prominent part in much classic theology. On this conception, the world is totally dependent on God and wholly external to him. Yet he is completely independent of it, being utterly unaffected by anything that occurs in it.

---

26. John B. Cobb and David Ray Griffin, *Process Theology: An Introductory Exposition* (Philadelphia: Westminster, 1976), p. 42.

27. Ibid., pp. 8–10.

3. God as controlling power. This is the idea that God is in absolute control of the world, determining every detail of what occurs within it. This is reflected in the conception that God has taken the life of a person who dies, or spared one who is delivered from a situation of danger. Process theology, however, asks what kind of God it is that favors one person over another in dispensing the circumstances of life.

4. God as sanctioner of the status quo. This is the idea that God is primarily interested in order. If God is the controlling power, then what is, is because he has brought it about. Therefore, obedience to God requires preserving the status quo.

5. God as male. Not only are the members of the Trinity regarded as male, but God is totally independent, powerful, and unresponsive. This dominant, inflexible, unemotional God is the archetype of the "strong" male.

Of each of these views, Cobb and Griffin say, "Process theology denies the existence of this God." Whether all of these qualities inhere in the orthodox understanding of God, it is clear that at least some of them do. There is therefore clearly a conflict between process theology's view of God and that of traditional or orthodox theology.

Hartshorne is similarly emphatic in his rejection of traditional theism. This comes out quite clearly, for example, in his discussion of the theistic proofs. Here he says, "I am convinced that 'classical theism' (as much Greek as Christian, Jewish, or Islamic) was an incorrect translation of the central religious idea into philosophical categories, and that consequently the failure of the classical proofs which accompanied that mistranslation is like the blowing up of the bridges on a route which at best was a detour and at worst led simply in the wrong direction."[28]

God as Creative-Responsive Love

The basic concept of God is that of creative-responsive love. Process theologians see their view as in contrast to and superior to the orthodox or classical view of God. On that view, God was beyond time and beyond any need of humans. He is totally unmoved by anything in their situation—impassible. Independence or absoluteness are, for the classical theist, positive qualities, while dependence or relativity are thought of as negative qualities. Since God is considered perfect, he must not possess this dependence or relativity.

Certainly, say the process theologians, there must be senses in which God is independent, and in which independence is admirable.[29] God must be ethically independent, for example, not deflected from his

28. Hartshorne, *Divine Relativity,* p. vii.
29. Ibid., pp. 47, 44.

commitment to do good by any passion. For such an ethical commitment, however, to be actualized in concrete situations requires respon-
siveness to the needs of others. What parent, for example, would be
considered noble who remained blissfully undisturbed while his or her
child was in agony? There is an admirable sense of absoluteness and
an admirable sense of relativism, and the god of process theism possesses both, not just the absoluteness characteristic of the god of classical theism.

God as Dipolar

As we noted earlier, in process metaphysics every concrete occurrence has both an eternal and a temporal pole. So, too, God has two
poles or aspects—his abstract essence and his concrete actuality. The
former is eternal, absolute, independent, and unchangeable. Included
here are such abstract attributes as omniscience. This means that at
any given point in time God knows everything it is possible to know at
that time. The concrete actuality of God, on the other hand, is contingent, dependent, temporal, relative, and in a constant state of change.
Here at any given point in God's life there are new and unforeseen occurrences, which only become known by him at that time. His knowledge depends on the decisions and actions of individuals within the
world. Thus, he is in this sense relative. His knowledge is a consequent
knowledge. This is what is meant by saying that God, according to process theology, is dipolar. Whereas classical theism thinks of God as having only one pole, the absolute and eternal, this theology conceives of
him as having two poles. Although the language used by Whitehead and
Hartshorne is somewhat different, they are asserting basically the same
thing about God. Whitehead speaks of the Primordial Nature and the
Consequent Nature of God, whereas Hartshorne's terms are the abstract essence and the concrete actuality.[30]

This characterization might be understood as God's knowledge
being merely a passive or indifferent cognition. It is, however, far more
than that. God not only knows the actions of concrete occurrences in
the world; he is also affected by them. He feels sympathy for the beings
in the world, all of whom have feelings. Thus, God is not merely dependent on the world and the actions of its inhabitants intellectually, but
also emotionally. He is acted on and reacts to the actions of concrete
occurrences.

This means, however, that God changes. For if one depends on others
emotionally through sympathy, then one changes when they change.
When these others grow in joy, so does God. This has seemed to some

30. Ibid., pp. 82–83.

theologians to indicate an imperfection of some kind in God, for it is thought that all change must be change either for the worse or for the better. If the former, then how can we admire God? If the latter, then God would seem to have lacked something, and thus to have been imperfect. Yet, Hartshorne defines perfect as completely worthy of admiration and respect, and so we do not admire a man less because he would be happier if his son who is wretched became happier. We do not admire the amount but the appropriateness of one's joy.[31]

God's Intentions for the World

A further important facet of the process view of God is the way he works in the world. As we noted, process theologians hold that God gives the initial aim to every concrete occurrence or actuality. This initial aim is defined by Cobb and Griffin as "an impulse, initially felt conformally by the occasion, to actualize the best possibility open to it, given its concrete situation."[32] The subject does not necessarily make this initial aim its own. Rather, it chooses its own "subjective aim." It may choose to actualize the initial aim, or one of the other numerous options open to it. What, then, is the role of God in this continuing eventuation of the concrete occasion? In traditional orthodoxy, God was the master in control of everything. He determined and knew the future in complete detail. This is most certainly not the process view of God's working. He certainly desires that each concrete occasion choose and actualize the initial aim he has given it, but he does not work coercively. While he seeks to persuade each occasion to actualize what would be best for it, he cannot control what it chooses and does. This means that there is a certain amount of risk in God's relationship to the world. As Cobb and Griffin put it, "the obvious point is that, since God is not in complete control of the events of the world, the occurrence of genuine evil is not incompatible with God's beneficence toward all his creatures."[33]

One final point is to note the nature of the good that God intends for his creatures. Traditional or classical theism pictured God as primarily concerned with the development of moral behavior and attitudes in human beings. Creaturely enjoyment was not, to say the least, his primary objective. At best he tolerated it, and at worst he was opposed to it. In the minds of process theologians, however, this put Christianity on the other side of the issue from Christ, who was accused of being a glutton and a drunkard (Matt. 11:19; Luke 7:34) and who said that he had

31. Ibid., pp. 45–46.
32. Cobb and Griffin, *Process Theology*, p. 53.
33. Ibid.

come to give life and to give it abundantly (John 10:10). The church, however, does not seem to promote enjoyment of the abundant life, but discourages most forms of enjoyment in favor of "being good." God has been understood as forbidding the desire of most experiences that people find intrinsically good in favor of being morally good. Moral goodness has been defined in negative terms as primarily involving the suppression of many natural forms of enjoyment.[34]

Process theology's understanding of God's concerns and activities is quite different. Cobb and Griffin put it very succinctly: "Process theology sees God's fundamental aim to be the promotion of the creatures' own enjoyment."[35] His creative influence aims at promoting what creatures experience as intrinsically good. This concern is for all creatures, not simply human creatures. The contrary view, that God's concern is for the morally good, means that the vast majority of history was given to preparing for beings who alone are capable of moral experience, the only kind of experience that really interests God.[36]

Does not this sort of concern, however, conflict with any emphasis on morality? Not so, says process theology. God wants everyone to experience enjoyment. Negatively, that means that we are to enjoy in such a way as not to prevent others' enjoyment. Positively, it means that our enjoyment is to increase others' enjoyment. There is a potential conflict between morality and enjoyment, such as between present enjoyment and future enjoyment, and between my own future enjoyment and that of others, but there are resolutions for such tensions.[37]

Evaluation

Having examined both the positive view of God held by the process theologians and the challenge they present to the orthodox view, let us now attempt some evaluation of this view, both positive and negative.

Positive

1. In process theology, we see a genuine attempt to construct a metaphysic. Metaphysics has suffered much of this century, at the hands of both analytical philosophy and neoorthodox theology. Yet theology of almost any type that holds to the reality of God and of human beings contains at least an implicit metaphysic. In the long run, this metaphysic must be worked out self-consciously and be justified. Except for

34. Ibid., p. 55.
35. Ibid., p. 56.
36. Ibid.
37. Ibid., p. 57.

a few Thomists, there had not been much effort by theologians to do so until the advent of process theology. Whether we agree with the conclusions of these theologians, we must commend their efforts.

2. Process theologians have correctly pointed out that at times theology has been so strongly influenced by Greek philosophy, particularly Aristotelianism, that the biblical tradition has been distorted. This is seen particularly in the doctrine of impassibility and some views of divine unchangeability. As such, process theology has performed an important prophetic role in purifying that tradition.

3. Process theology has reminded us of the necessity of logic and of objective truth if thought and communication are to take place. This is an important criticism of current subjective ideologies, such as deconstruction. This has formed part of Griffin's argumentation for the justification of this constructive metaphysic.

4. Process theologians have pointed out (correctly) that while we may well be seeing the demise of many features of the modern ideological synthesis, there may be more than one possible response. Thus, there may well be constructive, rather than destructive, postmodern theologies.

5. These theologians have taken seriously the existence of other, non-Christian, theologies. These are seen as drawing on the same set of natural data as Christianity, and thus not necessarily being totally in error. As such, the potential for a point of contact and genuine dialogue is justified.

6. Process theologians have endeavored to be genuinely contemporary in doing their theology. This means using categories that persons living and thinking in the present understand. This is part of the genuinely apologetic thrust of process theology, of attempting to make belief in God both intelligible and potentially acceptable to present-day humans.

7. Process theologians have sought to understand current physicists' conceptions of the nature of reality, and to build theology in conformity with this. They have realized that some understandings of God have been so tied to a Newtonian understanding of reality that they stood little chance of being accepted by those who are current in their understanding.

Negative

Despite these very commendable features of process theology, there are several defects in this theology, which in my judgment are considerably more significant than its strengths. These will consequently be developed at greater length than the discussion of the positive features of process theology.

1. Process thought rejects the idea of any sort of underlying substance that is the source of identity and continuity of any entity, and to which possibly changing attributes or accidents may attach. Instead,

there is a series of events that constitute the life history of anything or anyone. These succeed one another in some sort of connection, but there really is no "something" that persists throughout all this change. The process thinkers want to insist that there is an identity of a given occasion that is somehow transmitted to the next occasion, as the first perishes and the new arises. What is the nature of this transmission, however? As Royce Gruenler puts it, "no one in the process school has ever given a satisfactory account of how one occasion that perishes passes on its identity to the new occasion that succeeds it."[38]

This presents some serious questions when applied to human individuals. In what sense can I say that I am the same person I was twenty years ago, or even five seconds ago? What is the thread that connects the series of events that makes them *a* series? Why not simply say that these are unrelated happenings? On what basis can I say that I am the same person, not some other person who happens to think he has memories of his earlier existence? This is not to say that process theology cannot give an answer to this question. It is merely to say that it cannot appeal to the usual sources or guarantors of identity and continuity, and that it does not seem to have submitted a satisfactory answer thus far.

The same problem applies to God in this scheme of theology. What is the connection between these experiences or events in God's life? The answer, of course, is that one moment prehends other earlier events in God's life. The difficulty with this answer, however, is that there are other events, not claimed to be part of God's experience, which also prehend these past occurrences. Just what is the difference between the way these prehend the past events, and the way God's present prehends his past? On both the human and the divine levels, this is a problem needing attention.

2. There also is a major problem with how God can be actively related to all the events in this world. He must do this, for he is the one who supplies the initial aim to each and who continues to work by luring each of these to fulfill that initial aim. This, however, requires him to be constantly active everywhere within the creation.

How can this be, however? God is very much a part of the whole, obeying the same laws as does the rest of this creation. Being thoroughly immanent, this leaves us with the conclusion that God's ability to travel throughout the creation is restricted to the speed of light, as is everything else. But if this is the case, then how can he possibly be thus involved throughout the universe at the same time, in such a way as to be always "luring" everything?

38. Royce Gruenler, "Reflections on a Journey in Process," in *Process Theology*, ed. Ronald H. Nash (Grand Rapids: Baker, 1987), p. 341.

In the orthodox view, God was omnipresent, able to be everywhere at once. This was in part a function of his immanence, so that he was within everything, but also of his transcendence, in this case, to time and space, so that he was not limited to any one spot. He could be literally active at all places at the same time. In the analogy of cybernetics, he was understood as being like a computer with an infinite number of microprocessors, each of which could be running a different program simultaneously.

On this analogy, however, the process understanding of God makes him more like a computer that is multi-tasking. It has a single microprocessor that is simultaneously attempting to run several programs. In a sense, however, the simultaneity is not strictly literal. The computer runs all the programs roughly at the same time, but what it actually does is to switch back and forth among the programs rapidly. This is much slower than having an individual microprocessor dedicated to each of these programs, however, because there is not instantaneous switching, and when operating one program, the computer cannot be giving itself to another. This is like the process model of God. He cannot simultaneously give his attention and activity to every event. He must itinerate among them, and the practical limitation placed on the efficiency of his doing this is the speed of light. This, great though it be, is of course not infinite.

3. There is a lack of consciousness or at least acknowledgment of some of the basic controlling presuppositions. Certain features of the orthodox understanding of God are quite unacceptable to process theologians, as indicated by Griffin and Cobb's statement of the kind of God they rejected. The idea of an all-controlling, seemingly arbitrary God is quite anathema to them. Why is this, however? Underlying much of the objection, and thus much of the motivation for the contrary construction, is a strong belief in human freedom of a certain type and the necessity of formulating the understanding of God in such a way as not to conflict with this. But just what is this freedom? What is its relationship to determining or at least inclining factors, either in our past or in the present environment? It appears that a basically existentialist understanding of humanity is operating here. There must be freedom from any sort of undue influence by God, any suggestion that God may be determining the future, including my thoughts, feelings, choices, and actions. There certainly must not be coercion.

This idea of freedom is so crucial that Gruenler identifies the process theologians' effort as more an anthropodicy than a theodicy.[39] Hart-

---

39. Royce Gruenler, *The Inexhaustible God: Biblical Faith and the Challenge of Process Theism* (Grand Rapids: Baker, 1983), p. 31.

shorne identifies three criteria by which a conception of God either stands or falls. It must be free of logical contradiction; must appeal to an enlightened person; and must be of such a nature that such an enlightened person can judge him to be worthy of worship and service with the whole heart and mind.[40] Much, of course, hinges on the definition and identification of this enlightened person, who remains unspecified in Hartshorne's thought. Gruenler, however, claims that this is basically the Enlightenment ideal.

This conception of human nature, and of the exact nature of this basic freedom, deserves considerable elaboration and argumentation. It is fine to contend, as these process thinkers do, that classical theism has been influenced by Greek thought. There should, however, be similar acknowledgment of the sources of their own thought. To be sure, they would maintain that this has been done, and that their philosophy is designed to conform to the current understandings in science. Even the interpretation, adaptation, and application of these concepts, however, are influenced by these more philosophical and generally cultural presuppositions.

4. This leads us to a further problem: the ambiguity regarding the exact relationship between divine and human activity. The process theologians have insisted throughout that God works in strictly limited ways to bring about his objectives in human persons. He does this in two ways: by providing each such occasion with an initial aim, and by seeking to "lure" persons to make this initial aim their own subjective aim. Just what is the extent of this activity, however? To what degree is the initiative really that of the individual person, and to what extent is it that of God? These questions are not really addressed, but are highly important to the entire system. The vagueness regarding the nature and extent of human freedom is paralleled by a similar vagueness about the divine working in relationship to these human agents.

5. This leads to yet another problem. If God always works in such a way as to influence but never to determine or guarantee human response, what assurance is there of the outcome of the perpetual struggle between the forces of good and evil? The answer is that there is not, and cannot be, any such assurance. It may be that more persons will use their freedom to actualize bad ends and to reject the initial aim that God has given them than will use that freedom in the divinely desired, positive way.

We should note that on the surface of it, this is merely a pragmatic, not a logical, objection. It could even be called a religious problem. For if there is no assurance of the ultimate triumph of good over evil, then

40. Hartshorne, *Divine Relativity*, p. 149.

we really cannot have strong hope and confidence in that future. This in itself is a significant problem, of course. It should be noted, however, that one of Hartshorne's criteria for adequacy and acceptability of an understanding of God is that it call forth an enlightened person's full worship and service with his or her entire heart and mind. Can this limited God, who may lose the battle with evil, really evoke such a response, however? This seems unlikely. Such a God may deserve our sympathy, perhaps even our pity, our support and assistance, our respect, but hardly our full worship and service. For if this God who embodies good ideals is ultimately vanquished by the forces of evil, just what justifies those positive values, and why give oneself to the pursuit and advancement of them?

The word "process" gives an aura of progress to the whole scheme, for it stems from the same root as "proceed." Yet that ethos may not be justified by the outcome of history, and cannot be logically derived from the conception of the nature of the process.

6. Much of the force and appeal of this theology comes from its depiction of classical theism, with its impassive and uninvolved God. There is a natural desire to consider an alternative to such a view. It appears that the picture that has been drawn, however, is at best somewhat inaccurate and at worst an actual caricature. The theology described is actually classical Thomism, which represents one of the major and most influential theological syntheses in the history of Christian thought. Yet a rather large number of contemporary conservative theologians distance themselves from this view, acknowledging its indebtedness to Greek philosophy. An example of this would be Ronald Nash's *The Concept of God*, in which he contrasts and criticizes both Thomism and process theology, and then distinguishes his own orthodox view from both.[41] Thus process theology has been made more appealing by presenting it as the only real alternative to a rather extreme view.

7. A dilemma is present here with respect to Scripture. On the one hand, there is a claim that this view of God ultimately comports better with Scripture than does the classical view. Yet, when looked at closely, not only does this view of God seem very difficult to harmonize with Scripture, but it leads to other conceptions that at best involve distortion of the biblical witness. The choice of either alternative will alleviate the difficulty, but such a choice must be made, or at least the nature of the option chosen must be carefully elaborated.

8. The God described here turns out, in the final analysis, to be an impersonal God. He (if that pronoun can properly be used here) emerges

---

41. Ronald H. Nash, *The Concept of God: An Exploration of Contemporary Difficulties with the Attributes of God* (Grand Rapids: Zondervan, 1983), pp. 19–36, 113–15.

as more a metaphysical principle or force than a person with whom one can have some sort of communion. Again we look back to Hartshorne's criterion of ability to evoke complete worship and service. This type of God, who is actually something like the principle of concretion, can hardly fill that description.

This problem then contributes to the loss of the distinctiveness of this God. Process theologians are increasingly open to Theravada Buddhism, with its explanation of reality in terms of skeins of experience that come and go. Here again we must ask whether such a metaphysical reality can evoke that desired sort of commitment. It may well be that such is the case, but note that there is apparently a generic difference between the nature of this religious experience and that of the dominant tradition within Christianity throughout its history. Perhaps what has happened is that the adoption of process categories by Christian theologians has led to the transformation of that theology into Buddhism.

9. Finally, there is no real hope for individual personal immortality in this theology. Since each finite occasion perishes in passing over into the next occasion, there is the problem of identity within this life, and that problem becomes more severe with the cessation of ordinary life. There is no entity to survive death. There are only experiences to be passed on to other occasions, as they prehend the past. If there is any sort of immortality, it is that each occasion in some sense survives in the others. Yet that is scarcely basis for a real hope, and without hope, as Viktor Frankl pointed out, there is no real continuing basis for life either.[42]

---

42. Viktor E. Frankl, *Man's Search for Meaning: An Introduction to Logotherapy* (New York: Washington Square, 1959).

4

Free Will Theism

Recently a cluster of theologians, while continuing to refer to themselves as evangelical, have introduced a conception of God that significantly modifies the traditional view of God. While no official designation has really been assigned to them, these men most frequently refer to themselves as "free will theists" and to their view as "the open view of God." Each comes from an Arminian background, and the theology represents the extension of a major tenet of Arminianism: human free will. It is most fully presented and argued for in the symposium, *The Openness of God*, by its major proponents.[1] Clark Pinnock, probably the best-known member of the group, teaches theology at McMaster Divinity College, Hamilton, Ontario, a Baptist Federation of Eastern Canada school. Richard Rice is professor of theology at La Sierra University, Riverside, California, a Seventh-Day Adventist school. John Sanders is instructor in theology and philosophy at Oak Hills Bible College, a nondenominational institution in Bemidji, Minnesota. William Hasker is professor of philosophy at Huntington College, Huntington, Indiana, a school of the Brethren in Christ. David Basinger is professor of philosophy at Roberts Wesleyan College, Rochester, New York, a school of the Wesleyan Church. In addition to the major work mentioned, two other books, *God's Foreknowledge and Man's Free Will*[2] by Rice and *God, Time, and Knowledge* by Hasker argue for specifics of the doctrine of God.

1. Clark Pinnock, Richard Rice, John Sanders, William Hasker, and David Basinger, *The Openness of God: A Biblical Challenge to the Traditional Understanding of God* (Downers Grove: InterVarsity, 1994).
2. Richard Rice, *God's Foreknowledge and Man's Free Will* (Minneapolis: Bethany, 1985). The title of the original edition was *The Openness of God*.

Several other articles and book chapters by these men supplement their more systematic treatise.[3]

There are others who hold and have advocated a basically similar view of God in print. The view held by Paul Fiddes, a Baptist teaching at Regents Park College, Oxford, is similar to that of the openness theologians.[4] One who quite openly espouses the process understanding of reality is Gregory Boyd, professor of theology at Bethel College, a Baptist General Conference school in St. Paul, Minnesota.[5] Another who also attempts to build theology on a process basis is Stephen Franklin, former professor of theology at Wheaton College.[6] Basinger lists Gary Friesen of Multnomah College[7] as one whose view of God's will agrees with that of John Sanders as more open than the other free will theists.[8]

In the preface to *The Openness of God*, the authors indicate their reasons for writing the book. The first is because of the centrality of the doctrine of God, which greatly influences all the other doctrines of Christian theology. It also has significant implications for the various areas of practical Christian living. Second, for many Christians there is an inconsistency between doctrinal beliefs and the practice of the Christian life. They may believe that God does not change his mind, yet pray in a way that seems to require him to do just that, or they use the free will answer to the problem of evil but pray that God will override the free will of others. These theologians desire to see an integration between doctrinal theory and devotional practice. Third, while this view has been held and discussed on the scholarly level, they believe that it deserves to be expounded in a more accessible form than the technical theological and philosophical journals. Finally, two views of God, the

3. E.g., David Basinger, "Divine Power: Do Process Theists Have a Better Idea?" in *Process Theology*, ed. Ronald Nash (Grand Rapids: Baker, 1987), pp. 210–13; Clark Pinnock, "Between Classical and Process Theism," in ibid., pp. 313–27; Pinnock, "God Limits His Knowledge," in *Predestination and Free Will: Four Views of Divine Sovereignty and Human Freedom*, ed. David Basinger and Randall Basinger (Downers Grove: InterVarsity, 1986), pp. 141–73.

4. Paul S. Fiddes, *The Creative Suffering of God* (New York: Oxford University Press, 1988).

5. Gregory A. Boyd, *Trinity and Process: A Critical Evaluation and Reconstruction of Hartshorne's Di-polar Theism Towards a Trinitarian Metaphysics* (New York: Peter Lang, 1992). See also Gregory A. Boyd and Edward K. Boyd, *Letters from a Skeptic* (Wheaton, Ill.: Victor, 1994).

6. Stephen T. Franklin, *Speaking from the Depths: Alfred North Whitehead's Hermeneutical Metaphysics of Propositions, Experience, Symbolism, Language, and Religion* (Grand Rapids: Eerdmans, 1990).

7. Garry Friesen, *Decision Making and the Will of God: A Biblical Alternative to the Traditional View* (Portland: Multnomah, 1980).

8. David Basinger, "Practical Implications," in *The Openness of God*, p. 201, n. 25.

classical theistic and the process theistic, seem to assume that they are the only two options. Their adherents therefore argue at some length for their view and assume that if the other view can be successfully refuted, their view will emerge as the only option. This simply is not the case, however. There is a third option, which is superior to either of these, preserving the strengths of each while avoiding the difficulties of both. These men do not claim that their view is the only one that is philosophically and biblically tenable. There is some ambiguity in both sources of data. They do believe, however, that overall their view is the superior one when judged in light of all the relevant biblical, theological, philosophical, and practical data. They also realize that they have not said the final word on these matters. There is much research yet to be done, and they invite others to join them in the task.[9]

Exposition of the Open View of God

We will proceed through our examination of this view of God in several stages: exposition of the conception; analysis of the arguments; identification of the presuppositions; and evaluation, both positive and negative.

Depiction of the Classical View of God

A crucial part of the free will theists' presentation is the explanation of the view to which they are offering an alternative, the classical view of God. These men insist that they are seeking to present an alternative not only to classical orthodox theism, but also to process theism. It is, however, the former, not the latter, to which they are primarily reacting, for their background is orthodox Christianity. As they put it, the classical view is like a virus that has invaded the Christian doctrine of God, making it ill and causing the practical/theoretical dislocations described above. It has resulted from coupling biblical ideas about God with ideas taken from Greek thought. They consider *The Openness of God* an antibiotic to aid in the healing process, thus bringing about a healthier doctrine of God.[10]

The traditional view, according to these free will theists, has dominated the church's thinking throughout most of its history and is prevalent among Christians today. It emphasizes God's sovereignty, majesty, and glory. According to this model, God is the final explanation of everything that occurs. He has sovereignly created the entire universe, to

9. *The Openness of God*, pp. 8–10.
10. Ibid., pp. 8–9. It should be borne in mind, of course, that antibiotics are ineffective against viruses.

fulfill his purposes and exhibit his glory. His will being irresistible, everything that happens in the world is a result of his will and working. While God is supremely good, he is equally glorified by the destruction of the wicked, according to his will, and by the obedience and salvation of the righteous.[11]

This view holds God to be perfect, based on texts such as Matthew 5:48. On the traditional understanding of perfection, this means that God possesses every positive quality to the maximum degree. Such an approach, sometimes referred to as "perfect being theology," takes much of its inspiration from St. Anselm. God being perfect, he cannot change, for all change must be either for the better or for the worse. God cannot possibly change for the better if he already possesses the maximum degree of goodness in every respect. Any change for the worse would be inconceivable, for that would mean that he became less than perfect. Therefore, ability to change in any way is incompatible with divine perfection. This is the doctrine of divine immutability, that God does not change in any respect, at any time. Several biblical texts are cited in support of this view, among them, Malachi 3:6, Hebrews 13:8, and James 1:17. This idea of divine changelessness is also supported by personal religious experience, for God is depicted as never failing those who trust in him (Deut. 31:6, 8; Josh. 1:5; Isa. 43:1–2; 49:15–16; Heb. 13:5). Such faithfulness, however, requires an unchanging and unchangeable God, for if he could change, how could we trust him and obey his commands unreservedly?[12]

Just as God's immutability follows from the idea of his perfection, so other doctrines follow from this one. If God does not change, the content of his knowledge and experience must not change. He cannot discover anything about the world. Thus, rather than experiencing events as they occur, he must take in everything, past, present, and future, in one great fixed glance. In other words, God is timeless. He dwells in eternity, where everything is one timeless present. Thus the doctrines of God's perfect, omniscient foreknowledge and his timelessness are integral parts of the classical view of God.[13]

Since God is outside time, knows everything, and is not in any sense subject to change in himself, his plans and intentions never change either. What he does, he has planned and intended from all eternity. Consequently, God never has to change his mind, repent of what he planned to do, or alter the course of his activity. He is completely transcendent

11. Richard Rice, "Biblical Support for a New Perspective," in *The Openness of God*, pp. 11–12.

12. Rice, *God's Foreknowledge*, pp. 14–15.

13. Ibid., pp. 15–16.

over the universe and completely sovereign, unmoved by anything that transpires within it. He is timelessly eternal, immutable, impassible, and absolute in his foreknowledge, and everything comes to pass because he has planned it from all eternity.[14] This, the free will theists contend, is the view held by large numbers of Christians: "We may think of God primarily as an aloof monarch, removed from the contingencies of the world, unchangeable in every aspect of being, aware of everything that will ever happen and never taking risks."[15]

The Open View of God

Sharply contrasted with this view, the free will theists contend, is the open view of God. Here God is conceived not on the model of a metaphysical principle or an aloof monarch, but as a loving, caring, parent, who experiences the world, interacts with his children and consequently feels emotions, and takes risks and responds to developments in the world by changing his mind and his course of action as necessary.

There are several components of this view, corresponding to the several components of the classical view. Rice indicates that there are two basic convictions involved in this view: "love is the most important quality we attribute to God, and love is more than care and commitment; it involves being sensitive and responsive as well."[16] Not only does he act in relation to them, but they act in relation to him and he reacts or is affected by what they do. God's will is therefore not the sole cause of what occurs. History is a combined result of what God does and what humans do. We are partners with God in bringing about what occurs in the world.[17]

An important implication for this view is that God does not know antecedently everything humans will do. His knowledge is dynamic rather than static. He comes to know what occurs as it happens. He learns from what happens. This is truly an "open" view of God, for his knowledge and experience are open. They have not been fixed and closed from all eternity. Thus, God is dependent on the world in certain respects, but this dependence does not really detract from God's greatness; rather, it enhances it.

Having taken this brief overview, let us examine in somewhat greater detail the open view of God. The central claim, according to Rice, is that God's experience of the world is open rather than closed. He does not know all of time, past, present, and future, in one great timeless mo-

---

14. Rice, "Biblical Support," pp. 14–15, 12.
15. Pinnock, "Systematic Theology," in *The Openness of God*, p. 103.
16. Rice, "Biblical Support," p. 15.
17. Ibid., pp. 15–16.

ment. Rather, he becomes aware of developments in the world and responds to them as they occur. Thus, he is open to new stimuli and new experiences.[18]

This understanding of God should not be thought of as involving any imperfection. Rather, he knows infallibly the past and the present and all there is to know about the future. He allows humans the freedom to choose and act, and works in relationship to that freedom. Thus, he is a risk-taker, for he neither knows nor controls what those decisions and actions will be. There is, according to Rice, a twofold conception of the being of God. On the one hand, in relationship to the temporal world, God's experience is progressive, developmental, and, thus, open. There is, however, another dimension of God, in which he is unaffected by the world and incapable of or insusceptible to any type of development or change.[19] For example, with respect to his character, consider God's love. This is the way he is, and he cannot possibly be otherwise. It simply is part of his nature. This, and his other qualities, such as mercy, justice, and so on, are unaffected by anything that happens in the world.[20]

Let us now note how this view plays out in several relationships.

1. The openness of God and creation. The free will theists insist that at the beginning of time God created everything that came into being, including humans. It is important, however, if we would understand the total act of creation, to note something about the nature of the human that he created. A prominent feature of the account of the creation of humans is that God created them in his own image (Gen. 1:26, 27). What did this involve, however? Rice contends that most theologians today do not understand the image in terms of something substantive or structural within humans, some qualities they possess, but functionally, in terms of what they do, such as having dominion over the creation. If the image of God in the human means that the latter in some ways is similar to the former, then he agrees with Dorothy Sayers' observation that really the only thing said about God in the passage is that he creates. So the understanding of the image of God is that the human also has and is to exercise this creative power over the universe. Rice says, "In creating man in His image and endowing him with dominion over the earth, God was, in effect, inviting man henceforth to participate with Him in the work of Creation. Or perhaps we should say that God intended to continue His creative activity through the agency of his creatures. At any rate, Genesis 2 presents us with the God who creates

18. Rice, *God's Foreknowledge,* pp. 25–26.
19. Ibid., p. 26.
20. Ibid., p. 27.

a world and gives it the capacity for self-creation."[21] The openness of creation refers to the capacity of God's creatures for further creative activity. It should not, however, be thought of as any sort of imperfection on God's part, for he did not need humans to make up for some failure on his own part. He simply chose to do it this way.[22]

2. The openness of God and human freedom. God has given humans genuine freedom. They have the capacity to choose between genuine options. This means that God could not give humans the ability to obey without also giving them the ability to disobey. So the future of the world was not fixed in advance. God created a genuinely open world.[23]

Such a conception of human moral freedom is believed to give this view a great advantage over the traditional view, in terms of its ability to deal with the vexing problem of evil. A common response to the problem of how there can be evil in the world if God is completely powerful and completely good is the free will argument. This ancient response contends that God created free beings, and that having done so, there was no way to guarantee that they would not exercise their freedom by doing evil rather than good. If he had done so, they would be something less than free. If, however, God has perfect foreknowledge, then this solution may not really be a solution after all. For if God knew which humans would use their freedom to do evil and he still chose to bring them into existence, then he is responsible for the evil that they could have done. He could have prevented this evil, but did not. So we still have the dilemma.[24]

For the free will theist, however, this is not a problem. For if the future is genuinely open, then God cannot know it until it occurs. He knew that humans *could* rebel, but not that they *would*. He is therefore only responsible for the possibility of evil, not for its reality. That responsibility must be laid at the foot of humans. So the open view solves another intellectual problem—and probably the most serious of them all.[25]

3. The openness of God and the future. We have observed that these free will theists hold that the reason God does not know the future is because it is not yet there to be known. It is not fixed in advance. It is less like a rug that is unrolled as time goes by than it is like a rug that is being woven.

If God does not know the future in its entirety, is the belief in the omniscience of God compromised? The free will theists maintain that this

21. Ibid., pp. 36–37.
22. Ibid., p. 37.
23. Ibid., p. 38.
24. Ibid., p. 50.
25. Ibid., pp. 51–52.

can be understood better on the analogy of the correct understanding of divine omnipotence. It is now widely recognized that omnipotence does not mean the ability to do absolutely anything whatsoever (for example, to make square circles). This inability, however, is not really an inability. It is not failure to do something, for square circles do not exist, being logically contradictory. God cannot do the logically impossible, not because that lies beyond his power, but because it is not something "do-able." Omnipotence only means the ability to do things that are do-able, not to do things that are merely verbal sentences, but do not correspond to anything existing in reality.[26]

The same applies to omniscience, which does not mean simply "knowing everything." Rather, it means the ability to know everything that is knowable. The future is not something knowable, for it does not yet exist to be known. Consequently, not knowing the future does not mean that God's knowledge is lacking in anything. It simply means that "His knowledge corresponds precisely with what there is to know."[27]

This does not mean that God knows nothing about the future, however. His knowledge is partially definite, not totally indefinite. Many of the things that will occur in the future are the result of past and present causes. Since God knows the past and present exhaustively, he can know what will result. Further, God knows what he plans to do in the future. Thus, the fact that he does not know the future in detail does not mean that he is completely ignorant of it.[28] In addition, he knows the range of possibilities of persons' actions, and the consequences of each of these possibilities. So, although he does not know precisely what will occur, he knows what may, and on each of the scenarios, what the result will be. While the future is open to God, it is not wide open.[29]

4. The openness of God and providence. The free will theists believe that God is at work in the world, accomplishing his purposes. He supports the natural order, and sometimes even departs from his customary and familiar manner of working (natural laws) to perform the unusual, or miracles. Beyond that, God is especially involved with human history, and sometimes even responds to events that would seem to thwart his purposes to accomplish them nonetheless. The evil Joseph's brothers did to him and the stubbornness of Pharaoh are examples of this sort of working.[30]

26. Ibid., p. 54.
27. Ibid., pp. 54–55.
28. Ibid., p. 55.
29. Ibid., pp. 56–58.
30. Ibid., p. 62.

The nature of God's providential working is conceived quite differently on the open view of God than on the traditional view. In classical theism God is seen as controlling everything through an eternal decision to adopt a total plan. His relationship to the world and history is now a relatively passive one. According to the open model, however, the future becomes apparent to God as his human agents carry out their actions and he responds to those actions, adjusting his working accordingly. It is important to distinguish between God's ultimate intentions for the world, which have been planned from eternity, and the actions he takes to implement these within time. God's general intention for the human race is that everyone should be saved, but this only comes to pass in each individual case as specific individuals accept that offer.[31]

5. The openness of God and prophecy. Some critics of the open view have felt that predictive prophecy must present an insuperable difficulty for it. After all, if God is able to predict that which occurs, he must at least be able to know the future in all of its particularity, or even control it. How can God give predictive prophecy, if the future and his knowledge really are open?

There are various possibilities for accounting for given prophecies, according to free will theists. One is that the specific prophecy in question is actually an event God knows, on the basis of his exhaustive knowledge of past and present factors, will inevitably come to pass. There are other prophecies that are expressions of God's intention to act in a certain way, and God certainly knows what he intends to do. Some prophecies may be a combination of these two factors.[32] In addition, some of these may be conditional prophecies, or declarations of God's intention to act in a certain way if a particular course of action occurs or if people behave in a certain way. One of the clearest examples of this latter type of prophecy would be Jonah's prophecy to Nineveh. The prophecy was a real declaration of Jehovah's intention to destroy Nineveh, which would surely have happened *unless the people of Nineveh repented.* In fact, this warning was a means by which God would bring about that repentance. So, without knowing in advance what they would do, God was able to declare what he would do unless they changed their behavior.[33]

31. Ibid., pp. 63–64.
32. Ibid., pp. 77–79.
33. Ibid., pp. 79–80.

Support for the View

What arguments do the free will theists advance in support of their position? There are basically five different areas to which they appeal in setting forth their case.

Biblical Evidence

The first line of argument for these evangelicals must be the biblical evidence. Although present in a number of places, the most concentrated treatment is Rice's chapter in the *Openness* book.

Rice acknowledges that the proponents of the traditional view are able to appeal to Scripture passages, and in fact, to a rather large number of them. This is not really the crucial question, however. Rather, the issue is whether the view under consideration is faithful to the overall picture of God, the picture that emerges when all the evidence is examined. Rice's contention is that despite being able to appeal to a number of biblical statements, the conventional view "does not reflect faithfully the spirit of the biblical message." He does not intend to offer a point-by-point refutation of the conventional picture, but to identify some central elements in that biblical portrait and to show that this portrait is compatible with some of the passages that seem to call it into question.[34]

There is a variety of biblical material related to God, according to Rice. Most of the descriptions are metaphors. Some are more important than others. They bear a stronger resemblance to the divine reality, or they play a more prominent role in Scripture. Rice's aim is to restore some of these metaphors to the prominence they deserve in our thinking, especially such metaphors as divine suffering and divine repentance. "Giving such metaphors more weight will enable us to achieve an understanding of God that is much more faithful to the Bible than is the familiar alternative."[35] There are two lines of biblical evidence for the open view of God. One is the statements that affirm in one way or another that God is responsive to what happens in the world, that those events evoke certain emotions, a change in attitude or plans. The other consists of statements that appear to affirm the freedom of humans in one way or another.[36]

Rice begins with the most important affirmation in the Bible, that God is love (1 John 4:8). He believes this is as close as the Bible comes to giving a definition of the divine reality. It is the activity through which

---

34. Rice, "Biblical Support," p. 15.
35. Ibid., p. 17.
36. Ibid., p. 18.

God's nature is most fully revealed. It is not merely the most important of the biblical attributes of God; it is also more fundamental than all the others.[37] Rice says, "Love is the essence of the divine reality, the basic source from which *all* of God's attributes arise."[38]

When Rice examines the Old Testament material bearing on the question of divine openness, he notes two lines of evidence: regarding God's feelings and regarding God's intentions. Again and again the Old Testament attributes a variety of feelings to God, including joy, grief, anger, and regret. These are most prominent in the descriptions of his reactions to the unfaithfulness of his chosen people, such as the Book of Hosea.[39] Similarly, there are numerous indications in Scripture of God changing his mind, or, in the language of the Bible, "repenting." These are either cases where God is sorry for what he has done, as in creating the human race (Gen. 6:6) or making Saul king (1 Sam. 15:35), or repents of something he has said he would do or has started to do, such as his decision not to carry through on his threat to destroy Nineveh (Jonah 3:10).[40]

What about the two passages (Num. 23:19 NRSV and 1 Sam. 15:29) that seem to indicate that God does not repent? Some contend that these are general assertions of God's immutability, that he does not change. Rice makes four observations. First, in both instances, the word "repent" is used synonymously with "lie." The point is not that God does not change, but that he never says one thing while intending to do another. Second, these passages pertain to specific promises, not to general principles. Third, the assurance that God *will* not repent presupposes that he *can* repent. Fourth, one of the chapters that asserts that God does *not* repent (1 Sam. 15) contains two statements that he *does* repent (vv. 11, 35). On the basis of such considerations Rice concludes that this is not a statement of a general principle.[41]

But what about the contention that just as the references to God having a physical form must be taken as anthropomorphisms, so the references to his having emotions must be taken as anthropopathisms? Rice sees two reasons for taking these statements about God's thoughts and feelings at face value. One is their frequency and the other their strategic place, so that they have a defining function, indicating what it is that makes God God.[42]

37. Ibid., pp. 18–21.
38. Ibid., p. 21.
39. Ibid., pp. 22–23.
40. Ibid., pp. 26–27.
41. Ibid., p. 33.
42. Ibid., p. 35.

The third consideration is the divine actions, the fact that God does things. Rice summarizes this type of evidence by saying that "at times God simply does things, acting on his own initiative and relying solely on his own power. Sometimes he accomplishes things through the cooperation of human agents, sometimes he overcomes creaturely opposition to accomplish things, sometimes he providentially uses opposition to accomplish something, and sometimes his intentions to do something are thwarted by human opposition." God's will, therefore, must not be seen as an irresistible, all-determining force.[43]

Numerous New Testament texts also support the idea of the openness of God, especially as found in Jesus' life, ministry, and death. The very fact that God took human form and came to humanity in the incarnation is a powerful consideration. Jesus' life was characterized by service to and suffering with human beings, rather than power over them. His teachings about the Father picture a being who rejoices in the return and salvation of lost sinners. It is true that the Scriptures sometimes contrast God with humans, but it is with *sinful* humans, not with essential humanity as seen in Jesus Christ.[44] Jesus' death is a demonstration of the active part God takes in our salvation. Rice insists that the central New Testament truth is that God is always the subject and the agent of reconciliation, not its object and recipient.[45] Here, however, we see God suffering, "the antithesis of traditional divine attributes such as immutability and impassibility."[46]

But what about the problem passages? There are three types: affirmations of God's changelessness, prophecies, and statements of predestination and foreknowledge. Regarding the first group, Rice asserts that there is a changeless aspect of God, namely, his character, and that these passages refer to it. The prophecies are handled in the fashion we noted earlier. The foreknowledge and predestination passages seem to be the most difficult, but Rice has three responses. First, even when something is said to have been predestined, this does not mean that it could not have failed to occur. There are plenty of biblical accounts of God being disappointed and frustrated. Second, even if some events are determined, that does not mean that all of them are. Finally, the basic meaning of divine election does not primarily refer to a choice of individuals to salvation. Rather, the typical instances of this are a corporate call to service. The conclusion of all of Rice's discussion is that a broad selection of biblical texts supports the idea of the openness of God.[47]

43. Ibid., p. 38.
44. Ibid., pp. 39–43.
45. Ibid., p. 45.
46. Ibid., p. 46.
47. Ibid., pp. 46–58.

Historical Considerations

The historical section by John Sanders is both shorter and less central to the argument than the biblical discussion. It is introduced in relationship to the conclusion of Rice's chapter. If the Bible really does teach this view of the openness of God, why is it that most of us do not read it in such a way as to support these ideas? Sanders contends that when we become theologically informed, our more natural reading of the Bible is replaced by a reinterpretation of those passages in light of a "theologically correct" understanding of God, and that this conception of God has resulted from the absorption and adoption of Greek ways of thinking.[48]

Sanders sketches the picture of the Greek understanding of God, with his immutability and impassibility. He then shows in some detail how these ideas came progressively to be adopted by Christian theology, and became the orthodox understanding. The Reformers raised some questions about the biblical–classical synthesis, but in the final analysis it was not overcome. Jacob Arminius, however, significantly modified that synthesis, yet apparently never saw the conflict between some of these changes and the doctrine of impassibility.[49]

In the modern period, Sanders sees theology dividing into three groups. The progressives, such as Paul Tillich and the process theologians, made major modifications in the classical view of God. Conservatives, such as Carl F. H. Henry and J. I Packer, divide the scriptural evidence into two areas, the transcendent, or God as he is in himself, immutable and impassible, and the immanent, or God as he appears to us, namely, changeable and responsive. Conservative piety and hymnody are quite different, however, believing in a responsive God who answers prayer. A few conservative theologians, such as Charles Hodge and Millard Erickson, have begun to modify the classical view. The final group holds moderate views of God, much like the authors of the book. Their numbers are growing, including both philosophers and theologians.[50]

Theological Considerations

In the section on systematic theology, Clark Pinnock elaborates on many of the same ideas presented in Rice's chapter on the biblical basis of openness, and reaffirms Sanders' thesis that the classical view of God resulted from the amalgamation of Greek philosophy with biblical

48. John Sanders, "Historical Considerations," in *The Openness of God*, p. 59.
49. Ibid., pp. 60–91.
50. Ibid., pp. 91–98.

teaching. His major additional thrust is to show the theological problems that result from this synthesis.

Pinnock points out that the idea of divine timelessness presents many theological difficulties. First, it is hard to form any idea of timelessness, since all of our thinking is temporally conditioned. Second, timelessness creates problems for biblical history, where God seems to experience the flow of time and a future not completely settled. Third, it seems to undermine our worship, since we praise God for his actions in time. Fourth, a God who did not experience events as they occur would not be experiencing or knowing the actual world.[51] Similarly, the idea of God's perfect foreknowledge cannot be sustained biblically. There are passages where God seems to make discoveries, and others where he professes not to know something. It would be a serious limitation on God if he could not experience surprise and delight. Such a world would be boring. Finally, the idea of exhaustive foreknowledge must be rejected, because in such a world it would be certain what we are going to do, and this would conflict with real human choices and significant freedom.[52]

Philosophical Issues

In the chapter entitled "A Philosophical Perspective," William Hasker especially considers problems related to divine power, knowledge, and providential governance. He examines the views of these problems found in process theology, Calvinism, Molinism, and simple foreknowledge. He then examines the view of the openness of God. He concludes that this latter option is better able to avoid the difficulties of conflict with human freedom and of the problem of evil than any of its competitors.

Practical Implications

Finally, David Basinger considers the applicability of this view to certain practical issues of Christian living. With respect to petitionary prayer, he maintains that on what he terms "specific sovereignty," petitionary prayer cannot affect what happens, since God has already determined to do what he is going to do. Prayer can only affect the person doing the praying. Only openness-of-God persons can pray, believing that it makes any difference in what God actually does.[53] With respect to discerning God's will, specific-sovereignty persons really should conclude that whatever God wills occurs. The openness of God model, on

---

51. Pinnock, "Systematic Theology," in *The Openness of God*, p. 120.
52. Ibid., pp. 121–23.
53. David Basinger, "Practical Implications," in *The Openness of God*, pp. 160–62.

the other hand, allows for seeking God's insight, since only he knows all possibilities, but there is a significant sense in which it matters what we do.[54] Similarly, with respect to human suffering, evangelistic responsibility, and social responsibility, the openness model avoids the passivity that attaches to the specific sovereignty model, and both allows for and encourages us to do all we can to bring about the good that God desires for humans. Thus, this model more adequately justifies and motivates practical Christian living.[55]

Presuppositions of the Openness of God Model

It is helpful in understanding and evaluating a theology such as this to note the presuppositions from which it derives and which nourish it. In so doing, we must be careful to avoid committing the genetic fallacy: assuming that if we have discovered the causes of a certain view being held, we have settled the question of its truth. That, of course, is not the case. Several presuppositions bear significantly on these matters.

A Commonsense View of Human Will

One of the most basic contentions of the openness model is that the classical view allows humans no freedom. Freedom is the very basic starting point, almost the given, of much of this theology. This is why there cannot be foreordination or predestination in what they would consider the determinist form. It is also why there cannot be divine foreknowledge, in the sense of God knowing everything that will happen. If God knows what I am going to do, it is certain that I will do that and not something else. Thus, I cannot do otherwise, for if I did, God would be wrong. If this is the case, however, I am not free. Yet the one thing that cannot be denied is that I am free. If I am indeed free in this sense, however, it must not be true that God knows in advance exactly what I am going to do. Hence, foreknowledge, as defined above, is false.

This is the commonsense view of freedom. If asked why I do what I do, the answer usually given is because I decide to. But if the question is pressed further, in terms of why I choose or decide on this course of action rather than another, there really is no answer. I just do, that is all. Similarly, if asked how I know that I am free, no elaborate philosophical or psychological argument is given. I simply know that I am free, that is, that I could have refrained from taking this course of action. This seems to be an immediate, intuitive type of belief.

54. Ibid., pp. 166–68.
55. Ibid., pp. 168–76.

This is the Arminian view of the will and freedom. This view takes the argument one step further along the track of logical implications, however. The usual form of the Arminian position says that there is no inconsistency between God knowing what I am going to do and my being free in doing it, so long as it is I, not God, who determines it. This school of thought, however, takes the step of concluding that if I could not do otherwise, even without external compulsion, then I am not really free. Thus, in terms of the argument we noted above, the complete foreknowledge of God is rejected.

What is being assumed is that freedom must be of the incompatibilist or libertarian variety. The other alternative, compatibilism, is the idea that I may be free even if there are factors that lead me to choose as I do. That conception of freedom is not discussed or even acknowledged as a possibility by most of these persons, however. It is simply assumed that freedom must mean freedom of the incompatibilist type. In Hasker's case, he recognizes that there are these two options and describes them. He examines and criticizes both Calvinism and Molinism, showing the difficulties that attach to each, but does not show any difficulties in his own view. His criticisms of Calvinism and Molinism, however, assume the incompatibilist view of freedom. His use of expressions like "ventriloquist," "puppet-master," and "computer wizard-robot" reveals this assumption.[56]

This commonsense view of freedom is probably held by the majority of Americans, simply because this is how it seems to them to be. If, however, there is suspicion of common sense realism simply because it is commonsense and relatively uncritical, then one should also be critical of this view for the same reason. Part of the reason it seems so compelling is simply because it is so widespread.

Existentialism

A second assumption operating here is an existentialist view of humanity and God. Existentialism really originated as Søren Kierkegaard's reaction against a couple factors. One was "the system," the thought of Georg Hegel, which organized everything logically under one grand scheme: historical events, philosophy, and all. Everything fit into and was explained by the triadic pattern of thesis-antithesis-synthesis. Thus, all of reality was rational. The second was "the crowd." This included the church with its cultural Christianity; society, with its customary opinions; the newspapers, spreading the official view of things.

Kierkegaard objected to the logical organization and explanation of everything. Reality, to be treatable in this fashion, must be uniform, ra-

56. Hasker, "A Philosophical Perspective," in *The Openness of God*, pp. 142–43.

tional, law-driven, subsumable under logical categories. This, however, virtually requires that all of reality be of one type. This does not follow, however, according to existentialism. Individuals are unique; thus, treating them as specimens of a class results in distortion or over-simplification.

The individual, being free, breaks out of this subsumption, according to existentialism. Some try to justify or rationalize their behavior by appealing to any causative factors, whether genetic, psychological, sociological, or whatever. There also is what Heidegger called "the everydayness of the they." One does something because everyone else is doing it, or believes it because "that is what everyone says." All these kinds of behavior are what Heidegger referred to as "inauthentic existence." It is unwillingness to take responsibility for oneself and one's own actions. This type of conformity or self-excusing action degrades my humanity.

What I must rather do, says the existentialist, is exercise my own individuality, my power to choose to be myself. Freedom is virtually the essence of the human. It is the power to create oneself, one's own nature. Jean-Paul Sartre once said, "If there is a God, he is a limitation upon my freedom." He was, however, absolutely sure of his own freedom. Therefore, there must not be a God.

Most existentialisms are humanisms, as the title of one of Sartre's books declares regarding existentialism. This means that the human is the highest object of value in the entire universe. Humans come ahead of God in our concern. Attention, and all else, must center on him.

There are definite parallels to these existentialist themes in this theology. They are less extreme in the openness of God view than in non-Christian existentialisms, but they are there. So the freedom of the human leads to an objection to a plan in which everything is worked out and predetermined in advance. The objection thus is not to God, as in atheistic existentialisms, but to a certain kind of God, namely, the God of "specific sovereignty."

The humanistic dimension of existentialism can also be seen here. Human values are elevated to where God must conform to them. For example, God must not show partiality. He does not really have the right to determine anyone's ultimate destiny, to decide that someone should go to hell, for example. He also cannot morally overwhelm anyone. There seems as well to be something of an antithesis between human and divine acting. Something must be the result of one or the other of these. There also seems to be an objection to anything being too tight, too closed. A future that has already been worked out in detail is unacceptable, it appears. Perhaps without realizing it, these theologians seem to be saying that this is how reality is.

Semiprocess Metaphysic

Finally, there seems to be a semiprocess view of reality. Much contemporary thought regards reality not as fixed, but as changing, growing, and evolving. Reality, on such a view, is dynamic. Change, not fixity, is what is real. These characteristics are true of the whole of reality. In process theology, then, God also must participate in these same categories and thus also in this change.

In a number of places, this theology has taken pains to distance itself quite clearly from process theology. Nonetheless, it has a great deal in common with it. The openness of God theologians express strong objection to anything like divine timelessness, immutability, and impassibility. Yet their own objections are not made from some neutral position. It is one thing to criticize another theology for absorbing a foreign philosophy (in this case, Greek philosophy). One must ask, however, from what perspective these comments are made and what philosophy the commentators may have absorbed. Here one can notice a strong similarity between the statements process theologians make about the classical doctrine of God and the ones that these theologians make. So Rice, for example, acknowledges the commonality with process theology. He says, "The concept of God proposed here shares the process view that God's relation to the temporal world consists in a succession of concrete experiences, rather than a single timeless perception." This is not all, however. He adds, "It also shares with process theism the twofold analysis of God, or the 'dipolar theism,' described above. It conceives God as both absolute and relative, necessary and contingent, eternal and temporal, changeless and changing. It attributes one element in each pair of contrasts to the appropriate aspect of God's being—the essential divine character or the concrete divine experience."[57] He goes on to point out that there are significant differences between the two, but this certainly sounds like the acknowledgment of the presence of at least some process categories.

Evaluation

Our consideration of this theology would not be complete without an evaluation of its strengths and weaknesses. A number of points of strength and valuable contributions can be identified in this theology.

Positive

1. There is a genuine attempt to be biblical. Because these men claim to be functioning within the context of evangelicalism, which regards

---

57. Rice, "God's Foreknowledge," p. 33.

the Bible as its supreme authority, this is of great importance. They have sought to identify biblical themes that support their view.

2. These men have attempted to bring together the several fields of theology into a coherent doctrinal presentation. Biblical theology, historical theology, philosophical theology, and practical theology are all utilized in what should be a full-orbed systematic theology. This gives us a model of what should be involved in theological methodology.

3. These theologians have called attention to the fact that theological work is done in a context, and that this context can clearly affect what we do. We do not work in a vacuum, and it is incumbent on us to be aware of that context so that we can detect its possible influence on us.

4. These men have correctly pointed out the influence Greek thought has sometimes had on Christian theology, and that the view regarded by many as the synthesis of biblical teaching may actually contain a large amount of Greek philosophy read into the text.

5. There is a commendable desire and effort to relate the doctrinal view to practical issues of the Christian life, to make theology practical theology in the best sense of that word.

6. There is, for the most part, a desirable declared intention and an actual endeavor to treat coolly and rationally, rather than emotively, a subject on which obviously all of these men feel very strongly.

Negative

Despite these considerable strengths of the theology, there are some major weaknesses and flaws.

The use of Scripture is less than adequate. This is reflected in five manifestations.

1. There is a selective use of Scripture. Rather than a complete induction of the Bible's teachings, there is a concentration on those passages that support this view, but neglect of those passages that emphasize countering or supplementary perspectives. For example, much is made of the passages pertaining to the love of God, but little or no notice is taken of the passages that speak of his holiness, wrath, and judgment. This results in a rather one-sided understanding of God's love. Similarly, passages that speak of God's unchanging nature, or his complete power, his determination of the events of history or of persons' lives, and his complete knowledge of everything, including the future, are largely ignored or explained away. Rice even says that 2 Corinthians 5:18–20 "underscores the central New Testament truth that God is always the subject, and never the object, of reconciliation. He is the agent,

not the recipient, of reconciliation."[58] To make such a categorical statement about something which, to say the very least, is highly debated among biblical scholars and theologians, and to say that it is "the central New Testament truth" without consulting the other passages on the atonement, or the rich significance of the prepositions used for the relationship of Christ's death to our sins,[59] is quite amazing. Rice speaks of giving more weight to the metaphors that depict divine suffering and divine repentance, which he says "will help us achieve an understanding of God that is much more faithful to the Bible than is the familiar alternative." He contends that this is restoring these metaphors to the prominence they deserve in our thinking, but does not offer any real evidence that these are more prominent in the biblical testimony.[60] It appears that this may be a case of circular reasoning.

2. A hermeneutical device is employed whereby the specifics of Scripture are interpreted in light of "the broad sweep of Scripture, the overall themes." One must seriously ask, however, how something can be an overall or general teaching of Scripture without being related to the corpus of the Bible at specific points. Failure to do this arouses the suspicion that extraneous ideas are being imposed on the Bible and then being used to reinterpret the specific passages there.

3. When specific passages are employed, they are sometimes interpreted in ways that are suspect. For example, the passages that speak of God as love are understood as teaching that this is not merely an attribute of God, but virtually a definition of his essence. Nothing is done, however, with other passages that predicate other attributes of God in an equally qualifying fashion, such as the names of God, or the holiness of God (Isa. 6:3), or the jealous character of God (Exod. 20:5), or his identification by Jesus as Spirit (John 4:24). Further, in interpreting the incidents of Joseph's life, Rice comments that God is able to use even unpleasant circumstances, and cites Genesis 45:5–8. Verse 7, however, seems to indicate that this is not primarily God's reaction to something humans did, but rather part of his antecedent plan: "But God sent me ahead of you to preserve for you a remnant on earth and to save your lives by a great deliverance." This also seems to be implied by Genesis 50:20: "You intended to harm me, but God intended it for good to accomplish what is now being done, the saving of many lives." This casts

58. Rice, "Biblical Support," p. 45.

59. E.g., A. T. Robertson, *A Grammar of the Greek New Testament in the Light of Historical Research*, 2nd ed. (New York: George H. Doran, 1923), p. 573; G. B. Winer, *A Treatise on the Grammar of New Testament Greek*, 3rd rev. ed. (Edinburgh: T. & T. Clark, 1882), p. 479; George E. Ladd, *New Testament Theology* (Grand Rapids: Eerdmans, 1974), pp. 427–28.

60. Ibid., p. 17.

a rather different light on the whole matter. Finally, Rice's treatment of the apparent conflict between the descriptions of God's repentance and the statements that God does not repent is misleading. He maintains that in the two passages where God is said not to "repent," the word is actually used synonymously with "lie." Yet, on closer examination, the Hebrew text does not seem to bear out that contention. The word used in each case, is *nacham*, which appears not to bear the meaning of "lie."[61]

4. The interpretation of the broad sweep of Scripture is affected by the presupposition of the corruption of the tradition by the infection from the virus of Greek thought. This, however, rests on a strong distinction between Greek thought and authentically "biblical" (Hebraic) thought that was for such a long time a cliché in the Biblical Theology Movement but more recently has fallen into disfavor. The work of James Barr[62] was so influential on this concept that Brevard Childs spoke of the "cracking of the walls," one of which was the "distinctive biblical mentality," and said of Barr's book, "Seldom has one book brought down so much superstructure with such effectiveness."[63]

5. When these theologians consult secondary sources in the interpretation of the Bible, the exegetes and biblical theologians they use are frequently persons who do not share the usual evangelical understanding of the Bible. This immediately introduces some potential distortion, if conflicting presuppositions are at work.[64]

A major part of the case made by these theologians is their description and criticism of the classical view, against which their own theology is then developed. Its undesirable qualities constitute the major reason for their adoption of the openness view.

What these men do is trace the Greek model of God, as found in various Greek philosophers. They then show what this results in, if adopted by a Christian theologian and used in developing a model of God. In so doing, some of the most extreme examples of this from the history of Christian thought are taken as the norm. This is then assumed to be the standard orthodox or evangelical ("classical") view. The resulting depiction of the model they are opposing sounds like this: "We

61. Francis Brown, S. R. Driver, and Charles A. Briggs, *A Hebrew and English Lexicon of the Old Testament* (Oxford: Clarendon, 1955), pp. 636–37.

62. James Barr, *The Semantics of Biblical Language* (London: Oxford University Press, 1961).

63. Brevard S. Childs, *Biblical Theology in Crisis* (Philadelphia: Westminster, 1970), p. 72.

64. E.g., several works by Terence E. Fretheim, such as *The Suffering of God: An Old Testament Perspective* (Philadelphia: Fortress, 1986).

may think of God primarily as an aloof monarch, removed from the contingencies of the world, unchangeable in every aspect of being, as an all-determining irresistible power, aware of everything that will ever happen and never taking risks."[65] This God is described as being a metaphysical principle rather than as a person.

Is this a fair characterization of the orthodox doctrine of God, however? Two observations need to be made. The first is that the history of Christian thought does not follow this model as uniformly as these authors would lead us to believe. There certainly were doctrines of God held by mainstream Christianity that were not so uniformly aloof, mechanical, and unresponsive. Alister McGrath, for example, severely criticizes Sanders for his omissions, especially for failing to give adequate treatment to Luther's conception of the suffering God. He says, "A quick read of this volume, however, showed that the contributors seem not to realize that Luther has been down their road long before them. . . . I found myself outraged by this lack of scholarly familiarity with Luther and his background."[66]

The other observation is that a careful examination of contemporary evangelical theology would indicate that this picture of the classic view of God is something of a caricature. So, for example, any number of recent theology works clearly do not hold to the idea of impassibility as described here. Grudem, Lewis and Demarest, Erickson, and others clearly speak of the emotional dimension of God's experience, of his sympathetic suffering with and for his people. The idea of immutability also does not follow this stereotyped picture. God, according to these treatises, does not change in his fundamental character, but he certainly works in ways that vary from time to time. Finally, the idea of eternity as atemporal or timeless existence is not necessarily characteristic of all evangelical thinkers, although it certainly is of some. So, for example, conservative philosophical theologians such as Ronald Nash and Thomas Morris are unable to commit themselves definitely to either the timeless view or the endless extension within time, and do not consider this indispensable to the orthodox understanding of God.[67]

This is not so much a characterization as a caricature of the orthodox or classical view of God. Sanders, conceding that the picture is not as

65. Pinnock, "Systematic Theology," p. 103.

66. Alister E. McGrath, "Whatever Happened to Luther?" *Christianity Today* 39.1 (January 9, 1995): 34.

67. Ronald H. Nash, *The Concept of God: An Exploration of Contemporary Difficulties with the Attributes of God* (Grand Rapids: Zondervan, 1983), pp. 82–83; Thomas V. Morris, *Our Idea of God: An Introduction to Philosophical Theology* (Downers Grove: InterVarsity, 1991), p. 138.

uniform as might be thought, implies that this represents something of a compromise of or an inconsistency within the traditional view.[68]

When Pinnock describes the classical and the process views, he seems to be saying that the one is 100 percent one way, and the other is zero percent. His view and that of his co-authors represents a position between the two, for they certainly do not want to jettison all the features of the classical view. What he does not consider, however, is whether there are any other possible intermediate positions between these two. If, for example, his view is 40 percent of the way from the process to the classical view, what of the possibility of a view that is 60 percent of the distance, or 80 percent? If process theology in effect says, "All A is B," Pinnock's argument seems to be, "Some A is not B." This does not determine, however, how much of this A is not B, that is, whether it is "little of A is not B," "much A is not B," or "most A is not B."

There are a number of problems, both in the presentation of the case and in the internal structure of the view.

1. Much of the case rests on the perceived conflict between complete divine foreknowledge and human freedom, as we have noted above. What is significant, however, is that the conflict is between this foreknowledge and the incompatibilist view of freedom. The alternative, compatibilism, contends that foreknowledge requires only the certainty of a given event, not its necessity. This view would say that I am free to do A, but it is certain that I will not. Unfortunately, however, most of these men simply assume freedom (because it is indubitable, or indisputable, or something similar) of an incompatibilist or libertarian type, but do not really enunciate that. They simply proceed as if it is true. The partial exception to this is Hasker, who acknowledges and describes the difference between the two approaches.[69] Then, however, he does not argue for the truth or at least the superiority of the incompatibilist view. He simply states it and proceeds to evaluate Calvinism and Molinism, two views that generally presuppose the compatibilist view, but does so from an incompatibilist position. This begs the question, however, in effect criticizing a position by presupposing its contradictory. This is a clear shortcoming.

2. Hasker likens the Calvinistic understanding of the relationship of God and humans to that between a puppet-master and his puppet, a ventriloquist and his dummy, and a computer wizard and his lifelike robot.[70] This not only reveals the incompatibilist assumption, but uses language less descriptive than emotive and pejorative.

68. Sanders, "Historical Considerations," p. 96.
69. Hasker, "A Philosophical Perspective," pp. 136–37.
70. Ibid., pp. 142–43.

3. At times, inferences are drawn or transitions made that are not implied or required by the preceding evidence and premises. An example is found in Rice's discussion of the meaning and significance of the image of God. He moves from "These considerations suggest that . . ." to "Apparently, then, . . ." without intervening evidence.[71] A suggestion becomes a fairly definite conclusion without additional substantiation. Similarly, Hasker considers what he calls the proposition, "Susan was married last Sunday," and argues that this is true for just one week and God knows it for just one week. Actually, however, it appears that the sentence may well be, "Susan was married last Sunday," but that the proposition is actually something like "Susan [properly identified as this exact person] marries on Sunday, September 17, 1995." This proposition is always true, and God always knows it, although sentences expressing it may well change.

4. A further problem with the argument is that it in effect depends on historical conditioning and hence relativizing of the classical position. Because of the presence of the Greek thought of its time, the classical view developed as it did. What is disingenuous about the case being made, however, is the failure of these authors to admit to any similar conditioning of their own view. They acknowledge the presence of a certain kind of influence in the broad philosophy of the present time. Rather than relativizing their view, however, it is used positively. Pinnock says that this present-day culture is more congenial to dynamic thinking, which makes people more open to a dynamic, personal God. This makes it easier to recover the biblical witness today. But do they not see that if the classical theologians' reading of the biblical witness was colored by the intellectual milieu of their historical situation, so may that of himself and his colleagues. This seems to be a major blind spot or ad hoc exception in their thought.[72]

5. There may well be some "chronological snobbery" in assuming that the current philosophy is superior to Greek thought because it comes later. This is, however, a highly questionable assumption, especially outside the areas of the sciences, and one for which some justification ought to be given.[73]

6. Can the future be known, even partially, on this scheme of things? There are, according to these free will theists, two bases on which God knows the future partially and fragmentarily. He knows some of the things that he has purposed to do, and he is able to see the results of cer-

---

71. Rice, "God's Foreknowledge," p. 36.
72. Pinnock, "Systematic Theology," p. 107.
73. Thomas C. Oden, *After Modernity . . . What? Agenda for Theology* (Grand Rapids: Zondervan, 1990), pp. 41–42.

tain fixed factors in the past and present. Is this the case, however? For surely those factors depend on human responses for their outcome. The only exceptions would seem to be occurrences within a physical universe, which do not involve human wills and actions. And God's actions, because they also involve humans and their actions and reactions, cannot be fully known because those human components cannot be predicted. In other words, even God does not really know what he will do— he only knows the possibilities.

7. These theologians believe that their approach solves, or at least considerably alleviates, the problem of evil, by thrusting responsibility on the radically free will of humans. Is this really the case, however? Is not God at least indirectly responsible for evil, since he could presumably have created persons in such a fashion that they would not have had the free will to enable them to sin? Or is he not to be faulted for creating humans at all? Although shifted, and perhaps lessened somewhat, the problem has not been reduced as significantly as they wish and think.

8. There seems to be a contradiction, or at least a rather severe tension or dilemma, at the heart of this system. Just how does God know that good will finally prevail, rather than evil? What does he do when humans use their free will to resist his persuasion and loving entreaty? Hasker faces this issue with his illustration of the loving parent who seeks to affect the child's behavior by the use of persuasive power. Then he comments on the somewhat more extreme problem cases and the resources available to the parents: "The policy could well be described as the deliberate and intensive application of 'persuasive power'—though to be sure, coercive power is there in reserve, should the child start to run out into a busy roadway. Should not a similar account be given of God's control over us?"[74]

If I understand Hasker correctly, he seems to be suggesting that, in a situation of extremity, God may use "coercive power" to exercise his "control over us." But is this not the very thing with which the free will theists have charged the classical view: of holding that God coerces, or works irresistibly, thus robbing humans of their freedom? If he is actually suggesting this, however, then the difference between this view and the classical view is one of degree, not of kind. Actually, the Calvinist working with a compatibilist view claims that God does not coerce, he simply brings about cooperation or obedience, but that expedient is not

---

74. Hasker, "A Philosophical Perspective," p. 142. Similarly, Basinger says, "we who affirm the open view of God deny that God can unilaterally control human decision-making that is truly voluntary but affirm that God can unilaterally intervene in human affairs" ("Practical Implications," p. 160).

available to the free will theists, with their incompatibilist view. If, however, God does not do this, then there is no assurance that his desire to see good triumph will be realized. The dilemma, unless one adopts compatibilism, is either the loss of human freedom or of certainty of the ultimate outcome.

9. It appears that this understanding of God may reflect a precybernetic mind-set. The picture of a God who does not know the future and cannot guarantee it seems to be of a God who cannot know or cope with all the variables in such a complex world. That picture seems to reflect a time in which mathematics was done on an abacus, operators completed telephone connections manually, and notes were taken by hand. With the advance of powerful computers, which can recalculate thousands of cells in a spread sheet virtually instantly, we are beginning to get a slight glimpse of what a God who is infinitely wiser and more knowing than the most powerful computer could do. But the God pictured here is apparently much more limited than that.

10. Finally, it should be noted that this is an anthropocentric theology. It makes concern for the welfare or even the pleasant experiences of humans its major value. This God is the servant of humans, not their master. He is, as one critic said, a "user-friendly" God,[75] who seems to exist to glorify humans and to enable them to enjoy themselves forever. But to picture the divine–human relationship thus seems to significantly change the nature of Christianity from what has been its dominant interpretation over the many years of its existence. This may be not merely a quantitative, but perhaps also a qualitative, change from what Christianity has usually been thought to be.

All in all, although this is in many ways a creative theology, we conclude that the difficulties involved with it strongly outweigh its strengths. A number of important issues raised here will be examined more closely in succeeding chapters.

---

75. Timothy George, "A Transcendence-Starved Deity," *Christianity Today* 39.1 (January 9, 1995): 34.

Part 3

The Attributes of God

5

God and Change

The question of the relationship of God to change has taken on a special significance in the latter part of the twentieth century. The old Greek question of the one and the many has been given an added impetus. One reason is simply that change, at least in terms of cultural change, has become commonplace in our thinking. Whole books are devoted to the subject of change, such as Alvin Toffler's *Future Shock* and John Naisbitt's *Megatrends*. This change is the result of many factors. The accelerating capability of technology has meant that changes are more radical, more frequent, and farther-reaching. The knowledge explosion, together with radically improved means of communication, results in changes being spread over wide areas rapidly. Modern physics increasingly is coming to view reality not as static and fixed, but as dynamic and growing. Coupled with this is the rise and spread of process philosophy, with its emphasis on the basic unit of reality as being, not the fixed substance, but the much more evanescent event.

Interestingly, much of conservative theology has not really risen to the challenge to the traditional doctrine of divine immutability. Although there has been a real outpouring of new systematic theology texts from conservative theologians in the past fifteen years, most of them really do not give much attention to this subject. Among the exceptions are Wayne Grudem's *Systematic Theology*[1] and Carl F. H. Henry's *God and Revelation*.[2] Both volumes give major attention with respect to change and permanence in God's nature to the challenge of process theology.

1. Wayne Grudem, *Systematic Theology* (Grand Rapids: Zondervan, 1994), pp. 163–68.
2. Carl F. H. Henry, *God, Revelation and Authority*, vol. 5, *God Who Stands and Stays*, pt. 1 (Waco: Word, 1982), pp. 286–94.

At least on the surface, orthodox theology has much at stake in this issue, for it has traditionally maintained the doctrine of divine immutability. By this it meant that although everything else in the universe appears to undergo change, God does not. He is the unchanging eternal one. In light of the recent developments mentioned above, however, this topic needs fresh scrutiny and contemporary restatement.

Basis of the Doctrine of Immutability

Biblical

One source from which the doctrine of immutability has drawn inspiration is the Scriptures. Several passages seem to bear testimony to the fact that God is the unchanging one. Three passages in particular have come in for attention by theologians. The first is Psalm 102, where the context is the discussion of God's creation of all that is, and the contrast between him in his unchanging character and everything else, which is subject to alteration and decay.

> In the beginning you laid the foundations of the earth, and the heavens are the work of your hands. They will perish, but you remain; they will all wear out like a garment. Like clothing you will change them and they will be discarded. But you remain the same, and your years will never end (vv. 25–27).

Here the psalmist seems concerned to demonstrate to his readers that they need not be concerned as they see all that surrounds them deteriorating and changing. God is not like this. He remains the same, and he is endless and ageless.

A second passage frequently cited is Malachi 3:6. The context there is God's displeasure with his people, Israel. They have failed to live up to their part of the covenant that he made with them. He reminds them, however, that he is faithful to his covenant, both in terms of blessing as he has done in the past, when that is what they deserve, and of judging, when that is the proper response to their actions. As he has been in the past, he also is in the present: "I the LORD do not change. So you, O descendants of Jacob, are not destroyed." The emphasis is on God's unchanging action in the same situations, but underlying this is the fact that God is constant in his dealings. While there is not an explicit statement about metaphysical change and immutability, there is some implication that this is the basis of the behavioral consistency.

The final passage is from the New Testament Book of James: "Every good and perfect gift is from above, coming down from the Father of the heavenly lights, who does not change like shifting shadows" (1:17).

James is attempting to encourage his readers by pointing out that all good things come originally from God. These good gifts can be expected to continue to come and to be good, because the Father's character does not change at all. Of the three passages, this one seems to most directly address the issue of the constancy of God's being, in terms of not undergoing alteration.

Philosophical

The other source from which the doctrine of God's immutability derives is philosophy. As we noted, the earliest recorded philosophical treatises we have are from Greek philosophy, where there was early debate over whether reality was fundamentally fixed and permanent or changing and temporary. The eventual solution was to divide reality into two parts, one that was changing and the other that was unchanging. This unchanging component frequently played a role in the Greek philosopher's metaphysic comparable to that of God in a theistic view.

The two major types of Greek philosophy, at least during the period of influence on Christian theology, were Platonic and Aristotelian. Each had its own version of immutability of the supreme principle. The Platonic variety was first, both in terms of the development of the philosophy and the period of influence exerted on Christian theology.

The major discussion of this specific topic is found in the second book of Plato's *Republic*, in a dialogue between Socrates and Adeimantus. Socrates notes that all change of a thing is affected either by that thing itself, or by something external to it, and that the best of things are least liable to be changed by external influences. This is true of the influence on persons by meats and drinks, on plants by winds or sun, and on such manufactured things as furniture, houses, and garments. Everything good is least likely to suffer change from without. Since God is in every way perfect, he cannot be altered by the influence of external things. Might he not, however, asks Socrates, will to change himself? The possibility, however, is more apparent than real. Since God is perfect, not deficient in any quality, he cannot possibly change for the better, being already the ultimately good. If he is to undergo change, it must be for the worse. Why, however, would God or even a human ever will to change for the worse? Socrates' conclusion, with which Adeimantus agrees, is: "Then it is impossible that God should ever be willing to change; being, as is supposed, the fairest and best that is conceivable, every god remains absolutely and forever in his own form."[3]

There is a broader feature of Plato's understanding of reality that underlies this conception of immutability. For us, influenced by modern

3. Plato, *The Republic* 2.381.

empirical science, the visible or tangible, the perceptible, is most real, and the intangible things are less real. Plato understood reality in the exact opposite way. He expounds this in several places in his writings, but perhaps nowhere more clearly than in the *Republic*. He develops the scheme in his analogy of the divided line. The lower half of the line is the visible, and the other half (although the parts are of unequal length) is the intelligible. The lower part is in turn divided into a part composed of images, including shadows, reflections, and the like, and another part, which consists of things we see and everything growing and made. The upper part of the overall line consists of invisible but intelligible matters. The lower part of this higher half consists of ideals or forms, such as the absolute triangle and square that geometricians use. The higher part of this upper part of the line is the realm of the idea of the Good, where, unlike the hypotheses dealt with in geometry, one rises above hypotheses.[4]

The point is that the objects in the lower realm, subject to change, are less real than are the ideas or forms in the upper half of reality, which are absolute or pure and so do not change. While there has been much speculation among students of Plato as to the exact relationship in his thought about God and the idea of the Good, it is apparent that permanence and fixity are positively correlated with reality in his understanding. This analogy of the divided line is followed immediately by the myth of the cave. Here, persons are seated, bound from their childhood by chains that prevent them from turning and looking behind them. They can only see the wall in front of them. Behind them, unseen by them, are persons moving about, and behind these, a fire that casts its light on these figures so that their shadows and their movements are cast on the wall in front of the prisoners. Seeing only the shadows and never that which casts the shadows, they believe that the shadows are the reality. Actually, however, the shadows are inadequate representations of the real characters behind them. Again, the visible and the changing are less real than that of which they are images, and especially than the fire whose illumination makes it possible to see the shadows.[5]

Aristotle's approach to the matter is as different from that of Plato as is his general metaphysic from Plato's. Aristotle worked with a scheme in which potentiality and actuality were of great importance to understanding change. Change is from potentiality to actuality, when something becomes actually that which it is only potentially. Aristotle established, through his argument from motion, that for any motion to take

4. Ibid., 4.509–13.
5. Ibid., 7.514–18.

place, there must be some unmoved mover. Change of the type that we term motion is understood in terms of potentiality and actuality, for something can only move when it is capable of being elsewhere than where it previously was. God is unmovable because he is not potentially somewhere other than where he is. This is also true of other types of change besides motion. God, being fully actual, cannot change, because he has no potentiality not already fully realized.[6]

The philosophical arguments regarding the changelessness of God have also been developed more recently. Three of these are quite closely related. Each presupposes the basic doctrines of the creation and providence worked by God. The argument advanced then becomes almost a practical one: such a view of God cannot be maintained unless he is changeless. In other words, the argument is that certain activities of God, such as creation and providence, are inconsistent with the idea of change in him.

P. T. Geach has raised the question of the changelessness of God as it bears on the question of origins, both of himself and of other things. He contends that the question "Who made God?" does not apply to a changeless God. Such would presumably have always been as he is now. If, however, God changes, then he is one among many beings in the world. Even if it were possible to think of such a God as causing everything else, which Geach does not believe it is possible to think consistently, this God would still, like all other changing things, have to be caused. Geach says, "So I dismiss any 'rethinking' of God's changelessness; it can lead only to an alien and incoherent view of the Divine."[7]

A somewhat similar argument has been advanced by Keith Ward. He contends that divine changelessness is essential to divine providence, considered especially as preservation. If God is subject to change, then he might cease to be or to be the sustaining ground of the world. Thus we have a guarantee of the stability, regularity, and ordered continuity of temporal change only if there is a changeless God. The problem arises both on a theoretical and a practical basis. If God is changing, then he is not the God of preservation and providence. And if there is no such guarantor of the change in the world, we cannot really relate to the world on the basis of such expectations.[8]

A final philosophical argument for immutability has been advanced by Geach. He contends that the confidence in God and his promises that Christians have can only be experienced and justified on the basis

6. Aristotle, *Metaphysics* 12.5–9 (1071a–1075a).
7. P. T. Geach, *Logic Matters* (Oxford: Basil Blackwell, 1972), p. 322.
8. Keith Ward, *The Concept of God* (Glasgow: William Collins, 1977), pp. 153, 155.

of the immutability of God. This guarantees that God can and will fulfill his promises. If this is not the case, then Christianity as it has ordinarily been understood is destroyed.[9]

To summarize the several philosophical arguments:

1. Because God is perfect, he cannot change, because all change is either increase or decrease, improvement or decline, and perfection can neither be improved upon nor lost.
2. Because God is pure actuality, there can be no change in him, for all change is actualization of potentialities that are present.
3. If God could change, he would not be uncaused, and therefore could not be the cause of anything else either.
4. If God could change, we could not have confidence in his preserving all things that are, since his ability to do so might decline or alter.
5. If God could change we could not have confidence in him to keep his promises, thus losing an essential component of Christianity.

Definitions of Change

There are many definitions of change or varieties of change. It is helpful to look briefly at them.

1. There is change that might be called decline or deterioration. This is the loss, either partially or entirely, of positive qualities or the acquisition of negative qualities.
2. There is change that can be referred to as growth or improvement. This is the opposite of change of type 1.
3. There is locational change, the movement from one place to another.
4. Relational change involves no change in the thing itself, but in the relationship to another object or person.
5. Temporal change is aging, not in the sense of the deterioration that we usually associate with growing old, but the accumulation of a great number of years in existence.
6. Alteration is qualitative change, modifying the attributes or characteristics of that which changes. This could, however, be alteration that supplements, rather than contradicts, the qualities already possessed.
7. Reversal is alteration of such a radical nature as to involve actual contradiction of qualities previously possessed.

9. P. T. Geach, *Providence and Evil* (New York: Cambridge University Press, 1977), p. 6.

8. Change of mind involves coming to hold different beliefs or attitudes, or making different decisions than previously.
9. Change of action is a matter of behaving differently, or taking different action than previously, again either radically different and contradictory or supplementary and harmonious.
10. Change of knowledge is the acquisition of information or truth one did not previously possess. It could involve displacement either of ignorance or of error.

Which, if any, of these types of change can be appropriately attributed to God, and which are inconsistent with the concept of God or the biblical teaching regarding him? And which of these are under dispute in the current discussions?

1. Since God presumably is not spatial or spatially located, the sense of change as movement from one place to another does not apply to him.
2. Some cases of relational change are really not changes at all in the subject. The other, the object to which this subject is related, may have changed, thus changing the relationship. So, for example, if I am taller than my teenage friend and I remain the same height but he grows to be taller than me, I am now shorter than him, but this is not really a change in me. To be sure, the relationship can change through my becoming shorter than before and thus shorter than my friend. It would seem that change of the former type can be attributed to God without there really being any change in him.
3. Change as decline would certainly be genuine change in God, but this type of change is scarcely being argued for by any theologians today.
4. Change as increase or growth would also seem to be genuine change. Process theologians claim that God is changing in this sense.
5. Temporal change, or aging, is not a possibility if one holds that God is timelessly eternal. While those who think of God as of infinite duration within time might seem to be able to reconcile this kind of change with their concept of God, that may be questionable, since a God who is already and always has been infinitely old could scarcely somehow become older.
6. Alteration, in terms of either the strong or the weak sense, clearly conflicts with the more traditional view of God. It is under dispute at the present time, however.

7. Change of action seems to be clearly taught by Scripture. For example, God delivered the people of Israel from Pharaoh at one point in history, and sent his Son to the cross at another. Whether such actions represent real change or are only consistent outworkings of one unchanged and unchanging divine nature is debatable, however. To some extent, the answer here depends on the conclusion to the next variety below.

8. Change of mind is the issue currently being considerably debated, with not only process theologians but also free will theists claiming that God changes his mind and plan, often in response to the actions of human beings.

9. Change of knowledge, coming to know something he did not know before, would seem to be change in God, enlarging what he possessed within himself previously. This is also currently under dispute.

Arguments against Immutability

Biblical Arguments

One argument being advanced most vigorously is the contention that the biblical description of God is of a being who changes, in his attitudes, his decisions, and his actions.

1. Repentance passages. The first of these is Exodus 32:12. There Moses implores God to change his mind and his actions, not allowing his people to perish at the hands of the Egyptians. He says to Jehovah, "Why should the Egyptians say, 'It was with evil intent that he brought them out, to kill them in the mountains and to wipe them off the face of the earth'? Turn from your fierce anger; relent and do not bring disaster on your people." Moses certainly seemed to think that God was capable of changing his commitment to a course of action that presumably he had decided on.

Another significant instance is found in Jeremiah 26, where the possibility of God changing his mind is mentioned. So Jehovah says to Jeremiah, "This is what the LORD says: Stand in the courtyard of the LORD's house and speak to all the people of the towns of Judah who come to worship in the house of the LORD. Tell them everything I command you; do not omit a word. Perhaps they will listen and each will turn from his evil way. Then I will relent and not bring on them the disaster I was planning because of the evil they have done" (vv. 2, 3). This sounds like a clear declaration that God intends to bring judgment, but that he will change his mind, or literally repent, of that action. When Jeremiah goes to preach to the people, he repeats the message and says the same thing about God that God has said of himself: "Then Jeremiah said to all the officials and all the people: 'The LORD sent me to prophesy against this house and this city all the things you have heard. Now reform your ways and your actions and obey the LORD your God. Then the LORD will relent and not bring the disaster he has pronounced against you'" (vv. 12, 13).

A final example of God's repenting of judgment that he plans to bring is the case of Nineveh. The message Jehovah gave Jonah to preach in Nineveh, and which he finally did preach, was a categorical statement of judgment: "On the first day, Jonah started into the city. He proclaimed: 'Forty more days and Nineveh will be overturned'" (Jon. 3:4). When the king heard the message, he commanded everyone to turn from their wicked ways, and to show their repentance through the use of sackcloth and ashes, for he reasoned: "Who knows? God may yet relent and with compassion turn from his fierce anger so that we will not perish" (v. 9). This indeed proved to be the case: "When God saw what they did and how they turned from their evil ways, he had compassion and did not bring upon them the destruction he had threatened" (v. 10).

Nor is God's change of mind restricted to repenting of evil that he has purposed to do. The opposite change also takes place. In Genesis 3, God comes to regret having created humans, and resolves to negate his creative action by wiping out wicked persons. The Scripture writer reports, "The LORD saw how great man's wickedness on the earth had become, and that every inclination of the thoughts of his heart was only evil all the time. The LORD was grieved that he had made man on the earth, and his heart was filled with pain. So the LORD said, 'I will wipe mankind, whom I have created, from the face of the earth—men and animals, and creatures that move along the ground, and birds of the air—for I am grieved that I have made them'" (Gen. 6:5–7). This appears to be a clear indication of God reversing his plan and doing what negates, at least with respect to some persons, his earlier life-giving endeavor.

On their surface, these passages seem clearly to indicate a change of mind on God's part. Certainly, such a God must be subject to change, at least in terms of attitude, will, and intention, resulting in change of action from what he has already done and indicated he was about to do. Thus, for example, Richard Rice takes these passages quite literally:

> The biblical descriptions of divine repentance combine elements of emotion and decision to provide a striking picture of the divine reality. They indicate that God is intimately involved in human affairs and that the course of human events has profound effects on him. . . . God works toward his objectives in history in dynamic interaction with human beings. Their experiences and decisions affect his experiences and decisions. So

important is the notion of divine repentance in biblical thought that it deserves to be regarded as one of the central themes of Scripture. It represents "an important interpretive vehicle for understanding the divine activity throughout the canon."[10]

Rice does not think this is a problem in light of the sovereign nature of God or a contradiction of his nature. Rather than being isolated incidents, the accounts of divine repentance are actually characteristic of God. He repents, not despite the fact that he is God, but *because* he is God. It is his very nature to repent, or to relent of action he had planned to take, in light of human action and reaction. Rice finds repentance, or a willingness to turn from his determinations and actions, a defining characteristic of God, as found in lists of such qualities in Exodus 34:6–7, Jonah 4:3, and Joel 2:13.[11]

We cannot conclude our consideration of the question of divine repentance or change of mind at this point, however. For another set of texts seems to indicate that God does not, and indeed, cannot, repent, or change his mind. One of these is Numbers 23:18–20: "Then he uttered his oracle: 'Arise, Balak, and listen; hear me, son of Zippor. God is not a man, that he should lie, nor a son of man, that he should change his mind. Does he speak and then not act? Does he promise and not fulfill? I have received a command to bless; he has blessed, and I cannot change it.'" A second, quite similar, is 1 Samuel 15:28–29: "Samuel said to him, 'The LORD has torn the kingdom of Israel from you today and has given it to one of your neighbors—to one better than you. He who is the Glory of Israel does not lie or change his mind; for he is not a man, that he should change his mind.'"

Rice recognizes the difficulty of these two passages, but maintains that they do not ultimately teach the traditional doctrine of divine immutability or mean that God does not and cannot change his mind. He negates such an interpretation of these passages on four considerations:

1. Repent is used here as a synonym for "lie." Thus, the passages do not deny that God changes his mind, but rather, claim that he never deliberately says he will do something while fully intending to do something different.

---

10. Richard Rice, "Biblical Support for a New Perspective," in Clark Pinnock, Richard Rice, John Sanders, William Hasker, and David Basinger, *The Openness of God: A Biblical Challenge to the Traditional Understanding of God* (Downers Grove: InterVarsity, 1994), p. 34. The closing quotation is from Terence Fretheim, "The Repentance of God: A Key to Evaluating Old Testament God-Talk," *Horizons in Old Testament Theology* 10 (1988): 56.

11. Ibid., pp. 30–31.

2. These statements pertain to specific promises of what God intends to do. They do not declare general principles.
3. The assurance that God does not repent in these specific circumstances presupposes the general possibility that he does or can repent. It is not that God will not repent in such cases because he cannot, but because he does not choose to do so.
4. One of the very chapters (1 Sam. 15) that affirms that God does not repent actually says twice that he does (vv. 11, 35). "So," says Rice, "the scope of this denial obviously is very limited. It is not a statement of general principle."[12]

Is this rebuttal of contradictory passages successful, however? Although Rice makes a point of asserting that there are only two such passages, compared with more than forty that say that God does repent, he has not taken into consideration all of the pertinent passages. While counting every conceivable passage that asserts that God repents, he has disregarded several passages on the other side. Two of these refer to God's resolve with respect to Melchizedek: "The LORD has sworn and will not change his mind: 'You are a priest forever, in the order of Melchizedek'" (Ps. 110:4); "Others became priests without any oath, but he became a priest with an oath when God said to him: 'The Lord has sworn and will not change his mind: "You are a priest forever"'" (Heb. 7:20b–21). Another passage affirming the unchanging purpose and commitment of God is Jeremiah 4:27, 28: "This is what the LORD says: 'The whole land will be ruined, though I will not destroy it completely. Therefore the earth will mourn and the heavens above grow dark, because I have spoken and will not relent, I have decided and will not turn back.'" Finally, Ezekiel delivers a similar message to Israel: "I the LORD have spoken. The time has come for me to act. I will not hold back; I will not have pity, nor will I relent. You will be judged according to your conduct and your actions, declares the Sovereign LORD" (24:14).

Interestingly, these passages seem more susceptible to the interpretation Rice places on the other two, namely, that they could refer to God's particular purpose and action in these specific cases. That is less the case with the passages that he does treat, however. There the fact that God will not repent is tied to the fact that he is God, not a human. What he does or does not do is a result of who and what he is. The statements contradict Rice's interpretation. One of the principles for determining whether a particular or situational statement is to be understood as universal or as only applying to that situation is whether the statement made is dependent on or supported by a universal or doctri-

---

12. Ibid., p. 33.

nal statement. Here, that is indeed the case. God's action derives from who and what he is.

Rice's first point also deserves scrutiny. He does not support his contention with any discussion of the Hebrew words involved. Interestingly, the linguistic data do not support his contention of synonymity. In each of the cases (Num. 23:19 and two occurrences in 1 Sam. 15:29), the word for repent is the very common one, *nacham*. This basically means to be sorry, to console oneself, and is an onomatopoetic word used to mean to breathe pantingly, of a horse. In the niphal, as here, it means to be sorry, rue, suffer grief, or repent.[13] In the former case, the word translated "lie" is *kazav*, which means basically, to lie, to tell a lie, to disappoint or fail.[14] In the Samuel passage, the word translated "lie" is *shakar*, which means to do or deal falsely. Linguistically, *nacham* scarcely can be considered a synonym of either of these words. It may be that Rice is claiming that there is Hebrew parallelism in Numbers 23:19, so that the two statements are equivalent, but he does not say that, and this does not really seem to be poetry. Of further interest in 1 Samuel 15:29 is the word *natzach*. This can mean either preeminent or enduring. Many translators and commentators, basing their interpretation on a cognate meaning of illustrious or preeminent in Aramaic rather than that of pure or reliable or innocent in Arabic and Ethiopic, translate this as "the glory of Israel." Brown, Driver, Briggs also indicate that the word means enduring, everlastingness, and perpetuity,[15] and Keil and Delitzsch believe that in the context, the idea of permanence and unchangeableness make the best sense. They say:

> נֵצַח signifies constancy, endurance, then confidence, trust, because a man can trust in what is constant. This meaning is to be retained here, where the word is used as a name for God, and not the meaning *gloria*, which is taken in 1 Chron. xxix.11 from the Aramaean usage of speech, and would be altogether unsuitable here, where the context suggests the idea of unchangeableness. For a man's repentance or regret arises from his changeableness, from the fluctuations in his desires and actions. This is never the case with God; consequently He is נֵצַח יִשְׂרָאֵל, *the unchangeable One, in whom Israel can trust, since He does not lie or deceive, or repent of His purposes.*[16]

---

13. Francis Brown, S. R. Driver, and Charles A. Briggs, *A Hebrew and English Lexicon of the Old Testament* (Oxford: Clarendon, 1955), pp. 636–37.

14. Ibid., p. 469.

15. Ibid., pp. 663–64.

16. C. F. Keil and F. Delitzsch, *Biblical Commentary on the Books of Samuel* (Grand Rapids: Eerdmans, 1950), p. 158.

On the basis of all these considerations, we must judge Rice's second point inadequate.

Rice's third point is also questionable. He affirms that the statement that God will not repent assumes the general point that God does or can repent. That does not seem to follow, however. The assumption or hidden premise is that "If God promises that he will not repent in a given case, that means that he can or does at times." What is the evidence for this contention? It would seem equally possible that God is simply affirming that he has not changed, and just as he does not repent or alter his behavior, he has not and will not here. This is given as a practical encouragement, not a technical theological statement.

Finally, what of Rice's contention that 1 Samuel 15, which contains the statement in verse 29 that God does not repent, actually includes two statements (vv. 11, 35) that God did repent? Interestingly, Rice does not wrestle with the apparent contradiction. Logically, at least three possible interpretations of this phenomenon could be offered:

1. The statements in verses 11, 35, and 29 simply are in contradiction and must be understood as such.
2. The statement in verse 29 must be interpreted in light of those in verses 11 and 35.
3. The statements in verses 11 and 35 are to be interpreted in light of that in verse 29.

It would seem, in light of the consideration offered earlier, that the narrative statements (about what God did) should probably be interpreted in light of the doctrinal statement (about what and who God is). In any event, Rice's sliding past the issue is disturbing. It should be noted that the major sources cited in support of his view are not persons usually identified as evangelicals (i.e., Fretheim and Knight). Nonevangelicals do not necessarily feel a responsibility to reconcile biblical statements. Perhaps nonevangelical assumptions about the nature of biblical authority have crept in, or perhaps Rice is not conscious of or forthright about his biblical presuppositions.

What needs to be asked, however, is whether this rather literal approach to the discussion of the divine willing and acting is carried through consistently, or what the results would be if we were to do so. There are certain statements made in Scripture about God which, if taken literally, would produce some interesting results for the doctrine of God. For example, there is the statement by Jehovah in Deuteronomy 5:9, 10, "for I, the LORD your God, am a jealous God, punishing the children for the sin of the fathers to the third and fourth generation of those who hate me, but showing love to a thousand generations of those who love me and keep my commandments." Or take Malachi's statement attributed to God—"Yet I have loved Jacob, but Esau I have hated, and I have turned his mountains into a wasteland and left his inheritance to the desert jackals" (1:2b–3)—and repeated by Paul: "Just as it is written: 'Jacob I loved, but Esau I hated'" (Rom. 9:13). What would be the effect on the doctrine of God of interpreting these passages with the same literalistic hermeneutic employed with the repentance passages? Interestingly, Rice does not mention such data.

Is there a better way of understanding these statements about God's repentance? What if we look on those promises and warnings as being conditional in nature, so that the comprehensive form of statement would be: "I will reward obedience and righteousness, and condemn or punish disobedience and unrighteousness." Then, when God moves from promise to punishment, it is not because he has in any way deviated from his original intention, but because the *recipients* of those pronouncements have changed. This means that the changes to be found in God in these cases are actually relational changes. God is related differently to these persons than he had been, but not because *he* has changed. Rather, *they* have changed. Relational change, however, is considered by most philosophers not to be real change in the subject concerned.

To be sure, there are difficulties for the position we have outlined. One would wish, on this view, that there were not the direct statements that picture God as changing and repenting. One must, however, attempt to account for all relevant data, not simply those that fit one's theory. This view is able to take into account more of the data, with less distortion and greater consistency, than the alternative view.

2. The other type of biblical passage pertains to God's knowledge. Several passages seem to indicate that God has discovered something that he did not know. For example, after testing Abraham in connection with the command to offer his son Isaac as a sacrifice, God says to him, "'Do not lay a hand on the boy. . . . Do not do anything to him. Now I know that you fear God, because you have not withheld from me your son, your only son'" (Gen. 22:12). The clear impression one would get if coming to this passage without any other antecedent conception of God is that God needed this test to determine what Abraham would do, since he did not already have that information.

Much of this consideration will be examined in our discussion of omniscience, especially as it concerns foreknowledge. Here we must ask ourselves whether omniscience really is compatible with immutability. Norman Kretzmann has argued that the two are mutually contradictory. For if God is omniscient, he knows all things. In a changing world, therefore, God's knowledge changes. And to know the changing, to have one's knowledge change, is to change oneself.[17]

To be sure, God knows something different today than he did yesterday, namely, what is happening currently. To take a variation on a motif employed by various philosophers, God does not simultaneously know "Richard Nixon is president of the United States" and "Richard Nixon is not president of the United States." Since God knows truth and makes no errors in his knowledge, he knows the first statement from noon on Monday, January 20, 1969, to noon on Friday, August 9, 1974. Before and after those times, he knows the second statement. Does this mean, then, that he has changed?

Suppose, however, that God has always known, and perhaps has always intended, that Richard Nixon would be president during this period of time. If this is the case, then he has always known "Richard Nixon will be president of the United States from January 1969 [reckoned on the Gregorian calendar] to August 1974." He also, presumably knows what time it is on earth, that is, what is currently occurring there. Thus, at a given time, he knows, "it is now exactly 12:34:56 Eastern Standard Time, July 22, 1937"; "it is now exactly 16:32:19, Mountain Standard Time, November 4, 1962"; and so on. At the moment of this writing, he knows "it is now exactly 15:14:31, Central Daylight Time, July 16, 1996." He also knows that it is true that "Erickson is typing at his computer keyboard while looking out the window at the lake." But the content of his knowledge has not really changed. It appears that what has changed is something external to God, and he is conscious of that. This is, in other words, not greatly different from relational change.[18]

This observation grows out of P. T. Geach's discussion of what he has called the "Cambridge criterion," because it frequently occurs in discussions by Cambridge philosophers. According to this criterion, something changes if some predicate applies to it at one time and not another. Geach notes, however, that something may have a change of attributes without itself having really changed in the usual sense of the word.[19] Thus, as Swinburne illustrates, Socrates may at one time be thought about by Smith and at another time not be thought about by Smith, but without Socrates really having changed.[20]

17. Norman Kretzmann, "Omniscience and Immutability," in *Philosophy of Religion*, ed. William Rowe and William Wainwright (New York: Harcourt, Brace, Jovanovich, 1973), pp. 60–70.

18. Cf. Geach, *Providence and Evil*, p. 41.

19. P. T. Geach, *God and the Soul* (London: Routledge & Kegan Paul, 1969), pp. 71f.

20. Richard Swinburne, *The Coherence of Theism* (Oxford: Clarendon, 1977), pp. 212–13.

How does this analysis apply to the current question, however? When God knows something about someone and that person changes, is it not God who changes, just as in the preceding reference Smith, as the knower, changes but Socrates does not? Yet a closer examination may negate this supposition. For although God now knows that Smith is so and so, he has always known that this would be the case. In a sense, the content of God's knowledge has not changed, only the tense of the verb.

What, however, about the question of changes in God's action, so that he does something at one time differently than what he does at another? How are we to regard this? Does not this indicate some change in God? For example, at one point God looked with apparent favor on his children, the people of Israel, and delivered them from injustice and oppression at the hands of Egypt. Then, after their long-standing indifference, disobedience, and rebellion, Jehovah allowed them to be taken captive and carried off into a foreign land. When, however, there had been a sufficient amount of this experience, God intervened to bring his people back from captivity. Obviously, these were different actions by the same God at different times. Can we in some appropriate fashion argue that God has changed because he is acting differently?

One who thinks so is Steven Davis. He notes that the God revealed in Scripture does change in some ways. There are obvious cases in which he is at one point angry with someone who has sinned, and then at a later point forgives the person who has repented. He maintains that this should be considered change, but that it is not significant to the doctrine of immutability, as biblically maintained. It is only incompatible with the strong notion of immutability, of a God who does not change at all. Davis believes that the classical doctrine of immutability was designed to protect belief in a God who was faithful in keeping his promises, who did not act arbitrarily or capriciously. That faith can be maintained while allowing the sort of change we have spoken of here.

One way of responding to this question would be to frame it in terms of the question posed by Plantinga, "Does God have a nature?" If he does, then one possible response would be to say that God's actions change, but that what he is, as contrasted with what he does, does not change. There is another way of approaching the question, however. That is in terms of what it actually means to act. What if God has, from all eternity, chosen to take a certain action? If, then, the working out of this within time takes different forms at different points, can we say that there has been a change in God?

Richard Swinburne considers this possibility and feels that such a conception would indeed solve this problem, but at a high cost. He comments:

This difficulty could be avoided if one said that all that God brings about he has chosen "from all eternity" to bring about. The effects (e.g. the fall of Jerusalem, the fall of Babylon) which God brings about occur at particular times (587 B.C. and 538 B.C. respectively). Yet God has always meant them to occur at those times—i.e. there was no time at which God did not intend Jerusalem to fall in 587 B.C. When 587 B.C. arrived there was no change in God—the arrival of the moment put into effect the intention which God always had. This view would need to be made more sophisticated to deal with the suggestion that God's bringing out one state of affairs, say A, rather than another, say B, was due to his reaction to the behaviour of men (e.g. men may have behaved badly and so God gave them drought instead of rain). The view in question would have to claim that in such circumstances "from all eternity" God had intended that A-occur-if-men did so-and-do, and B-occur-if-men did such-and-such.[21]

Swinburne does not consider this an attractive solution, however, for it creates more problems than it solves. Such a God would be, he maintains, a very lifeless thing. He would not be a personal being who "reacts to men with sympathy or anger, pardon or chastening because he chooses to there and then." Yet this latter type of person, he feels, is the kind of God found in the Old Testament, which is the foundation of Judaism, Islam, and Christianity.[22]

It would appear that performing different actions at different times is not an indication of change in a person. Human beings do different things at different times and in different situations, but without being thought to have changed. It is only if a person acts in a way inconsistent with the earlier actions, or acts so differently that the whole pattern or tenor of the person's life appears changed, that we speak of the person as having changed.

Can this be said of Jehovah? Is it not rather the case that God's actions throughout the span of redemptive history are consistent with, and indeed are the unfolding of, the basic pattern he has revealed regarding himself from the very beginning? Examine the giving of the law, for example, where God's moral character and expectations for humans are spelled out in some detail. There is the threat of judgment on those who fail to heed God's commands, and a promise of mercy and forgiveness for those who refuse. Some have seen a change in the God described in Scripture from the Old Testament to the New. Marcion even posited that there were actually two different Gods involved. Yet there was always provision for the forgiveness of sin, mediated through the sacrificial system. Nor was there a change from salvation by works

21. Ibid., p. 214.
22. Ibid.

to salvation by grace through faith. Paul seems to make quite clear in Galatians 3:6–9 that Abraham was not saved by his works but by his faith, and presumably this was true of the rest of the Old Testament saints as well.

It appears that the strong objection to immutability has been motivated by a reaction to the Greek philosophical conceptions of static immobility. That kind of God, in the Aristotelian fashion, does not really act, and because thinking about what changes would itself entail change, does not really think about anything except himself. It is this static conception that is found objectionable. On these grounds, virtually any action is deemed change, and consequently, action is basically eliminated. Both those who hold such a view of God and those who reject it define change in such a way that it virtually excludes the idea of any significant activity.

Does immutability require this, however? Is it inconsistent with any action at all? It appears that what we are encountering is a confusion of stable with static. The God we find in Scripture is not a static being, as is Aristotle's God. He is rather an active, dynamic being, at work in the world. This dynamic activity, however, is stable, not unstable. His actions are in keeping with his fundamental nature, with his values, plans, and decisions. A human who acts at one time in one way and at another time in another way really can only be deemed to have changed if one or the other of these actions is in conflict with the fundamental values and moral beliefs of the person. There is nothing to lead us to believe that God acts at any point in conflict with his nature. Bear in mind that God is a much more complex being than we are, with beliefs, values, and decisions that take into account infinite possibilities. His plan will therefore be very complex, and may involve a great variety of activity as it unfolds.

The bigger issue seems to be the question of the constancy of God's nature. Is God actually changing in his essence, growing, altering what he is? Process theology, with its view of God as changing, has basically accepted the presuppositions of modern dynamic philosophy, and in addition holds to a rather radically immanent view of God. Thus, God participates in the same change that characterizes the rest of reality.

Process theology rather openly acknowledges its indebtedness to this modern dynamic philosophy. Interestingly, although vehemently (and accurately) disavowing the theology of process theologians, the "openness of God" or "free will theism" school of theologians also appears to have adopted the presuppositions of modern dynamic philosophical views of reality. Repeatedly, they criticize the traditional view, or classic theism, for adopting the Greek philosophy of a Plato or an Aristotle, but do not ask what philosophical view underlies their own theology. It may well be that modern dynamic or process philosophy is preferable to Greek metaphysics. That, however, is what must be debated, rather than simply criticizing the latter view while giving the impression that their view is not based on an alternative philosophy, but is simply the way things are.

6

God and Eternity

In many ways, one of the most disputed and difficult areas of theology is God's relationship to time. This is an area in which significant philosophers have difficulty deciding between the alternatives,[1] and one on which a number of philosophers have even reversed their positions.[2] These are clues that unusual difficulties of conception and of definition may be hidden within this area.

Biblical Data

The biblical writers at several points make clear that God is without beginning and end. He antedates not only human beings, but also everything else that exists. There are a number of types of reference to his eternal or everlasting nature. The first group simply applies the adjective "everlasting" to him. In Genesis 21:33, he is called "the Eternal God." In Isaiah 9:6 the reference is to him as "the Everlasting Father," in Isaiah 26:4 he is called "the Rock eternal," and Jeremiah calls him "the eternal King" (10:10). A second group of texts contrasts God to the temporary and fleeting nature of his creation. The psalmist especially conveys this thought: "Before the mountains were born or you brought forth the earth and the world, from everlasting to everlasting you are

1. E.g., Thomas Morris, *Our Idea of God: An Introduction to Philosophical Theology* (Downers Grove: InterVarsity, 1991), p. 138; Ronald Nash, *The Concept of God: An Exploration of Contemporary Difficulties with the Attributes of God* (Grand Rapids: Zondervan, 1983), p. 83.
2. E.g., Nelson Pike, *God and Timelessness* (London: Routledge & Kegan Paul, 1970), p. 189; Richard Swinburne, "The Timelessness of God," *Christian Quarterly Review* (1965): 323–37; 472–87; *The Coherence of Theism* (Oxford: Clarendon, 1977), p. 218; Paul Helm, "Timelessness and Knowledge," *Mind* 84 (1975): 516–27; *Eternal God: A Study of God without Time* (Oxford: Clarendon, 1988).

God. . . . For a thousand years in your sight are like a day that has just gone by, or like a watch in the night" (Ps. 90:2, 4); "My days are like the evening shadow; I wither away like grass. But you, O LORD, sit enthroned forever; your renown endures through all generations" (Ps. 102:11, 12); "In the beginning you laid the foundations of the earth, and the heavens are the work of your hands. They will perish, but you remain; they will all wear out like a garment. Like clothing you will change them and they will be discarded. But you remain the same, and your years will never end" (Ps. 102:25–27). The insignificance of passing time to God is expressed in Psalm 90:4 and repeated with the same imagery in 2 Peter 3:8: "But do not forget this one thing, dear friends: With the Lord a day is like a thousand years, and a thousand years are like a day." Finally, there are those passages which, without expressly stating that God has no beginning or end, stress his duration and that of his covenants and his people's praise of him: "Your throne was established long ago; you are from all eternity" (Ps. 93:2); "to him be glory in the church and in Christ Jesus throughout all generations, for ever and ever! Amen" (Eph. 3:21); "John, To the seven churches in the province of Asia: Grace and peace to you from him who is, and who was, and who is to come, and from the seven spirits before his throne" (Rev. 1:4).

The Issue

Essentially, the issue we are concerned with in this chapter comes down to something like this. Probably all Christian theologians agree that God is in some sense eternal. By this they mean that he will never come to an end, as many of them feel is also true of humans, at least those to whom God has given "eternal life." They also mean by this that God has had no beginning point. He has always existed. But when we ask what this means, the agreement begins to disappear. For two major understandings compete for our acceptance. One, which we may identify as "atemporal eternality," argues that God is completely outside time. Time does not in any sense apply to him. He holds all of his existence in one timeless point. There is no sequence, no before or after in him. Further, he holds all of history in one simultaneous glance. He knows the future and the past exactly as he does the present. There really is no qualitative difference in these for him. The other understanding we could perhaps term "endless temporality." This contends that time applies to God, just as it does to other beings. There is sequence within God, a before and an after. He also is aware of the sequence of events within human history. He knows the present, and he also has knowledge of the past and the future, but in a different sense. He knows the past as what has occurred, but he does not now experience these past events as currently occurring. He knows all that will happen in the future, but he knows it as not yet having occurred.

The differences between these two views are of considerable significance. In themselves, they may not seem to make a great deal of difference, since both see God as being without beginning or end. They appear, however, to have significant implications for other areas of doctrine and for other aspects of the doctrine of God. For example, the conclusion one comes to on this issue affects one's conclusion on the issue of immutability. For one who holds to the atemporal or timeless view will most certainly be committed to the position of complete immutability. On the other hand, the endless time position can be reconciled with either mutability or immutability ideas. Some theologians argue that if one takes the timelessness approach, God's personality is jeopardized, and the possibility of his really acting within history is rendered suspect, including creation, redemption, and numerous other important divine acts.

In light of such considerations, Nelson Pike argues that the issue of temporal versus atemporal understanding of God is of great importance. He contends that the position one takes on this matter of eternality "has a kind of controlling effect on the general shape and texture of his broad theological view about the nature of God."[3] This is especially true for one's view of the negative model predicates, such as "immutable" and "incorruptible," as well as for omniscience and omnipotence. In light of the pivotal character of this attribute, Pike bemoans the fact that theologians have not given it more attention. In addition, he notes that in the two decades or so preceding his writing of this book, there has been a protest, stemming from such philosophers and theologians as Whitehead and Bishop Robinson, that the very transcendent God usually thought of as the Christian God is not "religiously available." There is a desire to respond to these protests, but first there must be an understanding of what they are protesting, and he believes that the conception that God is timeless is the most emphatic expression of the transcendence of God.[4] Much of his book is devoted to tracing the relationship between divine timelessness and other negative and positive attributes of God.

Yet the assessment of the importance of the topic to Christian theology varies greatly. Despite Pike's statement he seems to conclude that the issue of divine timelessness is unessential to Christian theology. He indicates in the conclusion to his book that he began the investigation thinking that timelessness was of considerable importance, particularly

3. Pike, *God and Timelessness*, p. ix.
4. Ibid., pp. x–xi.

in the connection between it and other doctrines such as immutability. He found, in the course of his investigation, that the idea of timelessness came into theology through Greek thought and then took on a life of its own. His conclusion therefore turned out to be, as he puts it, "considerably more negative than I had anticipated it would be at the outset."[5] He closes by saying that he is not going to assert that the doctrine of timelessness should not be included in Christian theology, but he poses the question, "What reason is there for thinking that the doctrine of God's timelessness should have a place in a system of Christian theology?"[6] Kenny specifically endorses Pike's position, saying that "the doctrine of the timelessness of God is theologically unimportant and inessential to the tradition of western theism."[7] Wolterstorff, on the other hand, thinks that this issue is of the utmost importance. He would perhaps agree in part with Pike and Kenny in the sense that the idea of timelessness adds nothing positive to the doctrine. Where he would disagree, however, is in his sense that this doctrine is fundamental to a whole orientation to the doctrine of God, and as such, has had and continues to have powerful negative consequences.[8]

It is exceedingly important that we define these contrasting positions carefully, and especially that we let representatives of each position speak for their view, for there is a certain amount of discrepancy between the positions as stated both by adherents and opponents. This, of course, is found to some degree in all ideological disagreements, but the extent of this dissonance appears greater here than usual.

An unusual phenomenon is observable. Much of the argumentation tends to be criticism of the timelessness view on the part of the temporalists, and contentions by the atemporalists that their view is coherent. A sort of implicit advantage seems to be assumed for the atemporalist position. Probably this is because the atemporalist view has been the dominant one for much of the history of Christian thought, and therefore, its cogency needs to be challenged. This particular orientation to the debate does cast all of the discussion in a rather unusual light, however.

The Atemporalist View

The atemporalist position has had a long and hallowed history. It has been held by such significant theologians as Boethius, Augustine,

5. Ibid., p. 189.
6. Ibid., p. 190.
7. Anthony Kenny, *The God of the Philosophers* (Oxford: Clarendon, 1979), p. 40.
8. Nicholas Wolterstorff, "God Everlasting," in *God and the Good*, ed. Clifton Orlebeke and Lewis Smedes (Grand Rapids: Eerdmans, 1975), p. 183.

Anselm, and Aquinas. Many theologians and philosophers have held it over the years. These are persons who have given definite shape to the theological tradition and whose opinions are still influential. The most prominent recent defenders of the view include E. L. Mascall, Norman Kretzmann and Eleanor Stump, Paul Helm, and Brian Leftow.

Perhaps the classical articulation of the view set forth by Boethius, who wrote, "Eternity is the complete possession all at once of illimitable life."[9] He also contrasts this with what he calls "sempiternity," which is "the perpetual running resulting from the flowing, tireless now."[10]

Kretzmann and Stump point out four elements in this definition. First, anything that is eternal has life. This excludes from this designation such things as numbers, truths, or the world. One might say of the first two that they are atemporal and of the last that it is sempiternal.[11]

The second point to be observed is that the life of an eternal being is illimitable. While the natural interpretation of this is that of endless duration, infinitely extended both into the past and into the future, another interpretation is sometimes offered, namely, that this is like a point or an instant. It has no duration or extension, and so cannot be limited. It appears, however, that the more natural and probable interpretation of the passage is that it refers to infinite duration, because Boethius refers to God as "always" and because the tradition both before and after Boethius certainly preferred the idea of endless duration, without beginning and end. Boethius was working within the Platonic tradition (both Plato and Plotinus thought of eternity in that fashion), and the medieval theologians and philosophers who followed Boethius understood him in that fashion.[12]

The third element is duration. Although that may seem to be a necessary component of the life of any existing thing, Kretzmann and Stump think it necessary to emphasize this. The final element, and in some senses the key one, is the idea of the complete possession of life all at once. Everything in the life of a temporal being that is not present is not in its possession. The past and the future are not in its possession.[13]

It is important to understand that there is no denial of the reality of time, only of the idea that it applies to God. Boethius and other atemporalists are positing the existence of two separate modes of existence: time and eternity. Eternity is not reducible to time nor is it incompatible with the reality of time.[14]

9. Boethius, *The Consolation of Philosophy*, book 5, prose 6.

10. Boethius, *De Trinitate*, chap. 4.

11. Norman Kretzmann, and Eleanor Stump, "Eternity," in *The Concept of God*, ed. Thomas V. Morris (New York : Oxford University Press, 1987), p. 222.

12. Ibid., pp. 222–23.

13. Ibid., p. 224.

14. Ibid.

Having examined this definition of the atemporal view, we turn to the arguments advanced in its support by its advocates.

1. The atemporal view fits with and supports the idea of divine transcendence better than does the temporal view of God. Transcendence is a very important dimension of the doctrine of God. Yet how can a God be transcendent who is a part of time, who shares the same time-strand as his creatures, including human beings? That God is utterly separate from creation is seen very vividly in the fact that he is utterly outside the time chain, or is completely timeless. Thus, the danger of God collapsing into the created order and losing all distinctness, all difference, as happens in process theology, is avoided. As E. L. Mascall puts it as part of his defense of timelessness, "temporality is precisely one of the characteristics of finite beings which, when we pass from finite beings to God, needs to be transcended."[15]

2. The idea of timelessness is preferable to the alternative, because it means that God's relationship to time parallels his relationship to space. Space and time are usually thought of as the two distinguishing characteristics of the physical universe. God's relationship to space is that he is not in any sense spatial. He is not located at any point in space, and he does not occupy an extension spatially. Although he is present and active everywhere within space (omnipresent), it really is not appropriate to ask, "Where is God?" That would reveal a fundamental confusion regarding the nature of the person that God is. To be consistent, we should think of the relationship of God to time on the same model. He not only is not located within time, he does not have temporal location. He is as much outside time as he is outside space. If he is nonspatial, being a pure spirit, he must also be atemporal.

Paul Helm has argued this point at some length. He does so particularly by showing that some of the arguments offered against the timelessness of God cannot equally well be applied to the question of his relationship to space. Thus, for example, he considers what he calls the argument from simultaneity, as stated by Richard Swinburne:

(7) God exists timelessly.
(8) God exists simultaneously at all moments of human time (from (7)).
(9) God is simultaneously present at what I did yesterday, am doing today, and will do tomorrow.
(10) If time t_1 is simultaneous with t_2, and t_2 is simultaneous with t_3, then t_1 is simultaneous with t_3.

15. E. L. Mascall, *The Openness of Being* (London: Darton, Longman & Todd, 1971), p. 168.

(11) If God is simultaneously present at what I did yesterday and am doing today then yesterday and today are simultaneous (from (9) and (10)).

(12) But the idea that yesterday and today are simultaneous is absurd.

(13) Therefore (7) is incoherent.[16]

Helm then argues that a precisely parallel argument can be offered to show the incoherence of the idea of God's spacelessness:

(14) God is spaceless.

(15) God is wholly spatially present at different places.

(16) God is wholly spatially present at what I am doing here and you are doing there.

(17) If an individual A is wholly spatially present with another individual B, and A is wholly spatially present with a third individual C then B is wholly spatially present with C.

(18) Thus if God is wholly spatially present at what I am doing here and you are doing there then where you are and where I am are the same place.

(19) But the idea that this place and that place are the same place is absurd.

(20) Therefore (14) is incoherent.[17]

While not assuming that space and time are in all respects analogous, Helm nonetheless believes that he has succeeded in showing that if timelessness is incoherent, so is spacelessness. Most theologians and philosophers would not want to reject the idea of divine spacelessness. Therefore, Helm contends, there must be something fundamentally wrong with the argument.

3. Time is a created thing, just like matter. If it is an essential characteristic of the created universe, then it came into being at the time of the creation. The problem, then, as the atemporalist sees it, is what God was before the creation. Unless one is prepared to speak of something like time that is not actually time itself, it would seem that God would have to have been timeless before the creation. But if God was timeless, why need he be in time now?[18]

The essential point here, of course, is the contention that time is essentially tied to the created world, or at least, to the material part of it. Time is usually understood as being at least measured by the movement of material particles. If, however, there was no matter prior to the cre-

---

16. Helm, *Eternal God*, p. 45.

17. Ibid., p. 46.

18. Brian Leftow, *Time and Eternity* (Ithaca, N.Y.: Cornell University Press, 1991), pp. 275–76.

ation, in what sense could there be time? This is reminiscent of Augustine's assertion that God created the world not *in* time but *with* time.[19]

4. This atemporal view, it is claimed, is more in harmony with contemporary physics than is the temporalist view. The Newtonian view of time was of a river that "of itself, and from its own nature, flows equably without relation to anything external."[20] In the thinking of contemporary physicists, however, the paradox of simultaneity and the relativity of time as well as space, which constitute a key to the theory of relativity, seem to fit better with the atemporal view than with the temporal view and its seeming absoluteness of time. There is no single, absolute time to which God can be related, if one accepts the special theory of relativity.[21] In fact, Morris asserts that some theologians and philosophers believe that this discovery constituted something of a decisive development in the dispute.[22]

5. Not only the view of time found in physics, but also that in biology and psychology, supports the atemporal view of God. Mascall directs us to Bergson's *temps vécu*, according to which each sentient individual has its own process of time. This is intimately involved with its own vital rhythms, notwithstanding its complicated interrelation with the time processes of others. Mascall finds this to be a major weakness in Pike's book. Mascall feels that Pike assumes that there is one common time-process for all finite beings, which is at least logically antecedent to them. They are in time, rather than time being in them, in Pike's view.[23]

6. Mascall also contends that the atemporal view fits better than does its competitor with many of the statements made about God's attributes. Thus, for example, when we say that God is good or wise, we are not using the "is" to refer to a temporal present, inserted between past and future, but to a "'timeless present' before which the time-processes of all finite existents and the successive moments of each are uniformly and indifferently displayed and which would belong to God even if he had not created a world and was himself the only being in existence." It is similar to the status of statements like "The square of three is nine," as contrasted with the "is" of the empirical statement, "There is a wart-hog in the garden." This, of course, sounds like a reference to an omnitemporal fact, one that is true throughout all periods of time. Mascall contends, however, that the implied time reference arises from the fact that

19. Augustine, *The City of God*, 11.6.
20. Isaac Newton, *Sir Isaac Newton's Principles of Natural Philosophy*, 2 vols., trans. A. Motte, ed. F. Cajori (Berkeley: University of California Press, 1962), vol. 1, p. 6.
21. Leftow, *Time and Eternity*, p. 272.
22. Morris, *Our Idea of God*, p. 125.
23. Mascall, *Openness*, p. 164.

I am speaking about God from within my own temporal order of time. This does not mean that God himself is within that temporal order.[24]

Mascall suggests, as a parallel, that when we say, "God is good," in English, we are certainly not implying that God himself is English. The same statement could be made in another language, such as French. What is being ascribed to God is neither the English word "good" nor the French word *bon*, but what both words represent. So, he says, "Similarly, when several human beings in talking about God use the superficially temporal verb 'is,' the implied temporality belongs to the mode of existence of the speaker, not to the object denoted by the subject of the sentence, 'God.'"[25] Thus, his argument seems to be that the belief that God is in time is a mistake deriving from the fact that the person making the statements about God is in time and the statements themselves are made within time.

Mascall makes one other point in this connection. We should bear in mind that the different speakers do not even share the same time-scale, an insight derived apparently from the idea of time found in biology and psychology. Each has his own, although they are systematically connected, just as the Englishman and the Frenchman have their own languages, "though the two are connected in the ways described in grammar-books and dictionaries."[26]

We are not to think, however, that this insight pertains only to timeless statements about God, Mascall insists. It also applies to statements ascribing actions—specific historical occurrences—within the temporal process to God. Here the temporal element arises not from the writing or speaking taking place within time, but from the action described taking place within time. So the temporality is inside the sentence rather than outside it. However, at what Mascall calls the action's subjective pole, or God's end, it is timeless, although at the objective pole (that of the creature), it is temporal. So he says, "God timelessly exerts a creative activity towards and upon the whole spatio-temporal fabric of the created universe. This will be experienced as temporal by each creature who observes it and describes it from his own spatio-temporal standpoint; but no more implies that God is in time (even his own special grade-one time) than is the fact that I describe God in English means that God is English."[27]

One other attribute with which timelessness has especially been correlated is immutability. Helm has explored at some length the nature of

24. Ibid., pp. 164–65.
25. Ibid., p. 166.
26. Ibid., p. 166.
27. Ibid.

this connection. He argues that immutability implies timelessness, at least in the case of God. This is because if he is temporal, God must necessarily change. The argument runs somewhat as follows:

> God has acted, as is made clear from the creation of the universe.
> Every action in time must have a point before the act, and a time when the act is completed.
> An agent performing such an action must therefore change, from not acting to acting.
> Therefore if he is temporal, God must be mutable.
> However, God is immutable.
> Therefore, God is not temporal.[28]

Leftow, however, although also holding to divine timelessness, does not consider the argument sound. He does not believe that every act in time must have a point of beginning and a time of completion. Could it not be that a God within time nonetheless continually, at all points throughout time, sustains a universe in existence? Leftow does not see why time must have a first or a last moment, and consequently, God does not change from not sustaining the world to sustaining it, or vice versa.[29]

7. The atemporal view of God fits well with the metaphorical nature of language. It appears that the temporalist view of God assumes a rather literal character to our statements about God. If he is described as acting in time, he is literally within time. Mascall, however, asserts that temporal language is the only language we have. If, then, we are to talk about an atemporally eternal God, we will have to do so using temporal terms. That is the only way we can experience and speak about him. This does not mean that we cannot speak accurately about God, however. It merely means that to speak accurately we must speak using temporal terms. Because God is transcendent, he is also supremely mysterious. It is to be expected, therefore, that language about him would be metaphorical.[30]

8. One of the criticisms leveled against the atemporal view of God is that he is remote and unfeeling. He knows everything in one great undifferentiated present, and so does not feel anything with the force of being what is now transpiring. In fact, some say, God may not even know what is the present, what is happening at this exact moment. Mascall, however, turns this argument exactly around or upside down.

28. Helm, *Eternal God*, p. 90.
29. Leftow, *Time and Eternity*, p. 79.
30. Mascall, *Openness of Being*, p. 167.

He contends that precisely because God is timeless, he is able to be all the more concerned than a God entangled in history.

> For the latter kind of deity would be limited in his experience at each moment to the particular stage in its development that the world had reached at that moment, while the former, in his extra-temporal and extra-spatial vision and activity, embraces in one timeless act every one of his creatures and whatever its time and place may be. Difficult, and indeed impossible, as it is for us to imagine and feel what timeless existence is like, we can, I think, understand that a God to whom every instant is present at once has a vastly greater scope for his compassion and his power than one would have who could attend to only one moment at a time. Thus, in emphasising the timelessness of God, we are not conceiving him as remote but quite the opposite.[31]

9. The atemporal view solves or eliminates a whole host of problems. Among these are foreknowledge and predestination. In particular, the atemporalist view seems to resolve the thorny problem of foreknowledge and human freedom. For God knows everything that everyone will ever do, but in a sense he does not really *fore*know it; he simplies knows it. All time is present to him at once, so he sees the future as well as the past and the present. So, although God knows my action eternally, he does not know it temporally before the time that I do it.[32]

The Temporalist View

Quite different in many ways is the temporalist view, or the view of everlasting extension within time. To those who hold this view, God is everlasting. He is within time in the sense that there is a genuine sequence within his experience and his nature. There is a "before" and an "after" for him. He is also conscious of the sequence of events within history and knows what is currently occurring in a different fashion than he knows either the past or the future.

As we observed earlier, the arguments advanced by the temporalists are not so much arguments for their position as they are arguments against the opposing position, that is, attempts to show the inadequacy and even the internally contradictory nature of the atemporalist view. The structure of the argument seems to be as follows:

Either temporalism or atemporalism is true.
Atemporalism cannot be true.
Therefore, temporalism must be true.

---

31. Ibid., p. 172.
32. Richard L. Purtill, "Foreknowledge and Fatalism," *Religious Studies* 10 (1974): 321–23.

Consequently, several criticisms are raised against the atemporalist view, which conversely, then serve as arguments supporting the temporalist option.

1. The first is that timelessness is incompatible with God acting within time, performing the types of actions (such as creating) that the Bible depicts him as performing. Pike supposes that yesterday, on the prairies of Illinois, a 17,000-foot-high mountain came into existence, and that local theists claimed that this was a work of God. How can this be accepted as an explanation, however? Pike follows Schleiermacher's interpretation of such situations. He contends that a timeless God could not have done this, because an event such as creating or producing an object that has position within time would require God's activity to have occurred at a specific time. "The claim that God *timelessly* produced a temporal object (such as the mountain) is absurd," says Pike, in agreement with Schleiermacher.[33] Schleiermacher, who believed in divine timelessness, used the argument to refute creation within time. The argument works equally well in the other direction as well, however. If God creates within time, he must also be within time. With every other activity that we observe, we remark that the person uttered the sound or built the bird house or whatever at point T. So, the coming into being of something at point T through the creative activity of God must be described by saying, "God created x at T." If that is the case, however, then God is not timeless; he is within time.

2. A second argument is that a timeless being really could scarcely be called a person. The difficulty is outlined by Robert Coburn and elaborated on by Pike. In his reply to Professor Malcolm, Coburn attempts to outline certain activities essential to being a person and then shows that a timeless being could not do any of these. A person must be capable of doing at least some of these: remembering, anticipating, reflecting, deliberating, intending, and acting intentionally, says Coburn. He says, "To see that this is so, one need only ask oneself whether anything which necessarily lacked all of the capabilities noted would, under any conceivable circumstances, count as a person. But now an eternal being would necessarily lack all of these capacities inasmuch as their exercise by a being clearly requires that the being exist in time."[34]

Pike's analysis of Coburn's position is that reflecting and deliberating take time. Anticipating and intending require that the individual doing those actions have temporal location, since these involve thinking about events before they occur. Similarly, remembering involves thinking

33. Pike, *God and Timelessness*, p. 105.
34. Robert Coburn, "Professor Malcolm on God," *Australasian Journal of Philosophy*, v. 40–41 J (1962–63): 155.

about something after one has experienced it. Pike thinks that Coburn is on the right track, but that his conclusion is premature. What might qualify a being as a person even without these actions, in Pike's judgment, is knowing. When he examines the idea of a timeless being knowing, however, he finds that such a being could not act in the ways required of a person who knows, believes, or is aware of something. Until some sort of explanation or at least picturing can be given of the difference between a timeless being who has knowledge and one who does not, this does not seem to advance the idea of a timeless being as a person. Further, such a being could not be prompted or affected by another, and no action of such a being could be taken as a *response* to something else. Responses, after all, are located in time after that to which they are a response.[35] His conclusion is, "At this point, I think we should adopt the position set out by Coburn. An individual that is (in principle) incapable of all of these things could not be counted as a person."[36]

3. Nicholas Wolterstorff has contended that the God described in Scripture really cannot be the timeless God. Before engaging in his argument, he notes the heavy preponderance of theologians in the history of the church who have contended that God is eternal rather than everlasting. Why should this be? He believes there are two reasons, one of which appears to be psychological and the other cultural. He maintains that there is a powerful, deep-seated feeling that the flow of events into a fixed and irrecoverable past is a "matter for great regret." While the philosopher sees that regrets about the actual occurrence of events in history should not be allowed to produce regrets about temporality as such, but the average person is not as astute in this matter as is the philosopher.[37]

There is a further reason, however. Wolterstorff agrees with William Kneale that classical Greek philosophy has had a powerful influence on theology. He does not hold that everything the Greeks said is false. What he does maintain, however, is that "the patterns of classical Greek thought are incompatible with the pattern of biblical thought." He is convinced that the essential process of dehellenization of Christian thought "must fail unless it removes the roadblock of the God eternal tradition."[38]

After an extensive analysis of what it would mean to be a timeless being, Wolterstorff examines the actions of God. He sees that these are within time. As such, they involve sequence. But this performance by

35. Pike, *God and Timelessness*, pp. 122–28.
36. Ibid., p. 128.
37. Wolterstorff, "God Everlasting," p. 182.
38. Ibid., p. 183.

God of actions that take place within time must themselves participate in temporality. Consider knowing, for example. One can only know that something is occurring when it is occurring—neither before nor after. Thus a change takes place in the knowledge of anyone, even God. So Wolterstorff writes, "But surely the nonoccurrence followed by the occurrence followed by the nonoccurrence of such knowings constitutes a change on God's time-strand. Accordingly, God is fundamentally noneternal."[39] The same is true of God's remembering events and planning that he would bring about certain events.

> So in conclusion, if God were eternal he could not be aware, concerning any temporal event, that it is occurring nor aware that it was occurring nor aware that it will be occurring; nor could he remember that it has occurred; nor could he plan to bring it about and do so. But all of such actions are presupposed by, and essential to, the biblical presentation of God as a redeeming God. Hence God as presented by the biblical writers is fundamentally noneternal. He is fundamentally in time.[40]

4. A further objection to the timeless or atemporal view of God is that such a God really could know nothing that is going on in the temporal world. All he could know, strictly speaking, would be timeless truths, such as mathematical truths. He would not be able to relate knowingly to the contingencies of history. Arthur Prior has argued this point at some length. He says, for example, that although he knows that the 1960 final exams are now over, God cannot know that, for he is timeless, and to a timeless being it simply is not the case that the exams are now over, nor, in a sense, will that ever be the case. As a timeless being, he knows the timeless, and this is not a matter that is true timelessly. What we know when we know that the exams are over is not just a timeless relation between dates. That is not what we are pleased about when we are pleased that the exams are finally over.[41] Essentially, this is a variation of the contention that God does not know what time it is, but with a more specific application. The implication is that God cannot be both timeless and omniscient.

5. The idea of a timeless eternity, in which the whole is simultaneous with every part of time, is incoherent. Kenny argues this in his treatment of Aquinas's view of time. He raises the issue in connection with the question of prophecy. Aquinas believed that God, as the principal author of Romans, knew at the time of the writing of Romans that the

39. Ibid., p. 198.
40. Ibid., pp. 199–200.
41. Arthur Prior, "Formalities of Omniscience," in *Readings in the Philosophy of Religion,* ed. Baruch A. Brody (Englewood Cliffs, N.J.: Prentice-Hall, 1974), pp. 415–16.

Jews would be converted, and so foretold this. But, says, Kenny, if God is timeless we cannot attach to statements about his knowledge such adverbial clauses as "at the time when the Epistle to the Romans was written." That simply does not make sense.[42]

When we try to speak of a timeless God in terms referring to specific times, we get into paradoxes. Simultaneity is ordinarily understood as a transitive relation. If A is simultaneous with B and B is simultaneous with C, then A must be simultaneous with C. This, however, reduces history to nonsense, on the timelessness view of God: "If the BBC programme and the IRV programme both start when Big Ben strikes ten, then they both start at the same time. But, on St. Thomas' view, my typing of this paper is simultaneous with the whole of eternity. Again, on his view, the great fire of Rome is simultaneous with the whole of eternity. Therefore, while I type these very words, Nero fiddles heartlessly on."[43]

6. There also is the claim that the biblical view of time supports the idea of God as temporal rather than atemporal. In particular, much is made of Oscar Cullmann's view of time as stated and expounded in *Christ and Time*. The essential point of the book is that eternity is not thought of by the biblical writers as something qualitatively different from time as we know it. Rather, it is simply a quantitative extension, an extension of time back into the past and forward into the future. If this is the case, there is not some other, extratemporal realm for God.

The Biblical Concept of Eternity

This latter point is important enough to merit extended treatment, especially since many of the philosophers involved in this discussion are Christians, for whom the issue of the biblical understanding of time and eternity is an important consideration. Two important studies deserve special attention.

The Position of Cullmann: Eternity as Extended Time

One of the most influential treatments of the biblical understanding of time is given by Oscar Cullmann in *Christ and Time*. Cullmann was one of the most prominent members of the Biblical Theology Movement that flourished in the 1930s to the 1950s. In this work we see quite clearly exemplified the methodology of this school of thought. Much of his treatment is concerned with the examination of the terms

---

42. Anthony Kenny, "Divine Foreknowledge and Human Freedom," in *Aquinas: A Collection of Critical Essays,* ed. Anthony Kenny (Notre Dame, Ind.: University of Notre Dame Press), pp. 263–64.

43. Ibid., p. 264.

kairos and *aiōn*. His thesis is stated early in the first chapter: "The characteristic thing about *kairos* is that it has to do with the definite *point of time* which has a fixed content, while *aion* designates a *duration of time*, a defined or undefined *extent of time*. In the New Testament both terms serve, in a manner that corresponds remarkably well to the matter in hand, to characterize that time in which the redemptive history occurs."[44] For our purposes, it is especially his definition of *aiōn* that is significant. Cullmann is quite categorical. He claims that the word bears two meanings: "an exactly defined period of time and an undefined and incalculable duration, which we then translate by the word 'eternity.'"[45] He then goes on to say of this second usage, meaning "eternity,"

> Even here, however, the conclusion should be laid down that eternity, as meant in this linguistic usage, is not to be interpreted in the Platonic and modern philosophical sense, where it stands in contrast to time; it must rather be taken as endless time. . . . Thus in the New Testament field it is not time and eternity that stand opposed, but limited time and unlimited, endless time. Moreover, the thoroughly temporal manner of thinking is not surrendered even when the New Testament speaks of this endless time. This latter time is not different from the former. The difference consists only in the fact that it is limited.[46]

What arguments does Cullmann offer in support of this thesis? There seem to be four:

1. The word *aiōn* has a double meaning: a precisely limited duration of time (where it would be properly translated "age") and an unlimited, unmeasurable duration (where it would be rendered "eternity").[47] This is based on an examination of the New Testament usage.

2. The word can be spoken of in the plural, which "proves that it does not signify cessation of time or timelessness."[48]

3. The conception of time held by the primitive Christian community was gradually displaced by a view of eternity held by the Greeks. This does not enter the New Testament in the Book of Hebrews or in the Johannine writings. Rather, it can be traced back to Gnosticism.[49]

4. Certain biblical texts make clear that God is functioning within time as extended indefinitely both forward and backward, rather than

44. Oscar Cullmann, *Christ and Time: The Primitive Christian Conception of Time and History* (Philadelphia: Westminster, 1960), p. 39.
45. Ibid., p. 45.
46. Ibid., pp. 45–46.
47. Ibid., p. 45.
48. Ibid., p. 46.
49. Ibid., p. 55.

in some timeless realm. Among these are Hebrews 13:8, "Jesus Christ is the same yesterday and today and forever"; Hebrews 11:10, 16; 13:14, which speak of the future Jerusalem; Revelation 1:4, which speaks of God "who is, and who was, and who is to come"; Hebrews 4:9, which speaks of a "Sabbath-rest of God;" and 1 Corinthians 15:23–28, which includes a heaping up of references to time. Even Revelation 10:6, which speaks of there being no more *chronos*, is to be understood on the analogy of Hebrews 2:3 and Hebrews 10:37, so that it is translated, "There will be no more delay."[50]

Cullmann summarizes his view in several statements:

1. Time in its entire unending extension, which is unlimited in both the backward and the forward direction, and thus is "eternity."
2. Limited time, which lies between Creation and the eschatological drama, and which is thus identical with the "present" age or "this" age.
3. Periods of time which are limited in one direction but unlimited in the other, and specifically:
a. The period to which the phrase ἐκ τοῦ αἰῶνος, "out of the age" points back, i.e., the time that lies before the Creation. On the side of Creation it has an end and so a limit; but in the backward direction it is unlimited, unending, and only in this sense is it eternal;
b. The period that extends beyond the end of the present age (αἰῶν μέλλων, the "coming age"). It thus has in the so-called eschatological drama its beginning and so a limit; but in the forward direction it is unlimited, unending, and only in this sense is it eternal.[51]

James Barr's Criticism

As influential as this view has been, it has also been severely criticized, especially by James Barr in his *Biblical Words for Time*. In his earlier work, *Semantics of Biblical Language*, Barr criticized certain aspects of the method of the Biblical Theology Movement, and even the massive *Theological Dictionary of the New Testament*, which depended so heavily on it. In this book he proceeds to apply his criticism to a specific area, the Biblical Theology Movement's analysis of time, especially Cullmann's *Christ and Time*.

1. His first criticism is of Cullmann's argument that the use of the plural for "eternity" proves that continuance, not the cessation, of time is involved. But, asks Barr, "Why?" What logic is being followed here? He assumes that the reasoning is that the use of the plural implies some variety that is referred to, and that variety and change indicate time. This theoretical argument, however, takes no account of the dif-

---

50. Ibid., p. 49.
51. Ibid., p. 48.

ferent uses of the plural. In Hebrew there are numerous instances of plurals that have no singular, or do not indicate a plurality of the reality designated by the singular. This is particularly true of the Hebrew plural *olamim*, which has nothing to do with a plurality of an object denoted by *olam*.[52]

2. Cullmann's other main point was that the two meanings of *aiōn* both for an age or limited duration and for eternity of unlimited duration proves that the latter sense in the New Testament must mean not something different from the former but unlimited extent of the former. Barr says the fact that a word has two senses does not, however, mean that the two must be similar. It only means that they have some point of contact, which may lie in the past relative to the period under discussion. His basic criticism of Cullman's approach is that we cannot determine the meaning of a word in a given passage by appealing to the lexical stock, such as its etymology or something similar. The meaning is determined by usage, and the usage in a given instance indicates the meaning there. His comment on the contention that *aiōn* must mean age or ages in the passages where they have often been taken as meaning something qualitatively different from time is as follows: "To summarize: it is only in other syntactic contexts, and not in the ones quoted, that *aiōn* means a particular limited duration or 'age.' These phrases are therefore no evidence for the case that eternity differs from time only in being the unlimited entirety of time. The meaning has to be taken for the phrase as a whole."[53]

Based on such considerations as the preceding, Barr concludes that Cullmann's argument has failed to establish that eternity, as understood by the biblical writers, is simply qualitatively the same as time, but extended indefinitely, both into the past and into the future. It should not be concluded, however, that Barr feels that this establishes that eternity is qualitatively different from time. He is also quite critical of the methodology of John Marsh, who attempts to use lexical studies to establish that point, quite in opposition to Cullmann's conclusions. Barr's treatment does, however, leave open the possibility of either interpretation of the eternity of God.

A Mediating Position: Relative "Timelessness" or "True Temporality"

Recently, some philosophical theologians have attempted to slip between the horns of the dilemma of either atemporal eternity or infinite

---

52. James Barr, *Biblical Words for Time* (London: SCM, 1962), p. 64.
53. Ibid., p. 69.

temporality. One of these is the idea of the relative timelessness of God, proposed by Alan Padgett. This is the idea that God is not absolutely timeless (without any sort of succession within his nature.) Rather, he is not part of the same time sequence in which we and all other created beings participate. He has a time of his own, which is not simply physical time, measured by the movement of physical objects, but a transcendent time.[54] He acknowledges that this view's cogency rests on the adoption of a particular understanding of time, which he calls the process view of time, or A-time. This is the idea that events come into being, exist, and then pass away. This is contrasted with the stasis view of time, or time as untensed, also known as B-time. Based largely on a thorough critique of the stasis theory, Padgett finds the process view preferable.[55]

William Lane Craig accepts the basic elements of this view while adapting some of its concepts. He prefers to speak, not of "relative timelessness," but of "true temporality." In his view, there is not a true relativity of simultaneity within the universe. Rather, there is one absolute time frame, which Craig terms cosmic time and which is associated with cosmic expansion.[56] This conception depends on rejecting the positivistic dimensions of the Einsteinian interpretation of the Special Theory of Relativity. It also involves positing a "new aether wind" of approximately 360 kilometers per second. This cosmic time is not, however, real time. Real time, or ontological time, is God's own time, which, in Craig's judgment, coincides but is not necessarily identical with, cosmic time.[57] The universe does not merely act as a clock for God; it *is* God's clock. Craig says, "God is an unembodied Mind utilizing a physical clock.[58] Padgett holds that cosmic time is contingent, and that there may be possible worlds in which real time and cosmic time do not coincide.[59] Craig, however, is willing to say that both cosmic time and real time are contingent. A God existing without creation is timeless. He enters time with the creation of the universe. Craig seems to say, in effect, that God creates not only cosmic time but also real or ontological time.[60] The most natural meaning of this position is that the act of creation of a physical universe initiates, both cosmic time and ontological time, or world time and God's time. This seems to be sup-

54. *God, Eternity, and the Nature of Time* (New York: St. Martin's, 1992), pp. 122–37.

55. Ibid., pp. 82–121.

56. William Lane Craig, "God and Real Time," *Religious Studies* 26.3 (September 1990):340.

57. Ibid., p. 343.

58. Ibid., p. 345.

59. Padgett, *God, Eternity and the Nature of Time*, pp. 127–29.

60. Craig, "God and Real Time," p. 345.

ported by Craig's citation of his earlier article, in which, he says, "I argue that God existing without creation is timeless and that He enters time at its inception with His creation of the universe. Since creation is a freely willed act of God, the existence of real time is therefore contingent."[61] This seems, however, to conflict with his statement that "God's ontological time clearly exceeds cosmic time in that the former may have preceded the latter (imagine God leading up to creation by counting '1, 2, 3,. . . , *fiat lux!*')"[62] Perhaps the resolution is in saying that what Craig means to state is that ontological time comes into being *in connection with* the act of creation—not coincident with it, but rather immediately "prior" to it. This interpretation would be supported by his use of "1, 2, 3," rather than "3, 2, 1" (i.e., counting up rather than counting down).

This, then, raises the question of whether such a God can be independent of space. Padgett's approach is that God's time is not measured, by the clock of the universe or any other. Thus, just as he transcends cosmic time, he also transcends space, although Padgett finds no inherent conflict between the concept of God, including the properties of omnipotence and omniscience, and God's having a body, but accepts Swinburne's argument that the universe as a whole does not function as God's body.[63] Because Craig holds to the coincidence of both real and cosmic time, he responds by distinguishing between parameter time, as found in Newtonian physics, and coordinate time, as found in relativity theory, and contends (but does not elaborate on or argue), that the latter can also be reformulated entirely in terms of parameter time.[64]

One of the differences between Padgett and Craig seems to be in terms of epistemology. Craig rejects certain positions as based on a now-discredited positivism. Yet, while that earlier form of analytical philosophy disallowed the meaningfulness of any a priori synthetic statements, the later (or ordinary-language) form of analytical philosophy, while not being this categorically verificationist, asked for the basis of claiming that such statements are meaningful. Padgett seems more agnostic or at least more tentative in his conclusions about whether cosmic time may apply to other possible worlds and in challenging assumptions "about how God is in himself based upon how God seems from a limited temporal perspective (i.e. a particular frame of refer-

61. Ibid., n. 32. The article referred to is "God, Time, and Eternity," *Religious Studies* 14.4 (December 1978): 497–503.

62. Ibid., p. 343.

63. Padgett, *God, Eternity, and the Nature of Time*, pp. 129–30.

64. Craig, "God and Real Time," pp. 345–46.

ence)."[65] Craig seems to be more certain of some of this extrapolation, although his epistemology is not fully explained.[66]

We have an interesting situation here. The debate about temporality or atemporality turns out to be dependent on a more basic question, namely, the nature of time. So it hinges on whether one adopts an A-theory or a B-theory of time. One of the ways utilized to try to untie that Gordian knot, however, is by appeal to contemporary physics' understanding of time, particularly to the implications of the special theory of relativity. Here, again, however, we are faced with at least two different interpretations of the theory, which Craig designates as the positivist (the Einsteinian) and the Lorentzian. So we are faced with a series of at least three differences between the two theories. These differences are over issues that are so interlocked that if we were able to resolve one of them the other two would have to follow as well. In general, the approaches of Padgett and Craig, while they fall between the two positions of everlasting temporality and timelessness of God, have more affinity with the former, particularly in these secondary issues of A-theory versus B-theory time and the interpretation of the special theory of relativity.

A Synthetic Position

In the debate between the two major positions, we seem, in some ways, to have come to an impasse. Arguments can be proposed on both sides, and criticisms can be raised against either position. As Thomas Morris indicates, for each of the arguments advanced by one side, there is always a countering argument that can be raised.[67] It is not surprising, then, that Morris[68] and Ronald Nash[69] declare their inability to choose between the two views.

Such an impasse suggests, however, that we look for another solution, a third way that is more persuasive than either of these taken alone. When we have two views that are both logically possible and have strong arguments on either side, we perhaps need to take another

---

65. Padgett, *God, Eternity, and the Nature of Time*, p. 128.

66. In fairness to Craig, and somewhat ironically, it should be pointed out Craig's objection to Padgett's rejection of a physical clock measuring God's time is that "we have no reason, biblically or philosophically, to think that other universes exist. Parsimony justifies the assumption that ours is the only universe" ("God and Real Time," p. 345). This seems to make the contention that God's time coincides with cosmic time during the duration of the universe rest upon an argument from silence.

67. Morris, *Our Idea of God*, p. 138

68. Ibid.

69. Nash, *The Concept of God*, p. 83

look at the way we are approaching them. Some have argued that one view is logically incoherent, with this usually being alleged by the temporalists against the atemporalists. William Hasker, although clearly rejecting the atemporalist view, in an unusually fair and sympathetic chapter concludes that there is nothing logically incoherent about the idea of a God totally outside time being able to bring about effects within time.[70] His choice is based, not on logical consistency, but on the temporalist view's better fit of the significant facts.

Is it possible that the apparent deadlock between the two views is because they are not true contradictories? May it be that each of these views has seized on part, not the whole, of the truth? And if that is the case, can we blend the two views? Several considerations ought to be taken into account here.

1. It is customary to think of the attributes on some sort of scheme such as absolute and relative. The former refers to God as he is in himself, apart from his creation. This, presumably, is how he was prior to the creation, and, it is also presumed, the way he still is, independently of that creation. So, for example, God is pure love, which expresses itself in the mutual interrelationships within the Trinity. When, however, he creates, this also becomes transitive love, or love for his creatures. He is immutable, which, for the sake of the argument, we will restrict to his unchanging character. When, however, he becomes related to humans whom he has created, this becomes faithfulness, the fact that he will surely keep the promises and commitments he has made to his people.

What, however, about the issue of God's eternality? The absolute sense of this is that God is prior to (and, perhaps in some sense, independent of) the created order, which includes a time sequence. May there, however, also be a relative eternality, God's relationship to the entire span of the created universe's history?

2. This poses for us the particular issue of God's transcendence and immanence. By the former, we usually mean that God is in some way separate from or distinguished from the universe. By the latter, we also generally mean that God is nonetheless related to and active within that universe.

Here, however, we encounter an interesting phenomenon. In the contemporary discussion among philosophers, there is little discussion about God's relationship to space. In general, however, it seems to be the case that the discussants have no real problem considering God to be both transcendent to and immanent within space. He is not thought

70. Willliam Hasker, *God, Time and Knowledge* (Ithaca, N.Y.: Cornell University Press, 1989), p. 170.

of as being within space, in the sense of having location spatially, of having any sort of extension within space, or of moving from one location to another. He is, in other words, aspatial. He is not simply infinitely large, so that he spreads over the entire universe. He does not have a physical body. Yet there seems to be no objection to God's immanence, specifically, the idea that he is able to act within space, to effect occurrences in the realm of physical objects.

On the other hand, however, when contemporary discussions deal with time, the assumption seems to be that God must either be transcendent to or immanent within time. If God is truly atemporal, he cannot be aware of what time it is "now" on earth, for then what he knows would be changing. Further, he cannot act within time, for then there would be a sequence of not acting–acting–not acting. So the temporalist argues that God must not be atemporally eternal, while the atemporalist argues that God has one eternal will or one great act, of which the specific occurrences within time are effects. But is it possible that, just as with space, it is not *either* that God is timeless *or* that he is within time, but *both?* The apparent contradiction between being both transcendent to space and immanent within it is generally resolved by contending that God's relationship to space is in two different senses. He is not transcendent to it and immanent within it in the same sense. He is ontologically outside space, yet he is influentially present within it. While he himself does not have spatial location, he is able to act within space.

I am impressed with the arguments of Helm, Purtill,[71] and others that the same difficulties found with God's relationship to time also apply to his relationship to space, if the same arguments used in the former are applied to the latter. How is it that a nonspatial God can affect objects and events within space? Does this not require him to be spatial?

3. A further consideration is the nature of space and time in an Einsteinian universe. We have conducted this discussion as if the two were separable, and the debate whether the two are analogous often takes place. If, however, we accept Einstein's view of relativity, the two are not simply analogous; they are inseparable. Previously it was possible to think of three dimensions of space, plus time. For Einstein, however, reality is four-dimensional, involving length, breadth, width, and time.[72] Within our universe, reality is four-dimensional, and each dimension

71. Richard Purtill, "Foreknowledge and Fatalism," *Religious Studies* 10 (1974): 322.
72. Albert Einstein, *The Meaning of Relativity,* 5th ed. (Princeton, N.J.: Princeton University Press, 1956), p. 31. This connection was first called to my attention by Mr. C. Fred Smith, a Ph.D. student at Southwestern Baptist Theological Seminary.

must be taken into account. We are accustomed to speak of two-dimensional objects, having only length and width, for example, but not height. Yet in our world such objects do not actually exist. They are concepts, but they are more like Plato's Ideas than they are existing objects. What we usually think of as two-dimensional objects are actually three-dimensional, with the third dimension being very small, very thin, for example. So Stephen Hawkings' two-dimensional dog, if it had a true digestive tract, would fall apart.[73] While we may conceive of two-dimensional objects, they do not exist in our actual world, in which length, width, and height cannot be separated. We do not think of God as being transcendent to height, but not to length or width. And, from the perspective of Einstein, time cannot be separated from these either. They can be distinguished, just as height can be distinguished from length, but they are not separable in the created universe. If this is the case, then the question is not, What is God's relationship to time, and specifically, is it analogous to his relationship to space? Rather, it is, What is God's relationship to time-space? Is God both immanent within and transcendent to time-space, and what is the nature of such transcendence? Is it quantitative, so that God is infinitely large and infinitely old? Or is it qualitative, so that space and time do not apply to him in his transcendent aspect?

It may be helpful for us to look more closely at contemporary science's conception of time. Under Newtonian physics, "time was completely separate from and independent of space."[74] Since Newton, however, a major revolution has taken place within science, especially under the title of Albert Einstein's theory of special relativity and his theory of general relativity.

Whereas in Newton's thought space and time were considered absolute and separate from one another, in Einstein's theories the two are not independent concepts but are four dimensions by which everything is to be described and located. Einstein says, "we must regard x_1, x_2, x_3, and t as the four co-ordinates of an event in the four-dimensional continuum. . . . The circumstance that there is no objective rational division of the four-dimensional continuum into a three-dimensional space and a one-dimensional time continuum indicates that the laws of nature will assume a form which is logically most satisfactory when expressed as laws in the four-dimensional space-time continuum."[75]

73. Stephen Hawking, *A Brief History of Time: From the Big Bang to Black Holes* (Toronto: Bantam, 1988), p. 164.

74. Ibid., p. 18.

75. Albert Einstein, *The Meaning of Relativity*, 5th ed. (Princeton, N.J.: Princeton University Press, 1956), p. 31.

This inseparability of space and time can be seen in the fact that they vary together, both being subject to effects from the same natural forces. The theory of special relativity is the theory best known. It pertains to the effect of acceleration on space and time. It grew out of the paradox that although ordinarily there is addition or subtraction of velocities, this did not prove to be the case with the speed of light. That speed remained constant, regardless of whether the source of the light was moving toward or away from the observer. The only possible solution to this was that space is relative. Einstein performed some experiments and found that when an object is accelerated to 90 percent of the speed of light, its length in the direction of movement is half that which it is at rest. This also proved to be the case with time. This leads us to the "twin paradox" sometimes utilized in science fiction, whereby if one twin leaves earth, accelerates to 90 percent of the speed of light, travels for a time, and then returns to earth, he will have aged only half as much as his twin on earth, and his watch will have marked the passage of only half as much time as the identical watch worn by the twin on earth. This calculation was confirmed when physicists at the CERN laboratory in Europe accelerated muons to 99.94 percent of the speed of light and multiplied their life span by 30 times.[76]

Einstein's theory of general relativity pertains to the effect of gravity on time. Gravity is the attraction of one body of mass to another. Here it is well known that gravity affects the direction of movement of an object and its rate of acceleration. What Einstein's theory proposed was that gravity also affects the rate of passage of time. The closer an object is to earth, the greater is the force of the gravitational pull of earth and the more slowly time passes. This has been demonstrated through a series of experiments. In one of these, in 1975 and 1976, atomic clocks were flown high over Chesapeake Bay and then compared with identical clocks that had remained on the ground. When other factors were compensated for, it was found that the clocks in the air gained three billionths of a second every hour, as compared to the clocks on the ground.[77] In June 1976, another experiment was performed at Wallops Island, Virginia, in which an atomic clock was launched to an altitude of six thousand miles. It was shown to gain one-billionth of a second every second over a similar clock on the ground.[78]

Suppose we ask further how the unity of space and time works. We might note that temporal simultaneity is in part a matter of space as well as time. A being that is everywhere is also "everywhen." With re-

---

76. Nigel Calder, *Einstein's Universe* (New York: Viking, 1979), p. 1.
77. Ibid., p. 38.
78. Ibid., p. 39.

spect to visible occurrences in the physical universe, in effect all past events are still present somewhere. That each event emits light rays, which continue to emanate outward. So the sunlight that we see at the moment actually left the sun approximately eight minutes ago. The light from a star one hundred light years away left that star one hundred years before we see it. Thus, we will continue to see that star for one hundred years after it ceases to emit light. Barring difficulties such as lack of illumination and obscuration of the atmosphere, in theory every event in the physical universe is still current at some place in the universe. There are ways of cutting through the haze, as with a haze filter, and there are night glasses that employ infrared light. In theory, we could travel into space and observe the battle of Gettysburg, the launch of the first spaceship, or even the first sin in the Garden of Eden. Certain technical difficulties accompany our effort, of course. For one thing, as the cone of light emitted by the event extends, it also becomes wider at its more distant point. It therefore is necessary to cover a much larger area to observe it than would be true a few feet away. Further, because the light is traveling at the speed of light, one would have to travel faster than that to apprehend the outspreading light, which is technically impossible.

For God, however, this problem does not exist. For one thing, if he can travel at an infinite speed, he can be everywhere in the universe at any given time. Thus, the events that occurred at a particular place five minutes ago are present to him, as are those that happened ten minutes ago. Beyond that, God does not really have location. He does, however, if his transcendence of space also includes omnipresence, have access to every point of location in the universe. His having access to every moment is therefore correlated with this access to every point.

In short, we are proposing that God both transcends space-time and is immanent within it.[79] He is atemporal/aspatial in his fundamental nature, or is ontologically atemporal/aspatial but actively or influentially present within the space–time universe. This topic will be pursued at greater length in the chapter on immanence and transcendence, as we try to conceptualize how this can be. Most assuredly, this suggestion will meet with protest from both temporalists and atemporalists, for the discussion has been conducted in a sort of "winner-take-all" atmosphere. All arguments are marshaled on one side of the argument, the considerations advanced for the other side are rebutted, and the diffi-

---

79. In these references to time, we are speaking of time in the usual sense, within the space–time universe. It is this which God transcends. Whether he has another time of his own, a "real time" or "ontological time," as Padgett and Craig have suggested, will have to be deferred to a later chapter.

culties of one's own position are minimized, explained away, or "made to fit." Yet this endeavor sometimes seems to take a rather forced or artificial form. There are surely difficulties with the attempt to combine both concepts. I would contend, however, that they are not more numerous or more serious than the difficulties involved in holding either one position or the other with regard to time, nor the difficulties that would be found with respect to God's relationship to space, were the same sort of analysis applied to it that has recently been applied to his relationship to time. We will explore, in a subsequent chapter, how this transcendence and immanence are to be understood.

It would probably be desirable to formulate some new terminology for these aspects of God's relationship to time. The adjective "atemporal" is negative in orientation. If we followed the pattern of the other attributes of God, we would speak of him as "omnitemporal," although the idea of omnitemporality may be contained within the concept of omnipresence. And to capture the idea that time, at least thought of as cosmic time, does not limit God, we might speak of him as being "supratemporal."

7

God and Outside Influences

The topic of divine impassibility is an attempt to discuss the emotional life of God as it were. One aspect of this doctrine is the question of the extent to which God can be said to have an emotional life, or whether the word "emotion" should even be applied to God. It frequently is used of the possibility of God being affected by the created order. As such, it has both a strong and a weak sense. In the strong sense, God is completely unaffected or unmoved by anything taking place within the created order or any considerations based on it. The weaker sense of the word conceives of God as affected by the creation, but not being especially emotionally affected. This God is never perturbed, upset, or disturbed, in the fashion in which humans are. He never loses control of himself. He is completely cool and rational in his assessment of things and in his reaction to them. As we shall see shortly, the concept of impassibility is quite complex, and several different meanings are intended by those who use the term. It is sometimes correlated with a number of other doctrines or attributes of God, including eternity, immutability, simplicity, omniscience, and omnipotence. Sometimes it was part of a philosophical package, reflected in the particular formulation of each of these attributes, while at other times it has had its own unique grounds. Particularly the rejection of the idea of impassibility has often been tied to certain historical events, and the consideration of what God's part in or reaction to these might be.

The doctrine has not been popular in the twentieth century. Process theologians have been especially critical, seeing it as one of the worst perversions of the understanding of God wrought by the adoption of Greek metaphysics. Charles Hartshorne said of this doctrine: "The immutable, impassible God of classical theism has nothing in him conceivably analogous to love."[1] The free will theists have been somewhat milder in their dissent, with Clark Pinnock saying, "Impassibility is the most dubious of the divine attributes discussed in classical theism, because it suggests that God does not experience sorrow, sadness, or pain."[2] Others have been more emphatic. A. M. Fairbairn wrote, "Theology has no falser idea than that of the impassibility of God."[3] Douglas White said, "The doctrine of the impassibility of God, taken in its widest sense, is the greatest heresy that ever smirched Christianity; it is not only false, it is the antipodes of truth."[4] Considerably more restrained are H. P. Owen's words: "This is the most questionable aspect of classical theism."[5]

Richard Creel notes that much of this concern about the doctrine of divine impassibility seems to stem from what is perceived as a conflict between it and divine love. For, seemingly, impassibility means that God feels no emotions, including love. Yet this is an uneven competition: "Hence, for biblical theists, if there is a conflict between God being loving and being impassible, it is impassibility that must be modified or ejected. To go at the point another way, it is conceivable that one could affirm that God is love and deny that God is impassible yet remain a Christian, but it is inconceivable that one could affirm that God is impassible and deny that God is love, yet remain a Christian."[6] Whether thought of as the essence of God or a primary attribute, perhaps the supreme attribute, love is certainly thought of as an indispensable aspect of the divine nature.

We mentioned earlier the complexity of the concept and the definitions of it. Creel lists no fewer than eight:

I_1 "lacking all emotions" (bliss not an emotion)
I_2 "in a state of mind that is imperturbable"
I_3 "insusceptible to distraction from resolve"
I_4 "having a will determined entirely by oneself"
I_5 "cannot be affected by an outside force"
I_6 "cannot be prevented from achieving one's purpose"

1. *Philosophers Speak of God* (Chicago: University of Chicago Press, 1953), p. 152.

2. Clark Pinnock, "Systematic Theology," in *The Openness of God: A Biblical Challenge to the Traditional Understanding of God* (Downers Grove: InterVarsity, 1994), p. 118.

3. A. M. Fairbairn, *The Place of Christ in Modern Theology* (London: Hodder & Stoughton, 1893), p. 484.

4. Douglas White, *Forgiveness and Suffering: A Study of Christian Belief* (Cambridge: Cambridge University Press, 1913), pp. 83–84.

5. H. P. Owen, *Concepts of Deity* (New York: Herder & Herder, 1971), p. 24.

6. Richard E. Creel, *Divine Impassibility: An Essay in Philosophical Theology* (Cambridge: Cambridge University Press, 1986), p. 2.

I_7 "has no susceptibility to negative emotions"
I_8 "cannot be affected by an outside force or changed by oneself"[7]

Creel finds that the most common element in these several definitions is I_5, the insusceptibility to being affected by an outside force. Yet
this in itself will not be sufficient to enable us to answer adequately the
question, "Is x impassible?" For it is at least conceivable that God may
be impassible with respect to any of the following: his nature, his will,
his knowledge, or his feelings. When we then consider the possibility of
God being either passible or impassible with respect to these four areas
in various combinations, the result is a choice among as many as six-
teen different permutations. Further, although he has been using the expression "cannot be changed," Creel says that we must also admit the
possibility of the expression "will not be changed." Some would say that
God can be changed, but chooses not to be.[8]

There has been some variation in the general status of impassibility
over the years of the church's history. In general, impassibility was more
strongly held in the earlier centuries than in recent years. We will trace
this development in greater detail below.

The conclusion reached on this doctrine has some practical and
theological significant implications. To those who hold to divine impassibility, the doctrine seems important because it guards the transcendence of God. A God who experiences the same sort of emotions we do,
who is affected by all that transpires within creation, appears to be a
captive of forces beyond him. To the opponents of this view, on the
other hand, impassibility appears to make God remote, unresponsive,
unsympathetic, even indifferent. It seems to make him something less
than fully loving. Further, however, this doctrinal issue is very much en-
meshed with some other crucial issues, such as theodicy. It is one thing
to ask about the justice of God in allowing suffering in the world, if he
himself feels the suffering of people, in some sense. It is another thing
entirely to ask about the justice of such suffering being allowed by a
God who apparently feels nothing, who is simply indifferent or callous.
That would heighten the problem of evil considerably.

This issue also becomes a test of the philosophical profundity of
theological methodology. The issue is not one that can be settled on
purely exegetical grounds. If that were the case, then the relevant passages, if taken literally and applied consistently, would probably lead to
a picture of a God who is actually largely human. Hermeneutical considerations come into play in knowing how to understand these state-

7. Ibid., p. 9.
8. Ibid., pp. 11–12.

ments in a way consistent with the biblically revealed picture of the nature of God. There also is a challenge to our philosophical skill in detecting the nature of the presuppositions underlying particular views on this issue. This is sometimes done on a one-sided basis. It is common to contend that the impassibility view derives from Greek thought. What is not asked with equal persistence, however, is what presuppositions underlie the opposite version of the doctrine. Or, if such questions are posed, we must ask the further question: Why should one prefer one of these presuppositions and, therefore, one of these conclusions over the others? These philosophical skills are important and valuable in all areas of doctrine. In this one area, they appear indispensable.

Historical Background and Development

Much has been made of the influence of Greek thought upon Christian theology with respect to several aspects of the doctrine of God, but especially divine impassibility. It is important to gain an understanding of at least the contours of the major types of Greek philosophy that may relate to theology at this point.

The first major person in Greek philosophy was, of course, Plato, whose thought has had an impact down through many successive centuries since his time. His basic metaphysical principle is radically contrary to many of our current views, both philosophical and common sense, and hence seemingly counterintuitive for many of us today. Unlike our empiricism, intangible and unseen and, hence, more abstract, entities were, in Plato's judgment, more real than the visible and tangible objects around us. The imagery of the divided line makes clear that the Ideas, those pure forms or formuli of reality, are the most real. The objects in the bottom half of the divided line, the physical and perceptible objects, are mere shadows cast by the Ideas, which give the former their reality. The reason is in part because the Ideas are unchanging and perfect, while the physical objects, like anything else in the realm of the visible, are subject to variation. The Ideas are not, and cannot be, affected by anything that exists or occurs in the bottom half, the visible world. Thus, a God who could somehow be affected by anything in the world would be inferior to the Ideas. Consequently, God must be impassible.

Aristotle offered a somewhat different conception. He conceived of God as pure actuality, not potentiality. But if God is pure actuality, then there really is no possibility of change in him. And since the ability to be affected by anything in the physical world requires ability to change, this means that God must be impassible, in the sense of being insusceptible to being affected by the creation.

For both Plato and Aristotle, reason was considered the most noble aspect of human nature. So Plato, for example, in the *Republic*, says that no satisfaction is to be obtained in anger if pursued apart from reason and mind.[9] In Aristotle's view, the active intellect (νοὺς ποητικὸς) is the preeminent part of human nature, the one immaterial and impassible factor in the human. So Aristotle's God is primarily involved in thinking, not in feeling—and certainly not in feeling induced by the influence of the creation on him.[10]

It is in Stoicism that the most direct formative influence on the Christian doctrine of divine impassibility can be found. To the Stoics, the ideal of human life is the person who is completely imperturbable, who exists without any influence on him by the world. No circumstances that arise disturb him or influence his thinking, willing, or action.[11] What is the ideal for a human must, of course, also be the ideal for God as well. Thus, God must be unmoved or unperturbed by anything within the world.

One factor that moved the impassibility view into the church was the modalistic controversy. In the late second and early third centuries A.D., a movement arose that came to be known as Modalistic Monarchianism, although some forms of it were referred to as Sabellianism, named after the theologian Sabellius. This was an attempt to deal with the biblical testimony that God is one and that there are three who are God. As the church struggled to formulate what would be called the doctrine of the Trinity, one creative solution was proposed. Perhaps the three persons are not actually three different persons, but one person in three different appearances or playing three different roles. God, in other words, is not three persons, but one person under three different modes of existence or appearance. Although we do not have the original writings of the Modalists, we have reports of their teachings, written by theologians who opposed their views. So, for example, Hippolytus reports the modalist Noetus as teaching that "the Father and the Son so-called are one and the same. . . . One was He who appeared and underwent birth from a Virgin and dwelt as a man among men. . . . He also suffered, being nailed to the Tree, and gave up His Spirit to Himself, and died and did not die."[12]

This was a genuinely creative and in some ways ingenious solution to the logical problem of the Trinity. The church judged it to be untrue,

9. Plato, *The Republic* 8.586. C. E.
10. Aristotle, *Metaphysics* 1072b.
11. Philip P. Hallie, "Stoicism," in *The Encyclopedia of Philosophy*, ed. Paul Edwards (New York: Macmillan, 1967), vol. 8, pp. 21–22.
12. Hippolytus, *Refutation of All Heresies* 9.10; cf. 10.27.

however, concluding that although it fit nicely with the division of the Bible into Old Testament (Father), Gospels (Son) and Acts and Epistles (Holy Spirit), it failed to account fully for some of the texts in which two or more of the members of the Trinity appear simultaneously and even interact. Examples of this phenomenon can be found in all the prayers of Jesus and his references to the Father and the Holy Spirit, and most fully in accounts such as the baptism (Matt. 3:16–17). Consequently, the church rejected this view. The movement did, however, have the effect of heightening interest in the question of the possibility of God suffering.

Tertullian, in particular, raised the battle cry against the Modalist Praxeus. Tertullian did not deny that God has feelings. Indeed, he maintained that God alone experiences perfectly such feelings as gentleness, mercy, and goodness. Tertullian, however, was greatly influenced by Stoicism. Thus, the concept of the emotions being held in check and kept balanced so that the moral nature is not disturbed by any emotions is prominent in his thought. Most certainly the Scriptures attribute feelings of various kinds to God. These are not to be understood in such a way, however, that there is any mutability in the divine nature, inconsistent with its purity and perfection.[13] Rather, they are, in Mozley's words, "the varying expression of God's moral energy in its outgoing towards man."[14] Thus, while the form of Patripassianism represented by Modalism, in which the Father suffered in the Son's sufferings because he literally was the Son, did not present a major threat to the church in later years, it served the purpose of sensitizing the church to the general issue of Patripassianism.

In Augustine we find an adoption and adaptation of Platonic philosophy to theology. His definition of *passio* is helpful in understanding his general position. He maintains that it is derived from πάθος and means "a movement of the mind contrary to reason."[15] Consequently, it is incompatible with blessedness. It is not, however, the cessation of these movements, but the balanced harmony among them that is the source of blessedness: "this is a blessed and peaceful life of man when all its movements agree with reason and truth; then they are called joys and holy affections, pure and good. But if they do not agree, they tear the soul apart and make life most wretched, and are called perturbations and lusts and evil desires."[16]

---

13. Tertullian, *Against Marcion* 2.16.
14. J. K. Mozley, *The Impassibility of God: A Survey of Christian Thought* (Cambridge: Cambridge University Press, 1926), pp. 38–39.
15. Augustine, *The City of God* 8.17.
16. *De Genesi contra Manichees* 1.20.

The divine impassibility is seen in the absence of these weaknesses and flaws of the emotional life. Augustine recognizes the presence of scriptural expressions concerning God's feelings and corresponding actions. These apparent ascriptions of emotions to God must be recognized as expressions made using the speech available to us, with its limitations, and thus are analogical in nature.[17] In particular, we are not to understand these attributed emotions as involving any perturbation or change within God. "For as He is jealous without any envy, is angry without any perturbation, is pitiful without any grief, repents without having any evil in Him to correct, so He is patient without any suffering."[18]

Thomas Aquinas developed the concept of divine impassibility most fully. In many ways, his idea derives from immutability. God's perfection involves his complete immutability. He is not susceptible to any of the changes that exist in creatures. Neither his knowledge nor his will changes in any respect.[19] *Passio*, however, means the relinquishing of some natural quality and the influence of foreign and adverse quality, and this is inconceivable in the case of God.[20] Aquinas's objection is based in large part on the Aristotelian conception of potentiality and actuality. The divine being must be "pure action without the admixture of any potentiality, because potentiality itself is later than action. Now everything which in any way is changed is in some way in a state of potentiality, whence it is obvious that God cannot be changed."[21] He distinguishes two senses of potentiality. Active potentiality, the principle of activity directed toward something else, is found in God to the ultimate degree. This means simply that God is able to act, to do things that he is not currently doing. This is not a view of God as totally inactive. Passive potentiality, on the other hand, indicates some lack in the thing that possesses it. Because God is completely perfect, this cannot be found in him. Passive potentiality is "the principle of being acted upon by something else," and it cannot exist in God.[22]

What about the emotions Scripture apparently ascribes to God? How are they to be understood? Here Thomas distinguishes between two kinds of emotions. Love and joy can be understood to truly exist in God. Sadness and anger, on the other hand, are to be attributed to him only metaphorically. Love must be understood as the first action of the will. The type of love correctly attributable to God is that which does not

---

17. *City of God* 16.53.
18. *On Patience* 1.
19. Thomas Aquinas, *Summa Theologica* 1.14.5; 1.19.7.
20. Ibid., 2A.22.1.
21. Ibid., 1.9.1.
22. Ibid., 1.5.1.

stem from sense-desire but from intellectual desire, that is, the will. Because anger and sadness imply the presence of some imperfection, they can only be ascribed to God metaphorically. Love and joy, however, do not involve any such imperfection and thus can be properly predicated of God, but "without passion," that is, as involving only intellectual, not physical, desire.[23] It would appear that the difference is whether the emotion originates from God's activity, from his willing, or from the influence of something on him.

When we come to the Reformation theologians, we find ourselves on rather different ground. Particularly in Luther's thought, there is a strong emphasis on the passion and suffering of God. Luther strongly emphasizes God suffering in Jesus. This element is interpreted in different ways by different commentators. John Sanders and J. K. Mozley interpret these passages in light of the *communicatio idiomatum*, whereby the attributes of the divine nature are communicated to the human nature of Christ, and vice versa.[24] Thus, Jesus could suffer, but only in his human nature. Alister McGrath, on the other hand, believes the suffering of God must be understood in the light of the contrast between the *theologia crucis* and *theologia gloria*, the theology of the cross and the theology of glory.[25] As we noted in an earlier chapter, he is sharply critical of Sanders' research on Luther, in basing his interpretation on only one primary source and a secondary source. Regardless of the *communicatio*, the deity suffers. Further, there is definitely the idea of God suffering in Jesus. It is clear, however, that whatever the interpretation, Luther believed in divine passibility.

Calvin's position is less inclined toward passibility than is that of Luther. Much of his view is expressed in the *Commentaries* rather than the *Institutes*. So, writing on Genesis 6:6, he says, "The repentance which is here ascribed to God does not properly belong to him, but has reference to our understanding of him. . . . That repentance cannot take place in God easily appears from this single consideration, that nothing happens which is by him unexpected or unforeseen. The same reasoning, and remark, applies to what follows, that God was affected with grief." Calvin then appeals to his doctrine of revelation: "Certainly God is not sorrowful or sad; but remains for ever like himself in his celestial and happy response; yet because it could not otherwise be known how

23. Ibid., 1.20.1.

24. John Sanders, "Historical Considerations," in *The Openness of God: A Biblical Challenge to the Traditional Understanding of God* (Downers Grove: InterVarsity, 1994), p. 88; Mozley, *Impassibility*, pp. 121–22.

25. Alister E. McGrath, *Christian Theology: An Introduction* (Oxford: Blackwell, 1994), pp. 215–16. Luther's statement is found in "Heidelberg Disputation," thesis 21, in *Luther's Works*, ed. Harold J. Grim (Philadelphia: Muhlenberg, 1957), vol. 31, p. 53.

great is God's hatred and detestation of sin, therefore the Spirit accommodates himself to our capacity. . . . This figure, which represents God as transferring to himself what is peculiar to human nature, is called ἀνθρωποπάθεια."[26] Thus, as Calvin has put it elsewhere, God accommodates himself to human understanding by stooping down and lisping in our ear, the way a nursemaid does with a child.[27] Calvin appears to hold that God has emotions, but not quite the same as ours.

Impassibility of Will

What about impassibility of will? This issue brings very close together the ideas of impassibility and immutability, as well as the freedom of God. Although both immutability and impassibility involve change of God's will, there is a significant difference here that needs to be noted. Immutability means simply that God does not change his will, or in the stronger sense of the word, that he *cannot* change his will. It does not specify the source or influence of this excluded change. Impassibility of will, on the other hand, is the position that God's will is not affected by anything external to him. It does not exclude the possibility that God would change his will by his own initiative, only the idea of external cause or influence.

This issue is also very strongly correlated with the issue of divine omniscience, particularly foreknowledge. For if God knows in advance all that will occur, or at least all the possibilities that could occur, then nothing will take him by surprise and his will need not change in response to the changed situation; thus his will is not influenced by that external factor. This argument can work either on a Calvinistic view or on a traditional Arminian view in which God has complete foreknowledge. And it can work either on a view that God has complete foreknowledge of the actual events that will occur or on the view that while not knowing all the actual events, he knows all the possibilities and has determined in advance what he will do in each such circumstance.

The question arises because the biblical God appears to respond to human actions, situations, and, especially, prayers. Thus, since in the judgment of someone such as Nelson Pike, a response necessarily must follow temporally that to which it is a response, God must change his will.[28] Is this the case, however? H. P. Owen does not think so. He says,

26. John Calvin, *Commentaries on the First Book of Moses Called Genesis* (Grand Rapids: Baker, 1979), vol. 1, pp. 248–49.

27. *Institutes of the Christian Religion* 1.13.1.

28. Nelson Pike, *God and Timelessness* (London: Routledge & Kegan Paul, 1970), p. 128.

That God responds to men must be admitted by all Christian theists; for the admission is required by belief in petitionary prayer. But "response" does not imply "change." On the contrary, Christians are committed to the belief that God's response to their prayers is determined by his changeless desire for, and knowledge of, their good. Nothing that creatures do, and nothing that happens to them, can cause any increase (or decrease) in this desire and knowledge. Christian prayer presupposes that God's mind and will are immutable. Even if we say . . . that God does not know future free choices in their concrete actuality, he knows them perfectly as possibilities; he is (as the Creator) wholly sovereign over them; so that he is necessarily and timelessly adapted to them and to all their consequences.[29]

One illustration used to develop this is the idea of the game of chess. This is found in a number of theologians, although the first use of it may have been by the philosopher William James.[30] Theologians and philosophers who have more recently used this are P. T. Geach,[31] John Hick,[32] and Richard Rice.[33] In this illustration, an international grand master sits down to a chess game with a novice. Although the expert neither controls what moves the beginner makes, nor even knows exactly what those moves will be, he does know all the possibilities and in advance what response he will make to each move his opponent might make. Thus, the outcome is never really in doubt.

Thomas Morris has developed this view in an article written in response to a passibilist statement made by Richard Swinburne. Morris argues that the position he is presenting is quite consistent with God's intentions being indexed to or conditional on occurrences in the created universe, including actions of human beings. He puts it this way: "Why can't it always and immemorially have been the case that God intends to do A if B arise, or C if D comes about?"[34] This enables Morris to deal with instances in Scripture in which God seems to change his will. An example of this would be the Ninevites. God has not changed his will, but has eternally willed a change from "the Ninevites will be punished" to "the Ninevites will not be punished" if they repent. This

29. H. P. Owen, *Concepts of Deity* (New York: Herder & Herder, 1971), p. 87.

30. William James, *The Will to Believe and Other Essays* (London: Longmans, Green, 1897), pp. 181, 182.

31. P. T. Geach, "God's Relation to the World," in *Logic Matters* (Berkeley: University of California Press, 1972), p. 325; *Providence and Evil* (Cambridge: Cambridge University Press, 1977), p. 58.

32. John Hick, *Evil and the God of Love* (San Francisco: Harper & Row, 1977), p. 344.

33. Richard Rice, *God's Foreknowledge and Man's Free Will* (Minneapolis: Bethany, 1985), p. 66.

34. Thomas V. Morris, "Properties, Modalities, and God," *The Philosophical Review* 93.1 (1984): 47–48.

distinction is not original with Morris. Long before him, Aquinas had distinguished between willing a change and changing one's will, although he applied it in a somewhat different sense from that of Morris: "The will of God is altogether immutable. But notice in this connection that changing one's will is different from willing a change in things. For a person whose will remains unalterable can will that something should happen now and its contrary happen afterwards."[35] So, in Morris's judgment, the position he is taking does not involve any change in God's intentions, but a realization that God's intentions are, and always have been, conditional.[36]

Notice that on this interpretation, some theologians, who really claim to reject any sort of impassibility, hold to impassibility of will. Richard Rice, one of the "free will theists," uses the analogy of the chess game. Here the chess master neither knows nor determines every move that the amateur will make, but he knows all the possibilities and exactly what the amateur will do in each of those cases.[37] In order to preserve both the providence of God and human freedom, which requires that God not know all human actions in advance, he has adopted a view of the conditional will. The same is true of his treatment of biblical prophecy, of which this is also a case.[38] If, however, Creel's analysis of the situation is correct, then Rice also holds to impassibility of will in the sense specified. Although he does not emphasize God's intention to act in a certain way if a certain action is taken, it is there nonetheless. This may suggest that some persons in effect hold to an impassibility of will who do not acknowledge it.

Impassibility of Emotions

Here we are at the heart of the whole discussion about divine impassibility, for almost by definition passion, and thus passibility, seems to be especially a matter of emotions. Consequently, here is where much of the argument has developed. Process theologians and free will theists believe that the classical view makes God a completely unfeeling, unresponsive machine. A number of theologians and schools of thought have therefore argued for God's emotional passibility.

35. Thomas Aquinas, *Summa Theologia* 1a.q.19.a.7.
36. "Properties, Modalities, and God," p. 48.
37. Richard Rice, *God's Foreknowledge and Man's Free Will* (Minneapolis: Bethany, 1985), pp. 66–67.
38. Richard Rice, "Biblical Support for a New Perspective," in Clark Pinnock, Richard Rice, John Sanders, William Hasker, and David Basinger, *The Openness of God: A Biblical Challenge to the Traditional Understanding of God* (Downers Grove, Ill.: InterVarsity, 1994), pp. 51–52.

Jürgen Moltmann

Moltmann's *Crucified God* has been one of the more influential books in the area of divine passibility. His book grows out of his own experience in some ways. It is fundamentally an apologetic or answering theology in the sense that it is intended to speak to some of the questions people have today, which arise because of the circumstances of life. In his case, it arose out of both personal experience and observation. Moltmann served in the German army during World War II. Captured and imprisoned in a prisoner of war camp in Scotland, he saw his native country crushed in a war that had initially provided spectacular victories. Then he reflected on the holocaust and the immense loss of human lives therein, as well as the revelation of tremendous human cruelty to fellow human beings. Further, he subsequently taught on a university faculty that also included an articulate Marxist, Ernst Bloch. Consequently, he saw that Marxism, an atheistic philosophy, offered hope, whereas Christianity did not really seem to offer this to human beings. Part of this was the picture of an indifferent, aloof God, who could allow such immense suffering as had recently been seen in Europe, and apparently feel nothing himself.

Moltmann sees Jesus' death and resurrection as the key to this entire area of Christian doctrine. In particular, he emphasizes Jesus' experience of having been abandoned by God. Yet God also suffered in the sufferings of Jesus. After all, Paul wrote that "God was in Christ" in 2 Corinthians 5:19. Thus, the God who gave up Jesus to be crucified is also the God who suffered together with him. He is not impassible. He is capable of emotions.[39]

Kazoh Kitamora

In his book, *The Pain of God*, Kitamori, the leading post–World War II Japanese Christian theologian, describes God as suffering pain. Many commentators have seen this as growing out of his observation of the wartime and postwar suffering in his homeland of Japan, but Kitamori himself contends that this emphasis comes rather from his study of the Bible. The divine suffering is not so much a result of God's involvement in human history. Rather, it stems from internal conflict within his own nature. God is a God of love, who loves and cares about sinners. But he is also a God of wrath, who must punish sin. He is not, however, two gods, but one, and thus must somehow combine these emotions within himself. The result of this is conflict and pain. It is not

---

39. Jürgen Moltmann, *The Crucified God: The Cross of Christ as the Foundation and Criticism of Christian Theology* (New York: Harper & Row, 1974), pp. 200–290.

primarily that the pain is a function or a result of our sin against him, but is what he feels when he tries to love us, the objects of his wrath.[40]

Process Theology

The process theologians have especially emphasized the emotional dimension of God's experience. There are a number of reasons for this, growing out of their basic metaphysic. In process metaphysics, as we noted in an earlier chapter, the fundamental unit of reality is not substance but event. All events or actual entities have two poles, an abstract or mental pole and a consequent or physical pole. Each of these actual entities prehends or grasps or feels all of the others, so that there is an organic character to reality, whereby each entity is connected to every other, and is influenced and affected by every other. This dipolar character is also true of God. He persuades or lures everything toward his goal or intention for it. He is, however, also affected by everything. He is dependent on the world. He feels all that happens.

This is sometimes stated quite vividly. Charles Hartshorne put it this way: "God is not the being whose life is sheer joy and beauty, but the cosmic sufferer, who endures infinitely more evil than we can imagine."[41] This is because his knowledge of others' feelings and his sympathetic experience of them are the same thing. If this knowledge and sympathy were complete, they would not even be distinguishable by human beings.[42] The extent of this sympathetic experience is seen in his comment: "God cannot face his own death, whether nobly or ignobly; but he can face any and every death threat with full participation in the sufferings of those whose death is in question."[43]

John Robert Baker, a process philosopher, in interpreting Hartshorne, points out that the suffering God experiences is not merely the suffering of the human, felt sympathetically. It is also the pain he feels at the rejection of the love and lure that God exerts on the person. When such possibilities are spurned, it is "a misfortune both to the local agent and to God. . . . There is a resultant suffering and tragedy in the life of God. In this regard, we have moved beyond the first aspect of divine suffering, that of sympathetic participation. God does not merely suffer *with* us but *for* us."[44]

40. Kazoh Kitamori, *Theology of the Pain of God* (Richmond: John Knox, 1965), p. 21.
41. Charles Hartshorne, *Man's Vision of God* (New York: Harper & Row, 1941), p. 331.
42. Ibid., p. 163.
43. *Creative Synthesis and Philosophic Method* (LaSalle, Ill.: Open Court, 1970), p. 263.
44. John Robert Baker, "The Christological Symbol of God's Suffering," in *Religious Experience and Process Theology*, ed. Harry James Cargas and Bernard Lee (New York: Paulist, 1976), p. 100.

Liberation Theology

The various kinds of liberation theology—Third World, black, and feminist—make much of God's feeling for the predicament of his human creatures. It has sometimes been said that if Genesis 1–3 is the key passage for understanding the human predicament from the perspective of orthodox or evangelical theology, then Exodus 1–3 is the basis of liberation theology's doctrine of the human situation. The nature of theology is critical reflection on praxis, and the plight of the poor is the great concern of God, and consequently also of liberation theologians.

Similarly, black theologian James Cone speaks of God's concern for the plight of black persons. He sees God being highly involved in their situation. He goes so far as to say that God cannot be for blacks without being against whites. The God who is pictured in this theology is a God who feels strongly, who is angry about injustices.

Orthodox and Evangelical Theologians

The doctrine of divine impassibility was very much a part of the received or orthodox theological tradition. So, for example, in their original form the Thirty-Nine Articles of the Church of England assert that "God is without body, parts, or passions." As early as the Bishops' Conference of 1786, however, the word "passions" was omitted. The Westminster Confession, a major standard of Presbyterianism, retained the statement about divine passions.

In the past decade a large number of evangelical systematic theologies have appeared. The interesting feature of these, for purposes of our consideration here is that all of them either reject, revise, or omit the traditional doctrine of impassibility. A sampling of these theologies makes this quite clear. One of the most conservative and most Calvinistic of these is Wayne Grudem's *Systematic Theology.* He says, "But the idea that God has no passions or emotions *at all* clearly conflicts with much of the rest of Scripture, and for that reason I have not affirmed God's impassibility in this book."[45] Gordon Lewis and Bruce Demarest, in their *Integrative Theology,* say, "Unquestionably the Scripture speaks of God as passionately involved with sinners and repentant sinners. Even though its language be taken figuratively, it illustrates a nonfigurative point. God really suffers when people sinfully destroy his creation, and God literally rejoices when one sinner repents."[46] Alister McGrath has a lengthy discussion of divine suffering, including the

---

45. Wayne Grudem, *Systematic Theology* (Grand Rapids: Zondervan, 1994), p. 166.
46. Gordon Lewis and Bruce Demarest, *Integrative Theology* (Grand Rapids: Zondervan, 1987), vol. 1, p. 236.

thought of Luther and Moltmann, and seems to consider this part of the correct tradition.[47] James Leo Garrett raises two questions in connection with the doctrine: Can possibility be defended apart from the suffering of Jesus as the incarnate Son of God? Can one speak of the suffering of God without falling into Patripassianism? Nonetheless, he says, "Despite the attendant problems and questions, it seems to be necessary to affirm that God has the capacity to suffer, for he has participated in suffering."[48] Stanley Grenz does not overtly discuss the term *impassibility*, but he makes much of God's compassion and other divine emotions.[49] Carl F. H. Henry does not really address this as such. His emphasis is more on immutability and the idea of a God who changes in response to human actions. Henry interprets the references to divine repentance as instances of anthropomorphism, but he does not make a big issue of impassibility.[50] This survey of recent evangelical literature would suggest that the traditional doctrine of impassibility is not the current one, even among conservative Protestant theologians.

A Recent Defense of Impassibility: Richard Creel

Yet the doctrine of impassibility has not been without its defenders in our time. Probably the most thorough and competent defense of the doctrine is that of Richard Creel. Because he seems in some ways to be moving against the stream of recent theological thought, we will treat his view in somewhat greater detail than we have the other theologians. Creel observes that passibilists give seven basic reasons for their contention that God does and must feel with the persons whom he has created.[51]

1. Personality requires emotional passibility. A person must be capable of participating in the emotional life of other persons. That means to be subject to being influenced by what they are feeling, their joys and sorrows. This, however, is certainly emotional passibility.

2. God is a loving person, and love requires emotional passibility. Certainly the Bible in numerous places attributes love to God, and some would claim that the statement in 1 John 4:8, that "God is love," is not

47. Alister E. McGrath, *Christian Theology: An Introduction* (Oxford: Basil Blackwell, 1994), pp. 213–22.

48. James L. Garrett, *Systematic Theology: Biblical, Historical, and Evangelical* (Grand Rapids: Eerdmans, 1990), vol. 1, pp. 250–51.

49. Stanley Grenz, *Theology for the Community of God* (Nashville: Broadman-Holman, 1994), pp. 122–27.

50. Carl F. H. Henry, *God, Revelation, and Authority* (Waco, Tex.: Word, 1982), vol. 5, pp. 286–306.

51. Creel, *Divine Impassibility*, pp. 113–16.

merely the statement of an attribute of God, but a definition of him. Loving a person means caring for him or her, about what happens to that person, and that means being affected by what happens to that person. It is being happy when things go well for him or her, and being sad when things go badly for him or her. This certainly means, however, that God is emotionally passible.

3. Divinity requires emotional impassibility. God is worthy of worship. That is part of what being deity involves, practically. If, however, God were emotionally impassible, he would not be worthy of praise because he would be deficient in personality and love, as already noted. Furthermore, our worship, expression of gratitude, and devotion and service would be a waste of time, because he would not be affected by them in any way. The emotional impact on him would be no greater than that on a stone. But if this is the case, if he is not worthy of our worship, devotion, and service, he is not truly God.

4. Justice requires passibility in feeling. If God is emotionally impassible, he would not be moved by anything his creatures do. He would in no way be disturbed by sin. He would neither care about it nor be moved to do anything about it. He would not punish sin. But such a God certainly cannot be described as just.

5. Omniscience requires divine emotional passibility. Certainly God must know when his creatures suffer. It is not sufficient for him to know *that* we are suffering, however. He must also know our suffering itself. This means sympathetic suffering, suffering with us, experiencing the same feeling we are suffering. Therefore, if he is truly omniscient, he must be emotionally passible.

6. Morality requires emotional suffering. God has created us. He did so in such a way that we are capable of suffering, which we do, sometimes quite terribly. It consequently is only right that he should also share in our sufferings.

7. Redemption requires divine impassibility in feeling. The redemption of the human is possible only because of God's suffering love. God is not simply wrathful toward humans because of their sin. He is also grieved by it. We are not motivated to turn to God simply because of his wrath toward, and judgment on, human sin. Rather, it is when we realize that God is harmed and grieved by our sin that we are moved to respond to him. Thus, God's possibility relative to us is necessary for salvation really to occur.

Despite these strong considerations, Creel is not convinced that they require abandonment of the traditional view of impassibility. He formulates his own response to each of these arguments:

1. He asks whether personality really requires passibility in feelings. Is it necessary that a person's feelings be subject to alteration by what

occurs either to him or to others? In other words, to be a person, is it necessary that one's feelings be subject to being affected by stimuli external to oneself? Creel contends that for a thing to be properly termed a person, it must exist, have capacity for abstract thought and the use of symbols, and the power of will. He would further agree that a person must have some feeling for things—an emotional life.

Yet Creel does not see why this aspect of personality requires being subject to alteration by changing circumstances. He pictures an individual who is very concerned about injustice and other social evils, who works diligently to combat and remove these injustices, but who remains equally happy whether his or her efforts meet with success or failure. Similarly, the Stoics were not trying to cease to be persons, Creel contends, but rather were trying to develop the proper type of response to the vicissitudes of life. He cites Rose Fitzgerald Kennedy, who retained her tranquillity despite the tragedies that had entered her life. The essential point, then, is that God feels and feels appropriately, but his emotions are not controlled or even affected by external forces.[52]

2. What about love, however? Since on any interpretation of the doctrine of God, love is a very significant factor in his attributes, must it not require emotional passibility? Creel sees love involving three factors: caring about the welfare of a person, acting for that person's welfare, and taking pleasure in that person's welfare. The first two factors present no problem for him, but the third does. The way the issue is expressed seems to be very important to Creel. He asks, "Could an emotionally impassible being be rejoiced by the good fortunes of its beloved and distressed by its misfortunes?" His answer to that is "no," but he goes on to claim that "I do not believe that implies that such a being could not take pleasure in the welfare of its beloved."[53]

What Creel appears to do is to delimit the range of possible appropriate responses on the part of God to human adversity and good fortune. It surely would not be the case that, although he loves everyone including the demented or the mistaken, he must feel their same emotions in these situations. Further, there are situations in which it is unnecessary to feel the pain of others. Creel mentions specifically the difference between the suffering of a parent in her child's pain due to an incurable disease, and the happiness that parent feels, even though the child is suffering, as the result of the administration of a newly discovered medical cure for the disease. So it is with God. He may see humans suffering, but because of his omniscience he knows the good that this suffer-

52. Ibid., pp. 116–17.
53. Ibid., p. 117.

ing will accomplish and, consequently, need not be distressed despite unpleasantnesses. Creel asks, however, "But could there be circumstances that make it always unnecessary or inappropriate for God to suffer with his suffering creatures? God should sorrow for us, it seems to me, only when he knows us to have lost an irreplaceable good or to have suffered an irredeemable evil. He never will, however, because his omniscience and omnipotence enable him to replace every good and to redeem every evil."[54]

3. The argument that deity requires emotional passibility is an exercise in perfect being theology. Here a God who is incapable of responding to human circumstances is not the greatest of all possible beings, and therefore not deserving of human worship. Creel contests such a contention, however. He gives several responses.[55]

First, this position seems to presuppose that suffering adds some good to the existence of a thing. But that would require that suffering be either intrinsically or extrinsically good, that is, that it either be good in itself or that it be a means to a good end. But suffering itself is not a good, but an evil. Further, it cannot add anything to God. It cannot serve instrumentally to benefit God. It cannot be a corrective punishment, a warning of danger, or an incentive to greater sympathy for others. If he is completely good and all-knowing, these are either impossible or unnecessary. Suffering does not add to his moral wisdom or give him moral dilemmas that develop his character.

Second, Creel objects to the idea that suffering makes love admirable, saying that this puts things backward. It is love that makes suffering admirable. In itself, suffering is simply something evil. Suffering may reveal the depth of one's love, but does not cause it.

Third, if suffering made love more admirable, then clearly, the more suffering the better. The implications of this are mind-shaking: "since God is infinite love, he must suffer infinitely, or, if that be impossible because there is no maximal degree of suffering, he must be trapped in an endless vortex of ever increasing pain."[56] But the appropriate response to such a being would not be worship, but pity. Certainly, however, pity cannot be an appropriate response to a majestic and self-sufficient being.

Fourth, if suffering love were the highest love, then God would be indebted to sinners for his status as "suffering lover." He should therefore be glad that humans have sinned, and should desire that sinners sin all the more. However, says, Creel, "surely a position from which

54. Ibid., p. 121.
55. Ibid., pp. 122–24.
56. Ibid., p. 123.

such implications as these follow must be faulty in its basic conception of God. It is absurd to think that God depends on sinners for his virtue."[57]

Fifth, if God suffers with us, for us, and because of us, he shares emotionally in all the suffering of the entire world, as well as experiencing his own suffering over their waywardness. Then, however, God is the highest object of pity and even ought to pity himself.

Creel examines Brasnett's statements that "sin must cause to God an everlasting pain" and that people who turn away from God cause both themselves and him "unending pain and enduring agony."[58] Baker and Hartshorne give similar depictions of this type of suffering and pity. Creel concludes:

> The picture of God conveyed in these quotations strikes me as a portrait in sentimentalism. The religion of pity inspired by it should eventually dissolve into maudlin stupor because there is so little that any one person could do to relieve God's massive suffering. Moreover, it is obvious from centuries of human history that God's suffering is only going to get worse and worse. Poor God—and poor us, if we have no better concept of God than this![59]

If God is truly emotionally dependent on humankind, then Brasnett was right in saying that "Here God has given himself into our hands, we can wound and pain him, and make him suffer."[60] Creel concludes that if God possesses this type of suffering love, the human has the capacity to frustrate him eternally.[61]

4. Justice does not require emotion, specifically, anger, in order to act. Creel cites the fact that parents can punish wrongful behavior without doing so out of anger. Persons like Mahatma Gandhi and Martin Luther King Jr. opposed evil and injustice, not out of anger, but with love for the perpetrator of the wrong.[62]

5. Omniscience seems to pose special problems. Certainly, if God knows everything, then he knows what everyone is feeling. As we have seen earlier, in the judgment of such persons as Hartshorne, this means that if God knows that people are having a certain emotion, then he knows the emotion they are having. That in turn means that he must share that feeling with them or experience that emotion himself.

57. Ibid.
58. Bertrand Brasnett, *The Suffering of the Impassible God* (New York: Macmillan, 1928), pp. 71, 78.
59. Creel, *Divine Impassibility*, p. 125.
60. Brasnett, *The Suffering of the Impassible God*, p. 13.
61. Creel, *Divine Impassibility*, pp. 125–26.
62. Ibid., pp. 127–28.

Creel agrees that "it seems axiomatic that to know, intuit, or feel someone else's feeling is to have that feeling oneself in some sense."[63] He argues that this does not mean that one must necessarily feel happy, in pain, or whatever. We must distinguish between direct and indirect feeling, that is, feeling someone's emotion and feeling it as one's own. It is one's own in the sense that one is having it, but not of feeling that way oneself. It is to know that if one were that person, that is how one would feel, but that one does not necessarily feel that way oneself. Creel uses examples from physiology, such as feeling depressed as a result of an insulin shot—a chemical rather than an existential depression. He finds that even Hartshorne recognizes the problem when he asks how God can feel the joy of the sadist as his own. Creel contends that if God felt that emotion as his own, he would feel no ambivalence about it. Consequently, Creel concludes, "Hence, knowing the pain, depression, grief, etc. of another, God does not necessarily know himself as in pain, depression, grief, etc. Rather, I believe, he knows himself as eternally blissful and as knowing the pain, depression, grief, etc., of the other."[64]

6. Nor does morality require emotional passibility, according to Creel. Does a parent who is responsible for a child's suffering have to suffer that same pain for morality to prevail? Certainly not, he would insist. Yet, someone might respond by arguing that whereas the parents may not be aware of the unfortunate consequences their action will have, God is fully aware of these things. Creel's argument in effect requires a solution to the problem of evil. He contends that as long as it is logically possible for evil to be defeated, it is not necessary actually to solve it for this dilemma of the necessity of God's suffering to be removed.

7. Finally, redemption does not require emotional passibility. Creel contends that it is not necessary to know that our actions cause God suffering in order for us to be moved to accept redemption. We can be convinced of the wrongness of our behavior simply by seeing the harm we do to others. And if we are moved to repentance or abstinence from an improper behavior because we realize what pain it would cause God, that seems to give us undue power or control over God.[65]

A Synthetic Solution

Having now seen the varied positions and considerations, it is time to draw some tentative conclusions.

63. Ibid., p. 129.
64. Ibid., p. 132.
65. Ibid., pp. 153–57.

1. It seems indubitable, in light of the number and variety of biblical texts attributing emotions of several kinds to God, that impassibility in the sense of God being utterly devoid of any feelings cannot be accepted. However these emotions are understood, God is simply not without them.

2. If we take seriously the idea that God is both transcendent and immanent, then his emotions must in some sense be both similar to ours and yet to some extent different from ours.

3. It is apparent from even a cursory examination of the Bible that a number of anthropomorphisms are used of God. For example, bodily parts are attributed to him, but these references surely cannot be taken literally. It would seem likely therefore, in light of consideration of point #2 above, that to some extent the references to his emotions must be anthropomorphic, or more correctly, anthropopathic, as well. Actually, as is sometimes pointed out, since we are made in God's image, rather than he in ours, it would be more correct to say that the ascription of emotions to humans is theomorphic.

4. The issue is both what reactions are correctly to be attributed to God, and what sources or influences bear on his experiencing them. If it is the case that God has planned from eternity all that occurs, and that this includes the various events in the lives of all persons, then although God may experience certain emotions, make certain choices, and take certain actions in connection with those events, they really are not the cause of these events in God's life. Those actions and feelings are actually the result of his choices and plan, which is now being worked out within history. Passibility of will is not really an issue.

5. The issue then becomes the extent to which God genuinely feels emotions in conjunction with events in the lives of humans. Here a number of preliminary considerations need to be addressed or observed.

Much of the discussion of emotions is culturally conditioned. The picture of what it might mean for God to feel is affected by the temperament of cultures, subcultures, and individuals. In this connection, we should observe that in the United States a shift has been taking place in recent years. It involves what Ann Douglas called "the feminization of American culture," or perhaps it could also be called "latinization."[66] The terms designate a shift to greater emphasis on emotions, even in connection with decision-making. This shows itself in a number of ways, one of which is "relational theology."[67] This is in part a result of the widespread interest in and reliance on psychology, counseling, and therapeutic emphases in the church and its ministry.

66. Ann Douglas, *The Feminization of American Culture* (New York: Knopf, 1977), pp. 8–164.

67. Bruce Larson, *The Relational Revolution* (Waco, Tex.: Word, 1976).

In relational theology, the dimensions of human relationship and interaction become highly important, both in formulating the message and beliefs of the church and in the dynamics of carrying them out. Emphasis is placed on relationships rather than tasks. This has some interesting developments, however. It is easiest to feel emotions toward the person most immediately at hand, both temporally and spatially. In being relational with that person, one may neglect relational concern for many others in similar or even more serious need, but not immediately at hand. This is why the practice of triage was developed by the French medical personnel during World War I. This was the practice of separating the wounded into three groups: those who would survive and get well whether immediate medical attention was administered or not; those who would die whether immediate medical attention was administered or not; and those who would live or die, depending upon whether they received immediate medical attention. Emergency efforts were then concentrated on the third group. This required consciously overriding one's feelings toward the patient immediately at hand. The church's ministers are not always as wise in their work. One associate pastor told me that his senior pastor chided him for being too task-oriented, but the senior pastor himself poured countless hours into counseling one or two nearly hopeless cases at the expense of his preparation of the Sunday sermon that would be needed for the spiritual needs of three hundred people. If people are our task, then task-orientation is not contrary to people-orientation.

This emphasis on emotions has another serious consequence if not carefully managed. It can lead to decisions being made purely on emotional factors. This was the theme expressed in Debby Boone's song, "You Light Up My Life": "Can it be wrong, when it feels so right?" Some very immoral things have been done in the name of it feeling right or feeling good. It may even be a case of doing the right thing, of being moral but not being ethical. By that I mean doing what happens to be the right thing because of an emotional impulse, but not because of having reasons for the rightness of the action. This eventually produces Christians who only act when they feel like it.

In my first pastorate, one of my members said to me, "You must really like doing visitation, because you do it so regularly." My response was, "No it is not really my favorite ministry activity, so that if I only went visiting when I felt like it, I would probably make very few calls." I did that, not because I always felt like it, but because I knew it was part of what the Lord had called me to do.

This creeping inclination toward the emotional overriding the volitional then begins to color our understanding of God. God's actions are seen as motivated by what he feels toward and with humans. That may not be fully the case, however. That may be anthropomorphism, and even morphism of a specific kind of anthropos.

What does seem to be the case is that the closest analogy for understanding God is an emotionally mature person, one who experiences emotions but does not let them control him or her. One of the things that counselors have to learn is the ability to *empathize* with their clients without *sympathizing* with them—to be able to understand what their clients are feeling without actually personally experiencing those feelings themselves. This is a matter of experience in the practice of counseling. A counselor who does not acquire this ability will soon be overwhelmed by the emotions of his or her clients. Similarly, Creel uses the illustration of the emergency room doctor, who must learn not to be psychologically paralyzed by the trauma around her, so that she becomes unable to function. Weeping uncontrollably in the face of serious injuries is not a desirable quality in an emergency room doctor. The "loving" doctor, the one who actually ministers effectively, will be able to function in the midst of crisis. There has to be some ability to understand what the person is experiencing, a phenomenon that leads to what is sometimes called "medical student's disease," whereby when students study each disease, they think they have that condition. I recall reading a magazine article about thyroid condition. When I read the description of the symptoms of hyperthyroidism, I thought, "I have that disease." When, however, I read the symptoms of hypothyroidism, I was sure that was my condition. The two, of course, cannot co-exist. The point is that one knows what it would be like to have that condition, or knows the experience of the patient indirectly.

There is a further problem with the argument that God must directly experience everything that humans are experiencing. As we have pointed out, there are certain emotions God presumably cannot have. Beyond that, however, with several billion humans in the world at any given time, there are vastly different emotions being experienced. One person is experiencing great sorrow, another immense joy. One is experiencing hatred, another good will. One is feeling anger, another peace and contentment. On the model of passibility, which says that God must directly experience what he knows other humans are experiencing, God must simultaneously be feeling a whole host of conflicting emotions. How can this be? It could, of course, be argued that with an infinite God, whose emotions are quite different from ours, we cannot be certain that such a plethora of different emotions could not be experienced. That option, however, seems to have been forfeited with the adoption of a view of God that makes him very much like human beings.

That God cannot literally feel directly all of the emotions of everyone should be apparent. There are some emotions God has not, will not, and cannot experience. He cannot, for example, feel sexual lust. He cannot be hateful or sadistic. Thus, in these areas, certainly God does not experience the emotion.

Further, we should avoid the idea of God grieving, feeling great sorrow, to the point of depression, over those who reject his offer of grace and thus perish. If this were the case, then God would spend eternity grieving, mourning, over these persons. He would experience a perpetual and intense grief and pain. This would most certainly be inconsistent with the perfect bliss that many theologians believed was the nature of God's existence. It is perhaps this understanding of the passibility of God that has led to two adjustments to the eschatology of some otherwise orthodox theologians. One solution to this problem is universalism, whereby everyone is ultimately saved. Thus, there is no one for God to feel sorrow over. The other solution is annihilationism, whereby those who do not accept God's offer of salvation do not exist eternally in conscious suffering, but simply cease to exist. Thus, again, there are none in eternal punishment whose anguish God experiences. Yet annihilation is only a partial solution to this problem. If God really is passible, must he not experience a sense of loss over these who no longer are, who could have spent eternity in fellowship with him? He cannot, of course, experience their emotions, since they no longer exist to have emotions, but he can and should, if he is truly passible, experience a sense of loss.

We should, however, point out regarding Creel's statement about impassibility and redemption that genuine repentance cannot be evoked simply by realizing that one has done something wrong to another human. The nature of conviction of sin seems to involve the realization that God is wronged in such situations, and that apart from wrong done to the other person, there is wrong done against God. This is the thrust of David's prayer in Psalm 51, "against you, you only, have I sinned," even though he had sinned against Bathsheba and Uriah. This is not to say, however, that God's reaction to that sin need be one of anger, depression, or suffering, but that there is a realization that the person has not given to God that which he deserves.

8

God's Power

The topic of divine omnipotence has received less attention of late than the closely related topic of omniscience. Yet it is intimately connected with a number of other issues that are being heavily debated, such as the problem of evil and the question of human freedom. It is exceedingly important for several reasons.

The issue of divine omnipotence is important, first, because it is so crucial to the concept of God. In some ways, it seems almost essential to deity. In perfect being theology, of course, it is inseparable from the concept of God, because a perfect being would not have any limitations on his power or anything else for that matter. Even for those who do not necessarily identify with perfect being theology, God or the divine is the one who surpasses what we are. It seems most appropriate that he should absolutely surpass us. This conception is found in various types of informal religious ideas and expressions. The designation "the almighty" is widely used, even by persons who are not explicitly religious. A God who is limited in what he can do seems more like the gods worshiped by people surrounding Israel than like Jehovah.

Second, the concept of almightiness or omnipotence is important because it has great practical importance. It affects our religious practice. Only an all-powerful and generally infinite being seems to be the proper object of our worship. Other great persons are respected, admired, or even feared, but they are not worshiped. The type of veneration that Jehovah calls for is absolute, not to be shared with any other object, any other claimed "God" (Exod. 20:3). Only the almighty one can evoke such a response. If God is not unlimited in power, then other objects of worship, even though secondary, may exist.

Not only is omnipotence essential to worship, but only an almighty being can be a proper object of trust. Can we really be sure of salvation, if there is something that God cannot overcome, whether within or outside us? For that matter, if God is not all-powerful, may it be that not only the problem of evil is insolvable, but evil itself is? Perhaps evil will ultimately prove stronger than God and will be victorious. And what about God's promises in the Bible? Can they be relied on, because God is fully capable of doing anything he says he will do, or will they ultimately fail? Dare we stake our lives on God's commitment?

Biblical Basis of the Doctrine

We begin first with an examination of the biblical teaching on the extent of God's power. In general, there are two types of considerations: names or titles of God that convey the idea of power, and attributions of ability and power to him.

Old Testament

The primary name for God that relates to this issue of power is the compound name *El Shaddai*. The etymology of this word is shrouded in obscurity. It seems, however, to refer to powerful or mighty, but not necessarily almighty. And, as James Barr has pointed out, it is not possible to base one's understanding of the words of the Old and New Testaments simply on analysis of the word stocks or the derivation of the terminology. The meaning of the word must be determined from an examination of its usage in particular contexts.[1]

One of these usages is in the revelation to Abram in Genesis 17:1–18:15. The Lord comes to Abram and identifies himself as *El Shaddai* (17:1). The promise made to Abram involved his wife, Sarai. This required what must have appeared them—and to us as well—a miracle, for Abram was one hundred years of age and Sarai was ninety. She had been unable to conceive and give birth during the normal childbearing years and was now well past that age (18:11). It had been twenty-five years since God had first promised Abram descendants (12:2) and no child had been born. Abram and Sarai had consequently taken matters into their own hands, and Abram had fathered Ishmael by Sarai's handmaiden, Hagar. Now the promise of a child being born to Abraham by Sarah (17:16) seemed impossible. Abraham laughed and suggested that this would be Ishmael (17:18), whereupon God repeated the promise (v. 19). When Sarah heard the news, she also laughed to herself, at the idea that at this stage they would now have this pleasure (18:12). The Lord said to Abraham, "Why did Sarah laugh and say, 'Will

---

1. James Barr, *Semantics of Biblical Language* (London: Oxford University Press, 1961).

I really have a child, now that I am old?'" His next words were instructive to Abraham—and are especially instructive to us: "Is anything too hard for the LORD? I will return to you at the appointed time next year and Sarah will have a son" (vv. 13, 14). In this context, the name *El Shaddai* is linked with being able to do anything. Nothing is beyond the reach of God's power. Note, incidentally, that God was also apparently able to read the hearts of people who do not speak aloud (v. 15).

A second instance of the use of this word is found in the revelation to Jacob. In Genesis 28:3, his father, Isaac, the miraculously born son of Abraham, sends him from home into a situation of great uncertainty. His very life is in danger at the hands of his brother, Esau. He is virtually exiled from home. Isaac pronounces a blessing on him, and does so in the name of *El Shaddai*, God Almighty, invoking God's blessing on him, to make him fruitful and increase his numbers. Then in chapter 35, God appears to Jacob, commands him to be fruitful and multiply, and promises that a great community of nations will come from him. The same name is the one that Isaac had used of God. Although the context does not require almightiness, it does relate to his being powerful and doing very great things. Like his father, Jacob passed on this same name to his sons as well in Genesis 43:14, 48:3, and 49:25 (the last of these is simply *Shaddai*, rather than the compound name). In each case, it is in the context of God's great ability. For example, in 48:3, Jacob relates what God has done for him and what he is yet to do. This is told to the son whom he thought he would surely never see again.

This name is also used by God in his conversation with Moses. This reference comes in the midst of the plagues of Egypt. Pharaoh in response to those plagues has just increased the Israelites' task but decreased the available resources. The people complain to Moses, and he in turn complains to God. God responds that he had formerly revealed himself as *El Shaddai* to Abraham, Isaac, and Jacob, but not as the Lord (Yahweh), as which he now reveals himself (Exod. 6:3). This, of course, was the same name he had given to himself in 3:15. Yet here as well, God's power is being emphasized. It is as if God is telling him that he is no less, but rather more, than that which he was in the experience of his ancestors. The mighty works that Moses knew he had done there, would also be done here. God was the equal of any situation, including one that simply got worse rather than better.

Naomi also spoke of the Almighty and what he had done. She attributed to God Almighty the unpleasantness of what had occurred (Ruth 1:20–21). Although this is said virtually in bitterness, rather than gratitude, it was an indication that God was in control of all that occurs or, in this case, has occurred. It reflects the conception that God is the ultimate source and cause of the circumstances of life, and as such fits the omnipotence idea, even if it does not overtly express it.

In the Book of Job we especially find extensive or widespread use of the term *Shaddai* (Almighty). Indeed the word appears no fewer than thirty-one times. It includes the idea that God has both the ability and the right to do all things in relation to nature, justice, and the like. Frequently, it includes the idea that the human has no right to reply to God, or to question what he does. God has power over life and power to give it and to direct its details.

There are also several instances in the Old Testament where, without the use of the name "Almighty," God and what he does is described. One of these is found in Jeremiah 32. The context is that of the fall of the city of Babylon. The property is to be bought. God will bring his word to fulfillment. He is described as having power over nature: "Ah, Sovereign Lord, you have made the heavens and the earth by your great power and outstretched arm. Nothing is too hard for you" (v. 17). This is also related to the mighty works by which he brought his people out of Egypt (vv. 20, 21). He is also seen as sovereign over history. Not only has he delivered his people from the Egyptians, but he is bringing disaster on them for their disobedience, with the agents of his judgment being the Babylonians (vv. 21–29). The unlimited extent of his power is again expressed in verse 27: "I am the Lord, the God of all mankind. Is anything too hard for me?" It is because of this almighty power that he is able to assure them that he will bring his promises to pass (vv. 37–44).

Another declaration of God's omniability without the use of the name *Shaddai* is seen in Job 42:2, where Job says, "I know that you can do all things; no plan of yours can be thwarted." The import of this passage seems to be that there is no obstacle that can prevent God from reaching his goal, from achieving what he purposes to do. Although stated in a negative way here, this is what is usually being asserted by the doctrine of divine omnipotence. This is an amazing statement by Job, coming where and as it does. He indicates to God his understanding of him, even after all that had happened to him. Nothing that he had experienced deterred him from this conviction and confession. God had the right over his life and had the ability to take it.

One additional, somewhat different, note is found in Psalm 115:3: "Our God is in heaven; he does whatever pleases him." This assertion pertains not to his capability, but to the fact that he does whatever he pleases. This carries with it the sense of freedom from limitations or restraints. Similar ideas are expressed in Psalm 135:6 ("The Lord does whatever pleases him, in the heavens and on the earth, in the seas and all their depths") and Daniel 4:35 ("All the peoples of the earth are regarded as nothing. He does as he pleases with the powers of heaven and the peoples of the earth. No one can hold back his hand or say to him: 'What have you done?'").

We may, then, summarize the Old Testament teaching by saying that God is the absolute Sovereign. He has both the authority and the ability to do whatever he chooses. No task is too hard for him, even that which humanly speaking was regarded as impossible, and its achievement therefore as miraculous. There is nothing that forms an obstacle to his plan and work that he cannot overcome.

New Testament

When we come to the New Testament, we find once again a name or title for God and the ascription of certain powers or accomplishments to him. The one dominant word for God used here is *pantokratōr*. This is a compound word, formed from two words meaning, respectively, "all," and "to be powerful," and meaning roughly the same as *El Shaddai* in the Old Testament. The word appears ten times in the New Testament, of which nine occurrences are in the Book of Revelation. The one instance outside Revelation is in 2 Corinthians 6:18, where God, identified as the Lord Almighty, promises to be a Father to them. In Revelation, three of the instances (11:17; 15:3; 16:7) are instances of worship or commitment, based on recognition of God's greatness and accomplishments. In one of the occurrences, God identifies himself by the name of almighty: "'I am the Alpha and the Omega,' says the Lord God, 'who is, and who was, and who is to come, the Almighty'" (1:8). Two of these references are expressions of praise to him (4:8; 19:6). Three are attributions to God of greatness (16:14; 19:15; 21:22). There are, of course, many interpretations of the Book of Revelation, but on virtually any of them, it is regarded as asserting God's lordship over the events of history.

A narrative passage where the all-powerful nature of God is taught, but without the use of the name or title, is the annunciation to Mary in Luke 1. The angel appears to Mary and announces that she will give birth to a child, the Son of the Most High. Mary, of course, being a virgin, expresses amazement: "How will this be, since I am a virgin?" (v. 34) The reply is in terms of the source from which this comes, that it is a supernatural matter, the Holy Spirit overshadowing her (v. 35). Then the angel, as if to show that God can do not just one, but two miracles, tells her that her relative Elizabeth is pregnant as well, even though she is old and was considered barren. The concluding statement, apparently covering both these situations, is: "For nothing is impossible with God" (v. 37). Here is a declaration of God's power in the biological realm, such that nothing cannot be overcome by this all-powerful God.

An incident from Jesus' ministry shows us his understanding of the extent of God's power. It involves the rich young man who came to Jesus and was told to sell all he had, give to the poor, and come and follow Jesus. He went away sad. Jesus then gave his teaching about how it was easier for a camel to pass through the eye of a needle than for a rich man to be saved. The disciples expressed wonderment, asking, "Who then can be saved?" Jesus' reply was, "With man this is impossible, but with God all things are possible" (Matt. 19:26) or "What is impossible with men is possible with God" (Luke 18:27). Here the power of God was related not simply to physical natural laws, but to the ability to change a human heart.

We may also note Jesus' prayer in the Garden of Gethsemane, where he asked the Father to take this cup away from him. His statement to the Father was, "*Abba*, Father, everything is possible for you. Take this cup from me. Yet not what I will, but what you will" (Mark 14:36). He had no doubt about the Father's ability to do it or anything else. It was merely that he wanted to declare his desire that the Father's will be done.

In Ephesians 1:19, we find this statement by Paul: " his incomparably great power for us who believe. That power is like the working of his mighty strength." This passage underscores our inability to measure the extent of God's power. This in itself may mean simply human inability to measure, and would not necessarily mean that God's power is truly unlimited. It could be just the idea of human incomprehensibility. It implies more than that, however, suggesting that it is inherently beyond any measure, or in other words, infinite.

Finally, we have one additional statement of a rather limited type. In Romans 8, Paul speaks of God working in all things for the good of those whom he has called (v. 28), of his ability to fulfill his purpose of creating in his children the likeness of his Son, Jesus Christ. Then, in concluding the passage, he states the inability of any of the supposed sources of power to separate them from this love: "For I am convinced that neither death nor life, neither angels nor demons, neither the present nor the future, nor any powers, neither height nor depth, nor anything else in all creation, will be able to separate us from the love of God that is in Christ Jesus our Lord" (vv. 38–39).

Here, in the New Testament as in the Old, a title is applied to God that seems more clearly to mean "all-powerful." Beyond that, however, there are the assertions of God's ability to do anything, whether that be a miracle in the realm of nature, the ability to change the human heart, the whole course of history. The combined teaching of the Bible is that God is the almighty one, able to do anything, and nothing or no combination of things is able to resist or frustrate that one.

Specific Problems of Omnipotence

We turn now to the discussion of certain problems that have been raised by philosophers and others regarding omnipotence. We may regard these in various ways. One would be to view them as simply as annoyances, to be ignored. If they do not present an immediate problem to our own faith, we need not concern ourselves with them. A second approach would be to consider them as challenges to our understanding of God, to be disposed of in the most vigorous way. Apologetics (the positive arguments) and polemics (the negative arguments) are to be mustered against these. Or, we may regard these as of potential assistance in understanding the nature of omnipotence. Because these statements of Scripture are not entirely explicit and admit of different interpretations, the issues raised may be of help to us in understanding exactly the nature of divine omnipotence. They may serve to point out erroneous conceptions we may have held. They may point out refinements in the doctrine, carrying our understanding to a new level. They may help us define omnipotence by showing us what issues must be addressed.

We may identify some of these issues before we begin to address them individually. One is whether God is bound by the laws of logic. Do these rules limit what God can do, and if so, is this a genuine limitation of God? A second is the paradox of the stone: can God make a stone so large he cannot lift it? The third is the problem of evil: if God is completely good, he would want to eliminate evil. If he is all-powerful, he is able to eliminate evil. Yet there is abundant evil, both natural and moral, in our world. Therefore, unless we are prepared to reject the idea of God's complete goodness, we must concede that he is not all-powerful. The fourth relates to sin. It is often believed and stated that God cannot sin, something that humans can do. But if this is the case, then he must be limited. A fifth problem is God's apparent inability to change the past once it has occurred. Finally, there is the issue of subsequent freedom. Is God bound to honor his previous promises and commitments? If so, he is not now free to do the contradictory of those or to abstain from those.

The Paradox of the Stone

This is an old question, which continues to receive attention from various philosophical theologians. The statement of the problem is actually quite simple. Can God create a stone so large that he cannot lift it? If he cannot, then there is something he cannot do, namely, make such a stone. If he can, there is also something he cannot do, namely, lift such a stone. Either way, there is something God cannot do so that he is not all-powerful or almighty. Several varied responses have been given. These break down basically into three groups.

1. The internal contradiction solution. According to this approach, the problem is failure to see that this is a contradictory concept. The solution, therefore, is an adaptation of the solution to the question of God's ability to do the contradictory, or defy the laws of logic. What this calls for, according to Mavrodes, is that "a stone too heavy for God to lift" is actually "a stone which cannot be lifted by Him whose power is sufficient for lifting anything."[2] This, however, is self-contradictory. Self-contradictory acts are not proper objects of power. So God is unable to perform a self-contradictory act, but the inability to do this is not an actual lack at all.

2. The conditional omnipotence solution. This seems to assimilate the solution to that of the problem of God making promises he then must keep. Essentially, this approach says that God can at some point create a stone too large for him to lift. He need not actually choose to make such a stone, however. He may simply abstain from such an action. Swinburne contends that an omnipotent being has the ability to choose to make himself no longer omnipotent, a power that he may or may not choose to exercise. As long as he never exercises this ability, he remains omnipotent.[3] Note that this somewhat redefines the meaning of "omnipotent." Its usual meaning is "not capable of failing or being frustrated." Here it seems to mean not actually ever failing or being frustrated. It is like the difference between a boxer who is undefeated because there is no one capable of defeating him, and one who is undefeated because he only accepts fights with fighters whom he can defeat.

3. The meaningless description solution. Savage claims that creating a stone too large to lift does not actually describe any act that an omnipotent being cannot do. The phrase "cannot create a stone" seems to imply that there is a task that God cannot perform, and that, consequently, God is not all-powerful. Rather, however, we need to see that the statement "x cannot create a stone which x cannot lift" actually means, "If x can create a stone, then x can lift it."[4]

My own solution to the problem is in some ways a blend of the first and third solutions above, but with more emphasis on the approach of Savage. We should note, first, that there are different ways to describe actions. One is to describe them in terms of the direct object of the ac-

2. George I. Mavrodes, "Some Puzzles Concerning Omnipotence," in *The Power of God: Readings on Omnipotence and Evil*, ed. Linwood Urban and Douglas G. Walton (New York: Oxford University Press, 1978), p. 132.

3. Richard Swinburne, *The Coherence of Theism* (Oxford: Oxford University Press, 1977), pp. 157–58.

4. C. Wade Savage, "The Paradox of the Stone," in *The Power of God*, p. 141.

tion. This is probably the most common. Another, however, is to describe them in terms of the relationship of the object to another object or the reaction to it by another person. An example of the former would be, "I can paint a picture that is asymmetrical, discordant of color, poorly represents what it presents," and so on. On the other hand, an example of the latter would be, "I can paint a picture which no one would want to see." The difference is this: the former describes an intrinsic quality; the latter, a relational quality. It could, of course, be contended that there is also a relational quality to some of the qualities mentioned in the former sentence, such as discordant color, but there is at least some objectivity involved in those factors. Further, there is a problem with the latter sentence, in that it is a universal statement and thus insusceptible of verification. There might be someone who likes the grotesque. The sentence can, however, be reworded in such a fashion that this problem is avoided: "which many persons would not want to see," or "want to buy," or by limiting severely the sample being described, such as, "most persons in the Rotary Club of Left Overshoe, Montana, would not want to see or buy."

It appears to me that the present problem, the paradox of the stone, represents the use of sentences such as the latter. Note that the stone is described not by how heavy it is, but as "a stone that God cannot lift." That, however, is a relational description. It does not describe the stone, telling us how heavy it is, but what the effect of making a certain stone would be, namely, that someone could not lift it.

It is possible to approach the problem of describing the stone in a somewhat different fashion, however, by describing it simply in terms of what is done, or the nature of the object that is created, rather than the effect of making such a stone. The statement describing such an action would then be, "God can make an infinitely large stone." Paired with this would be the statement, "God can lift an infinitely large stone."[5] There is no limit to the size of the stone either that God can make or that he can lift. There would seem to be no inherent contradiction between these two statements, however.

There is, however, another way of putting the original statement involved in the paradox: "An omnipotent God must be capable of contradicting himself or negating himself or frustrating himself." That is an interesting but unverifiable sort of statement. Such an action would not

---

5. Strictly speaking, an infinitely large stone would be weightless, since it would comprise all the matter in the universe, and there would be no other object with which it could have mutual attraction. Thus God could lift an infinitely large stone, but this might not be true of very large but not infinitely large, stones. This insight was first suggested to me by a Truett Seminary student, Dr. Neal Scogin, formerly of the faculty of Louisiana Tech and Texas A and M universities.

seem to be a proper object of power. On either of these approaches, then, we conclude that the paradox of the stone is actually a pseudo-problem.

Ability to Do the Contradictory

Can God do that which is logically contradictory? Usually the examples of such action are drawn from the realms of mathematics, including geometry. Must an omnipotent God be able to construct squares with three angles, or circles, not all points on the circumference of which are equidistant from the center? Most philosophers have replied that this is not necessarily a part of omnipotence, so that lacking the ability to do the self-contradictory is not a threat to omnipotence. There have, however, been those who contend that God is not or was not bound by the laws of logic. Descartes, for example, maintained this:

> But I do not think that we should ever say of anything that it cannot be brought about by God. For since everything involved in truth and goodness depends on His omnipotence, I would not dare to say that God cannot make a mountain without a valley, or that one and two should not be three. I merely say that He has given me such a mind that I cannot conceive a mountain without a valley, or an aggregate of one and two which is not three, and that such things involve a contradiction in my conception.[6]

To Descartes, God is dishonored by making him subject to something else, namely, in this case, the laws of logic. Most theologians, including Thomas Aquinas, have disagreed: "As a consequence, anything containing a contradiction cannot be conceived. . . . Hence it is not contrary to the message of the Angel if it is said that God cannot violate the law of noncontradiction."[7]

To many who reject the problem of inability to do the contradictory, the laws of logic are simply part of the very way in which reality is structured. It could not be otherwise. The ability to contradict oneself would not be real. Swinburne, for example, says that while these words have the apparent grammatical form of something that could be done, they do not really describe anything that is anything, that is, that could be a possible object of power. Morris says that logically impossible tasks are not just very esoteric or very difficult tasks. They are things that simply cannot be candidates for power ascriptions. The two terms "married" and "bachelor" in a statement such as "God can create a married bachelor," for example, simply cancel each other out, so that it is like writing

---

6. René Descartes, "God Can Do the Logically Impossible," in *The Power of God*, p. 39.
7. Thomas Aquinas, "Are Those Things Which Are Impossible in Nature Possible for God?" *Quaestiones Disputae, De Potentia Dei* q. 1, a. 3. Reprinted in *The Power of God*, p. 45.

something and then immediately erasing it.[8] This is therefore not even logically conceivable.

What about the idea that God being bound by the laws of logic is a restriction on him, and thus dishonoring to him? This assumes that God could choose to violate the laws of logic. That would mean that reality would then be structured on a different basis than it currently is. Appealing as it is, this is an irrefutable theory, like the theory that biological life could be organized on some basis other than the carbon-based form that we know. We do not know what other ways of organizing reality might be possible. We do not know what the things are that we do not know. Beyond that, however, Ronald Nash contends that "since any sound argument or refutation must begin by presupposing certain rules, it is impossible to argue against someone who rejects the most basic rules of reasoning."[9] J. L. Mackie expresses the same idea:

> Now if anyone holds that there is an omnipotent being in this sense, then he need never be disturbed by any reasoning or any evidence, for if his omnipotent being could do what is logically impossible, he could certainly exist, and have any desired attributes, in defiance of every sort of contrary consideration. The view that there is an absolutely omnipotent being in this sense stands, therefore, right outside the realm of rational enquiry and discussion; once held, it is so unassailable that it is a waste of time to consider it further.[10]

Nash's and Mackie's point does not appear to be telling, however. It assumes that because God could have created the world with other logical patterns, it is impossible to debate the issue with someone who holds such a view. Note, however, that Descartes merely is asserting that God could have created the world in such a fashion, not that he actually did. What he did was to create the world as we now know it, within which these logical laws apply. Therefore, we may proceed to discuss these matters, assuming the validity of these laws of logic for our purpose. Only in one of the other possible worlds that God might have created would this be a problem. Those are not the worlds that God has created, however, or at least not the one in which we are located.

More serious is Nash's objection on biblical grounds. Those who believe that God is all-powerful, able to do anything, and who also believe in the authority of the Bible, must reckon with the fact that the Bible says that there are certain things God cannot do. Among these are to lie

8. Morris, *Our Idea of God*, p. 67.
9. Ronald Nash, *The Concept of God: An Exploration of Contemporary Difficulties with the Attributes of God* (Grand Rapids: Zondervan, 1983), p. 39.
10. J. L. Mackie, "Omnipotence," in *The Power of God* p. 76.

or swear on something greater than himself (Heb. 6:13, 18). So it would seem that omnipotence does not require God's ability to do absolutely anything.[11]

Many philosophical theologians contend that the problem may be resolved simply by recognizing that the problem is illusory, because a description of a self-contradictory action does not really describe any *thing*. It is a collection of words, but there is no reality corresponding to the symbols. Swinburne says that those who claim that God should be able to do the logically impossible are mistaken in regarding

> a logically impossible action as an action of one kind on a par with an action of another kind, the physically impossible. But it is not. A logically impossible action is not an action. It is what is described by a form of words which purport to describe an action, but do not describe anything which it is coherent to suppose could be done. It is no objection to A's omnipotence that he cannot make a square circle. This is because 'making a square circle' does not describe anything which it is coherent to suppose could be done.[12]

Mackie similarly states that "a logical contradiction is not a state of affairs which it is supremely difficult to produce, but only a form of words which fails to describe any state of affairs."[13]

Finally, we should note the religious significance of this issue. Nash claims that a supralogical God, one not bound by the restrictions of logic, would have devastating implications for religion. He says:

> If God can do self-contradictory acts, then there is no inconsistency in His *promising* eternal life to all who trust in Christ but actually condemning to everlasting damnation all who trust Christ. Such duplicity (inconsistency) would be entirely in character for a God not bound by the law of noncontradiction since, in a world where the law does not apply, there is no difference between eternal life and eternal damnation. But if there is a difference, if things are what they are and not their contradictory, then the law of noncontradiction holds.[14]

It appears, therefore, that God's inability to do the self-contradictory is not an actual instance of weakness, especially if the laws of logic are not thought of as something external to God, to which he must conform, but as part of his very nature. This simply says that God cannot frustrate himself. He is not a God of nonsense. Because he is as he is, believers can confidently place their trust in him.

11. Nash, *The Concept of God*, p. 39.
12. Swinburne, *Coherence of Theism*, p. 149.
13. Mackie, "Omnipotence," p. 77.
14. Nash, *The Concept of God*, pp. 40–41.

The Ability to Sin

One thing that God cannot do is sin. Indeed, he cannot even be *tempted* to sin (James 1:13). This, however, is something God cannot do, which his highest creatures are capable of doing. Is this not a weakness or a limitation on him? If he lacks this capability, which humans possess, how can he be the highest of all beings, the greatest conceivable Being?

There are, of course, some sins of which God is incapable simply by virtue of being God. For example, not having a body, he cannot commit fornication, adultery, or even gluttony. The incarnation made this possible for at least one person of the Trinity for a certain period of time. What about the rest of the godhead and for the rest of time?

One approach treats this problem by an appeal to logical consistency and contradiction. This is used, for example, by Ronald Nash. This view contends that the very nature of God is contrary to sin or evil. So the ability to sin cannot even be discussed independently of the other attributes of God, including justice, goodness, and power. Actions can only be performed in the light of these. To commit sin would be to contradict this nature. Even God cannot do this. Contradictions can be acted as well as spoken, so this is a case of an acted contradiction.[15]

A somewhat different approach to this problem is described by Thomas Morris. He notes that one way of dealing with the problem is to define omnipotence rather carefully. This would lead us to a definition something like the following: God has every power that it is logically possible for a being perfect in every other respect to possess. This will only successfully enable us to reconcile ascriptions of both perfect goodness and perfect power to God if we place three restrictions on that power:

1. There can be no independent, externally determined constraints on God's power.
2. The internally determined structure and scope of God's possibilities of action (the limits on divine action set by God's own nature and decisions) are not, and cannot be, such that he lacks any power that otherwise would be ingredient in perfection.
3. God is the sole source of all the power there is or could be.

Under these conditions, we could say that the nature of God is such as to preclude his sinning, but that is no restriction on the concept of his true omnipotence.[16]

15. Ibid., p. 43.
16. Morris, *Our Idea of God*, pp. 77–78.

Morris, however, believes that there is a better solution to the problem. This is to deny that there is some discrete causal power to sin. To deny, then, that God can sin is not to deny that he lacks some power, termed "the power to sin." Morris points out that our language, our vocabulary, is much richer than the underlying metaphysical realities having to do with power. He states two phrases, which he calls power locutions:

A. The power to lift a blue two-ounce pencil
B. The power to lift a yellow two-ounce pencil

There is no real difference of power involved in the actions referred to by these two statements. Rather, only one basic power is referred to by the two phrases. The power involved in performing these two acts has absolutely nothing to do with color. So, although superficially they seem to state two different things, they are not really referring to different powers at all.[17]

Morris cites Anselm's statement, that to say of a certain man that "he cannot lose in battle" does not attribute any lack of power to the man, but only to his enemies. Likewise, Morris says, "to say of God that he cannot sin, should not be taken to imply on God's part any lack of power. It only indicates a necessarily firm directedness in the way in which God will *use* his unlimited power."[18]

There is, in Morris's judgment, no discrete power referred to by the phrase "the power to sin." There are various powers involved in sinning. For example, he says, suppose Jones wrongfully hits Smith in the face, with the intention of causing him pain. This requires certain physical capabilities, such as the power to make a fist, the power to swing one's arm, and so on, but there is no additional power such as the power to sin involved in addition to the other powers. What is lacking is not some power.[19]

To understand what is involved in this "incapability," it is necessary to look at something Morris writes earlier in the same chapter. He notes different meanings of the statement "can do X." He believes this involves three different components: ability, determination, and capability. Under ability, "able to do *x*," he includes power; skill in the use of that power; opportunity to exercise it; and practical knowledge regarding how to use that power. Determination is will power, the determination or persistence to pursue a line of action that requires time or action

17. Ibid., p. 79.
18. Ibid., p. 80.
19. Ibid.

to achieve. The third component, however, is the moral capability, or just plain capability, of performing a given act. Some persons are incapable of certain acts, such as cruelty or thoughtlessness. Sometimes we say something like, "He just doesn't have it in him to do that." This, however, is not a weakness on the part of the person, but a moral strength. So it is with God. He may have all of the abilities, the power, skill, and so on, to do the acts that comprise sin, but doing them is not consistent with the kind of person he is.[20]

Morris here has summarized well God's positive goodness. For him to be God and unable to sin is not a weakness but a strength. Goodness is a positive force; sin is not.

The Paradox of Creating Uncontrollable Beings

Another question concerns God's creation of humans as free agents. The question is whether God can make a being he subsequently cannot control, and whether this is consistent with divine omnipotence. Mackie has stated the paradox in a classic article:

> It is clear that this is a paradox: the questions cannot be answered satisfactorily either in the affirmative or in the negative. If we answer "Yes," it follows that if God actually makes things which he cannot control, or makes rules which bind himself, he is not omnipotent once he had made them: there are *then* things which he cannot do. But if we answer "No," we are immediately asserting that there are things which he cannot do, that is to say that he is already not omnipotent.[21]

There have been a number of responses to this problem. One is that of Bernard Mayo, who contended that "things which an omnipotent being cannot control" is a self-contradictory phrase. Consequently, making such things is logically impossible. Therefore, "failure to bring about logical impossibilities does not count against omnipotence."[22] This constitutes an argument for the answer, "No."

In a later article, Mackie recognized the force of the Mayo type of argument. He contended, however, that there are two types or levels of omnipotence. The first is the ability to control everything, to determine all outcomes. Second level omnipotence, on the other hand, is the ability to limit first order omnipotence. This, however, is still omnipotence: "But if instead we start by saying that God has second order omnipotence, we infer that he can assign first order powers that limit his own, but that his first order powers thus limited can still count as omnipo-

---

20. Ibid., pp. 70–72.
21. J. L. Mackie, "Evil and Omnipotence," in *The Power of God*, pp. 28–29.
22. Bernard Mayo, "Mr. Keene on Omnipotence," *Mind* 70.278 (April 1961): 249–50.

tence."[23] Even if we grant this, however, the additional comment is necessary: "God can only make beings which are beyond control by his first order power. Their independence, being constituted by an exercise of second order power, is still subject to this."[24] In other words, God still has the power to revoke the limitation on his omnipotence, to remove their uncontrollability, presumably either by altering them or by destroying them. Urban and Walton agree with Mackie's description of alternatives, but believe that "a being who can both create a world over which he is in complete control and also a world over which he has only partial control has greater general control over the outcome than a being who can create only a world in which he can determine every outcome which does not entail a contradiction and which is such that an omnipotent being could bring about and control."[25] The paradoxical conclusion is thus that a being who can create uncontrollable beings has a greater measure of control than one who cannot.

Is this so, however? It appears that Urban and Walton are using "general control" in a somewhat unusual fashion. It might be more accurate to say that such a being exercises control over a wider range of possibilities, but not to say that he exercises a greater measure of control.

In summary, it can be said that whether an omnipotent being, as omnipotent, can create beings over which he has no subsequent control will depend on the definition of control being used. It would seem that there is no essential compromise of God's power if he had the power to create or not to create such beings, and has the power to rescind that decision, or at least to nullify its effects. This would be a voluntary limitation of his omnipotence, not greatly unlike that involved in the incarnation. But if one holds that God had that power but did not actually use it, in other words, did not make creatures he cannot control, then omnipotence would seem to be in no way compromised.

Ability to Cause the Past

One final question remains: Does God's omnipotence include the ability to change the past, or to cause the past not to have been, or at least, not to have been what we may currently understand it to have been? Here we may note the interesting psychological tricks we play on ourselves in connection with the question, Do we pray about something that has already happened? I do not mean in terms of praying about the effects that the event will have, but, rather, praying about what has hap-

---

23. J. L. Mackie, "Omnipotence," in *The Power of God*, pp. 83–84.
24. Ibid., p. 84.
25. Linwood Urban and Douglas Walton, "Freedom within Omnipotence," in *The Power of God*, pp. 206–7.

pened. I suspect that many of us may tend to pray after the event, when we do not yet know has happened. While some would not, others do. Presumably the explanation that would be given if one were asked for justification for the practice would be on the grounds that God, when he acted, foreknew that we would pray and so took that into account. Thus, it had an effect on what happened. Yet once we know the outcome, we certainly do not continue to pray. We know that it is past, and know what that past now is, and proceed on the basis that it therefore cannot be changed. Actually, of course, the fact that we know what the past is should not really make a difference, for if it is now past, it should be unchangeable regardless of the epistemological fact that we know it.

Here is the dilemma, then: either God is unable to change the past, in which case he is not omnipotent in the fullest sense, or he is able to change the past, in which case it is not fixed and we cannot rely on it. Aquinas considered this dilemma, and in his customary fashion first considered three arguments that some propose to the effect that God has the power to change the past. The first is that since God has the power to do that which is considered impossible, such as raising the dead, there seems to be no inherent reason why he cannot also change the past. The second is that since God's power does not diminish, and he had power in the past to determine these things to happen, he must now be able to do whatever he did in the past. The third is that if a woman has lost her virginity, the only way God can restore her virginity is through a change in the past. But if God can restore people to charity when they have lost it, and if charity is more important than virginity, then God must also be able to restore virginity.

Aquinas's response essentially is that to change the past is contradictory. Just as it is contradictory to say that Socrates is sitting and not sitting, so it is contradictory to say that he sat and did not sit. It may be only incidental to Socrates' sitting or running that it was in the past, but it is not incidental to the past that what is past cannot be undone. Second it is not God's power that is diminished, but the number of things possible to do. Third, while God can restore a sinner to charity, he cannot make it be the case that he never sinned. So, similarly, he cannot make a non-virgin never to have lost her virginity.[26]

Another, more recent contribution to the question of God's power over the past is that of P. T. Geach, in his essay, "On Praying for Things to Happen." He contends that one cannot rationally pray for things to have happened at the time of prayer. The question is not what God knows or can do, but what we can say. By using an imperative in our

---

26. Thomas Aquinas, *Summa Theologia*, part one, q. 25, art. 4.

prayer, we speak of a situation as if it is still to be brought about, but that is incompatible with representing it as a fait accompli.[27]

Anthony Kenny, however, objects to this argument of Geach. He contends that if imperatives are normally concerned with the future that is because they normally are directed to humans, but that does not mean that imperatives addressed to God must concern the future. Further, prayers need not be given in the imperative mood only, but may also be in the subjunctive or optative mood. Finally, praying for past events is not as unusual or even eccentric as Geach represents it to be. The Tridentine Mass included the prayer, "Deliver us, O Lord, from all evils past, present, and to come."[28]

A rather different approach has been offered by Michael Dummett in a paper entitled, "Bringing about the Past." He insists that he is not talking about God changing the past, but bringing it about. If he reads in the newspaper that there has been a shipwreck of a ship on which his son was a passenger, he could pray, not that if his son has drowned, God would now cause it to be the case that he has not drowned, but that at the time of the shipwreck, God would have made it to be the case that he had not drowned.[29]

There seem to be two possible interpretations of what Dummett is proposing. One, based on his imaginary story of an Indian chief dancing in order to cause the braves to act bravely, even after their acting is over, seems to be that the report of what happened may not be true.[30] The other possibility is that he is speaking here of what Aristotle referred to as final causation—causation for the sake of or for the purpose of something that lies in the future. If it is the latter that he has in mind, then this would seem to be a matter of God acting because of foreknowledge of the prayer that was to be made.

It appears that the cogency of Dummett's argument will turn on the definition of cause, for as Kenny says, "if Hume's account of cause is the correct one, the notion of backward causation is a contradiction in terms; what distinguishes effect from cause is that of two events linked by constant conjunction the cause is the earlier and the effect the later."[31] Yet he notes that there is nothing incoherent in the idea of an effect being simultaneous with its cause.

In Kenny's judgment, three unfortunate consequences follow from the idea of backward causation. The first is that it becomes unclear how

27. P. T. Geach, *God and the Soul* (London: Routledge & Kegan Paul, 1969), p. 89.

28. Anthony Kenny, *The God of the Philosophers* (Oxford: Clarendon, 1979), p. 103.

29. Michael Dummett, "On Bringing about the Past," *Philosophical Review* 73 (July 1964): 341–42.

30. Ibid., pp. 348–57

31. Kenny, *God of the Philosophers*, p. 107.

to distinguish cause and effect. Second, we conversely do not know how to distinguish between earlier and later, since these cannot be correlated with cause and effect. Finally, we do not then know how to distinguish between past and future. Much of this turns, of course, on our understanding of the nature of the past and the future. Time is sometimes seen as a book, with the present being the pages that are open; the past, the pages preceding; and the future, the pages that follow. On one view, the future pages are already written, but are not known until they are turned. The other view sees the future pages as being written only when that page is turned. Kenny then points out that, on Dummett's view, the past pages are not entirely written yet either. There is not a universal two-way causation, on Dummett's view. There is a single cause working backwards while other causal relations operate in the normal manner. The difficulty with Dummett's view is seen as less formidable, he believes, if finite causes are seen as all working in one direction—forward—and there is just one finite eternal cause that can effect the past.[32]

In summary, it seems that the concept of present causation of the past is incoherent if one is referring to efficient causation, the most common use of that term. If, however, one thinks of final causation as a legitimate variety of cause, then there are senses in which a present factor can affect the past. And if God is timeless, then his acting is, from God's perspective, simultaneous with the effect of that action, even though causes may occur at a point in time which from our perspective is subsequent to the effects.

Conclusion

We have noted that the initial definition of omnipotence, namely, the ability of God to do absolutely anything, has necessarily been modified. We have first concluded that the limitation "logically possible" must be attached. Second, we must add the qualification "in keeping with his being," in light of the fact that he is pure spirit and perfectly good morally. Thus, the definition can be stated as, "able to do all things logically possible, that are consistent with his perfect being."

---

32. Ibid., pp. 108–9.

9

God's Knowledge

The doctrine of omniscience parallels that of omnipotence in its insistence that God knows everything. This appears to be a function of his being God, for this would seemingly be a natural accompaniment of being the ultimate person. Of the several attributes of God, perhaps this has come in for the most discussion and debate of late. For just as the doctrine of omnipotence must be qualified by saying that there are some things that are not proper objects of power, such as doing the self-contradictory, so omniscience means the ability to know all things that are proper objects of knowledge.

Importance of the Doctrine

This is a doctrine whose importance can be seen from several perspectives. The convergence of these considerations makes this a topic that we cannot disregard.

Biblical Considerations

There are numerous passages in the Bible that seem to assert that God knows everything, including us, and knows what he knows exhaustively and accurately. While a number of these will be examined in some detail later, their existence gives us reason to pursue the topic at greater length.

Theological Implications

Jonathan Kvanvig has pointed out that several of God's activities assume or require his omniscience. One of these is his activity in forming our character. This is sometimes referred to as "soul-making" and sometimes as "sanctification." In order to avoid error in this process of character formation, however, God must know certain things completely and accurately. He must know what we are and what effect certain events or actions will have on our characters. Further, for his actions to be perfectly just, he must not lack any knowledge that relates to his judgments. Thus, the actions of God in his dealings with humans require extensive, if not complete, knowledge.[1]

Religious Significance

Christians regularly pray for God to intervene in certain situations in life. They also pray that God will guide them. Both types of requests, however, assume divine knowledge. For confidence and trust that God will do the good, what ultimately needs to be done, assumes that he knows what is good and what the future will be. Further, trust in God's guidance of believers for conducting their personal affairs assumes that he rightly knows the good for them and the consequences of his actions. Thus, much of the believer's trust in God derives from a belief in his omniscience.[2]

Psychological Significance

Kvanvig also points out another important dimension of a practical nature. He maintains that there is a deep human need to be loved unconditionally. With humans, this is never quite completely possible. The difficulty is that no other human knows us completely. Perhaps if they did, they would not love us. God's love can be unconditional, for he alone can know all about us, our negative as well as our positive qualities. If, however, God is not truly omniscient, then it is possible that his love is also not unconditional. Perhaps there is some terrible truth about us, which, if God were to discover, he would cease to love us. The quality of God's love is directly related to the extent and accuracy of his knowledge.[3]

Biblical and Theological Support for the Doctrine

Having seen the reasons why this is an issue of great importance, let us now examine some of the most significant arguments for the view. These will both enable us to understand the doctrine and supply evidence for its truth. There are a number of biblical witnesses to this fact. These can be grouped into several types of evidence.

1. Jonathan L. Kvanvig, *The Possibility of an All-Knowing God* (New York: St. Martin's, 1986), pp. ix–x.
2. Ibid., p. x.
3. Ibid.

Direct Biblical Evidence

There are a considerable number of passages that address the nature and extent of God's knowledge. These include several varieties of assertion.

1. *God's knowledge compared to that of humans.* One group of passages simply compares the greatness of God in so many respects, including his knowledge, as compared to us as limited human beings. One of these is the great transcendence passage, Isaiah 55. The loftiness of God is compared with the height of the heavens above the earth. So are the ways of God beyond our ways and hence beyond our understanding, and his knowledge beyond ours. Verse 9 puts it most succinctly: "As the heavens are higher than the earth, so are my ways higher than your ways and my thoughts than your thoughts." Another is found in Job 28, repeating a frequent theme found in that book—the idea that God knows what we do not, and that therefore one should submit to him. "But where can wisdom be found? Where does understanding dwell? Man does not comprehend its worth; it cannot be found in the land of the living" (vv. 12, 13). Then, after speaking of the costliness and unattainable nature of wisdom, Job says, "God understands the way to it and he alone knows where it dwells, for he views the ends of the earth and sees everything under the heavens" (vv. 23, 24).

To the extent that wisdom requires knowledge, this wisdom is present with God because of the surpassing nature of his knowledge compared to ours. Some of these references emphasize our inability to comprehend God's knowledge. One of these is David's testimony that God's great knowledge (in this case, of him) goes beyond anything he can generate himself: "Such knowledge is too wonderful for me, too lofty for me to attain" (Ps. 139:6). In Job 9:10, Job says of God, "He performs wonders that cannot be fathomed, miracles that cannot be counted." More explicitly referring to the knowledge of God is Romans 11:33–34: "Oh, the depth of the riches of the wisdom and knowledge of God! How unsearchable his judgments, and his paths beyond tracing out! 'Who has known the mind of the Lord? Or who has been his counselor?'" A final example of this type of witness is found in Isaiah 46:9–10: "Remember the former things, those of long ago; I am God, and there is no other; I am God, and there is none like me. I make known the end from the beginning, from ancient times, what is still to come. I say: My purpose will stand, and I will do all that I please."

2. *God's knowledge of us.* Several passages witness to God's great knowledge of us, his human creations. In Psalm 139, the psalmist praises God for the greatness of the Creator, including God's knowledge of him and all that he does: "O Lord, you have searched me and you

know me. You know when I sit and when I rise; you perceive my thoughts from afar. You discern my going out and my lying down; you are familiar with all my ways. Before a word is on my tongue you know it completely, O LORD. You hem me in—behind and before; you have laid your hand upon me" (vv. 1–5). At least in part this knowledge stems from the fact that God has created him: "For you created my inmost being; you knit me together in my mother's womb. I praise you because I am fearfully and wonderfully made; your works are wonderful, I know that full well. My frame was not hidden from you when I was made in the secret place. When I was woven together in the depths of the earth, your eyes saw my unformed body. All the days ordained for me were written in your book before one of them came to be" (vv. 13–16). He then puts in poetic form his estimation of the greatness of God's knowledge: "How precious to me are your thoughts, O God! How vast is the sum of them!" (v. 17). He concludes this song of praise with a prayer: "Search me, O God, and know my heart; test me and know my anxious thoughts. See if there is any offensive way in me, and lead me in the way everlasting" (vv. 23, 24). Another is found in Jesus' words of encouragement in Matthew 10:30, where, after assuring his hearers that nothing happens to even the smallest of God's creatures without their Father's knowledge and permission, he says: "And even the very hairs of your head are all numbered." This information is, of course, not of great importance, either to God or to us, but it illustrates how comprehensive God's knowledge of us and all of his creatures is. The final instance is found in Hebrews 4:13, and applies to every creature, but specifically to humans: "Nothing in all creation is hidden from God's sight. Everything is uncovered and laid bare before the eyes of him to whom we must give account."

3. The greatness of God's knowledge. A third group or classification of passages are those that speak of the great extent of God's knowledge, but without necessarily asserting his omniscience. Paul spoke of the Spirit's knowledge: "but God has revealed it to us by his Spirit. The Spirit searches all things, even the deep things of God. For who among men knows the thoughts of a man except the man's spirit within him? In the same way no one knows the thoughts of God except the Spirit of God" (1 Cor. 2:10–11).

Some of these passages refer to God's knowledge being unmeasurable: "Great is our Lord and mighty in power; his understanding has no limit" (Ps. 147:5) This verse speaks of greatness of power, but without an explicit commitment to omniscience per se. It declares that God's knowledge is, from our perspective, such that we cannot measure it, but that in itself does not necessarily mean it is unlimited. The context, however, is one in which God's naming activity is mentioned. He creates truth, thus presumably knowing it. "He determines the number of the stars and calls them each by name" (v. 4).

4. The infinity of God's knowledge. The final and in some ways most persuasive texts are those that indicate not simply that God knows the things that are very difficult to know, but that he knows everything, or that his knowledge is perfect. One of these is Job 28:24. Here Job says, "for he views the ends of the earth and sees everything under the heavens." Later in Job (37:16), we have the statement, "Do you know how the clouds hang poised, those wonders of him who is perfect in knowledge?" Finally, in 1 John 3:20, John writes, "For God is greater than our hearts, and he knows everything." These passages seem to indicate that God's knowledge is not simply unmeasurable; it is unlimited. Yet these are not highly refined philosophical statements about God's intellectual capabilities. The exact implications of these statements for some of the complex or marginal issues will need to be reflected upon philosophically.

5. God's knowledge of the future. It is important, in light of some of the issues that we will be examining shortly, to observe that there are specific statements about the relationship of God's knowledge to matters that at the time of the writing or speaking were still future. Indeed, the entire phenomenon of prophecy seems to rest on or presuppose this fact. In Isaiah 42, for example, God says to Isaiah: "I am the LORD; that is my name! I will not give my glory to another or my praise to idols. See, the former things have taken place, and new things I declare; before they spring into being I announce them to you" (vv. 8–9). Four chapters later he says, "Remember the former things, those of long ago; I am God, and there is no other; I am God, and there is none like me. I make known the end from the beginning, from ancient times, what is still to come. I say: My purpose will stand, and I will do all that I please" (46:9–10). Nor is this a matter of mere general trends or broad occurrences that God refers to. Jesus is able to predict that one of his disciples will betray him, and even identify which one it will be: "And while they were eating, he said, 'I tell you the truth, one of you will betray me.' . . . Then Judas, the one who would betray him, said, 'Surely not I, Rabbi?' Jesus answered, 'Yes, it is you'" (Matt. 26:21, 25). He is able to foretell in great detail that Peter will deny him exactly three times: "'I tell you the truth,' Jesus answered, 'this very night, before the rooster crows, you will disown me three times'" (Matt. 26:34). It appears that this knowledge even extends to the possibilities of what may occur. So Jesus said: "Woe to you, Korazin! Woe to you, Bethsaida! If the miracles that were performed in you had been performed in Tyre and Sidon, they would have repented long ago in sackcloth and ashes. But I tell you, it will be more bearable for Tyre and Sidon on the day of judgment than for you. And you, Capernaum, will you be lifted up to the skies? No, you

will go down to the depths. If the miracles that were performed in you had been performed in Sodom, it would have remained to this day" (Matt. 11:21–23).

Indirect Biblical Evidence

Here we are referring not to statements about God's knowledge, but rather to the actual functioning of that knowledge. This is inductive material about his knowledge rather than deductive or didactic material. The knowledge of God is inferred from the description of what he does or says.

The prime example of this, of course, is biblical prophecy. Simply put, how could God prophesy anything that was going to occur, unless he knew what would happen? This is the function of knowledge as foreknowledge. Rather than simply knowing eternal truths (such as mathematical truths) or current empirical facts, God knows what will come to be the case historically. Again and again this occurs in Scripture. At times and points, the prophecies are quite detailed and minute. While this does not necessarily require omniscience, it certainly seems to involve a superhuman kind of knowledge that exceeds the usual human capabilities.

Inferences from Other Doctrines

There are other aspects of God, or attributes, which imply omniscience. One of these is God's omnipresence. If God is everywhere, or is active everywhere, then there must be nothing he does not observe—or, to put it less anthropomorphically, of which he is not aware. He also is universally present with respect to time, if his relationship there is both that of transcendence and immanence temporally. Nothing is hidden from God because of when it occurs.

The doctrine of omnipotence also implies omniscience. If God is able to do anything, then he must also know everything, or there would be areas with respect to which he could not do something, because he would not understand what needed to be done or how it might be done. This is particularly seen in God's work of providence. How could God, for example, plan to use Joseph as he did if he did not know what the future would hold? How could he anticipate Joseph's greatness and the dependence and subservience of his brothers and parents (as expressed in the two dreams), without knowing what was to come to pass?

Problem Areas

There have been, in recent years, a number of problems related to the idea of divine omniscience. These have tended to fall into two major groupings: problems concerning the internal coherence of the doctrine of God, and problems related to conflict between divine omniscience, particularly foreknowledge, and human freedom.

Problems of Internal Coherence of the Doctrine of God

A number of philosophers have contended that if we hold to the idea that God is absolutely omniscient, we encounter difficulty squaring this idea with other aspects or attributes of God. Although most of the concern has been generated in recent years, some of the discussion, of one of these conflicts in particular, goes back to ancient Greek times.

1. Omniscience and immutability. The major statement of this dilemma in recent years was presented by Norman Kretzmann. If God knows everything, then he must know everything in our world as it currently is. If this world is unchanging, there is no problem. Our world, however, is constantly changing, so God's knowledge must be changing as well. Therefore, if he is omniscient, he *cannot* be immutable.

Specifically, the argument Kretzmann presents states that certain propositions can only be known at certain times or by certain persons. So, in terms of the first of these aspects (pertaining to certain times), he claims that a being who always knows what time it is first "knows, that it is now t_1 (and that it is not now t_2), and then knows that it is now t_2 (and that it is not now t_1). To say of any being that it knows something different from what it used to know is to say that it has changed; hence (4) [A being that always knows what time it is is subject to change.]"[4] Swinburne states Kretzmann's argument as that "at any instant any agent will be necessarily ignorant of a truth expressible at another instant by stating that it is 'now' that instant."[5]

The kinds of statement that Kretzmann is referring to here are what are known as "indexical references." These refer to times, persons, and places in terms of their spatial or temporal relations to the speaker. So, "now" means the instant at which the speaker is saying this, "you" is the person to whom he is speaking, and so on. So, when the speaker says, "Today is Tuesday," the speaker is predicating the property of being Tuesday of the day on which he is speaking. In his classic response to Kretzmann's article, Castañeda contrasts these indexical expressions with what he calls "quasi-indexical expressions." They differ from true indexicals by referring to their objects in relationship, not to the speaker, but to the subject of the sentence. So the statement uttered by John, "Jones knows that he is ill," is quasi-indexical because the refer-

4. Norman Kretzman, "Omniscience and Immutability," *Journal of Philosophy* 63.4 (July 14, 1966): 410, n. 4.

5. Richard Swinburne, *The Coherence of Theism* (Oxford: Clarendon, 1977), p. 164.

ence is indexed to the subject of the sentence rather than to the speaker.[6]

Castañeda then offers, in response to Kretzmann's examples, the following principle:

"(P) If a sentence of the form 'X knows that a person Y knows that . . .' formulates a true statement, the person X knows the statement formulated by the clause filling the blank.'"[7]

Castañeda goes on to contend that if John knows that Mary knows that $2 + 2 = 4$ or that George is ill, then John knows that $2 + 2 = 4$, or that George is ill. If these statements are expressed in quasi-indexical form, then when the sentence is shifted from the former to the latter, certain other references will have to be shifted in light of the change of subject of the sentence, to make sure that the second statement expresses the same meaning as the former. So, for example, if "John knows that Mary knows that her own house has four bedrooms," it does not follow that "John knows that her own house has four bedrooms," but rather that "John knows that Mary's house has four bedrooms."[8]

What is being done here is to distinguish between propositions and sentences. What we have in the case of "Today is 2 October," and "Yesterday was 1 October," is really the same proposition, but expressed in different sentences. They are not asserting anything different regarding what day it is. In Castañeda's terms, if A knows, "it is 2 October," then it is certainly quite possible for B to know on 3 October what A knew on 2 October. Thus, the statement, "it is 2 October" is not true on 3 October, but that does not mean that B now knows something different from what A knew on 2 October.

Ronald Nash has attempted to spell this out in somewhat greater detail, applying it to the question of the time of Christ's birth. Let us assume that Christ is born at point T, and that T_1 precedes T_2 and T_3 follows it. Then we could describe what God truly knows at each of these times as follows:

God knows that at T_1, "Christ will be born" is true.
God knows that at T_1, "Christ is born" is false.
God knows that at T_1, "Christ was born" is false.

God knows that at T_2, "Christ is born" will be true.
God knows that at T_2, "Christ will be born" will be false.
God knows that at T_2, "Christ was born" will be false.

6. Hector-Neri Castañeda, "Omniscience and Indexical Reference," *Journal of Philosophy* 64.7(April 13, 1967): 204–7
7. Ibid., p. 207.
8. Swinburne, *The Coherence of Theism*, p. 165.

God knows that at T_3, "Christ was born" is true.
God knows that at T_3, "Christ will be born" will be false.
God knows that at T_3, "Christ was born" will be false.[9]

2. Omniscience and personality. In the article we have been considering, Kretzmann advances yet another contention. This deals with the question of the compatibility of God's omniscience with theism, which is the belief in a personal God. His contention here is that certain propositions can only be known by certain persons. If God is not that person, then he cannot know that proposition. He offers, as an example, two statements:

s_1. Jones knows that he is in the hospital.
s_2. Jones know that Jones is in the hospital.

Now, says Kretzmann, anyone can know the fact stated by s_2, but only Jones can know what s_1 describes Jones as knowing. His conclusion is: "The kind of knowledge s_1 ascribes to Jones is, moreover, the kind of knowledge characteristic of every self-conscious entity, of every person. Every person knows certain propositions that no *other* person *can* know. Therefore, if God is omniscient, theism is false; and if theism is true, God is not omniscient."[10]

To take another example, consider the fact that I am typing at my computer while looking out at the lake. What do I know when I reflect upon this fact? It can be expressed as, "I am typing at my computer while looking out at the lake." God does not know that sentence. What he knows is, "Erickson is typing at his computer while looking out at the lake." That, however, Kretzmann would insist, is not the same thing that I know. The dilemma then becomes this: either God knows what I know or he does not. He can only know what I know if he is I. So either he knows everything I do and must then be identical with me, in which case God being a separate or distinct individual person is false. Or, he is not identical with me, so he cannot know as a first-person statement what I know. In that case, he is not omniscient.

Is this really the dilemma that Kretzmann suggests it is, however? It appears to me that if we approach this, again with the sentence/proposition distinction in mind, something of the difficulty disappears. For although the statements "I am typing at my computer while looking out at the lake," and "Erickson is typing at his computer while looking out at the lake," are two different sentences, they are the same proposition.

9. Ronald Nash, *The Concept of God* (Grand Rapids: Zondervan, 1983), p. 70.
10. Kretzmann, "Omniscience and Immutability," p. 421.

God knows what I know, but he knows it in third-person, rather than first-person fashion. God is not experiencing sitting at my computer, but he knows that I am experiencing that. The claim that s_1 and s_2 are two different pieces of knowledge seems to be a parallel in the realm of knowledge to Morris's illustration in the realm of power of the ability to lift a blue two-ounce pencil and the ability to lift a yellow two-ounce pencil.[11]

There is another dimension to this issue, which may be of some help—the difference between personal experience and knowledge. One sentence that I might truly utter would be, "I know that I am lying in my bed, in bedroom number one of my home, because I am experiencing that." I may be looking at the walls, seeing the hallway outside the bedroom, and so on. Consider, however, another sentence: "I know that I am lying in my bed, in bedroom number one of my home, because I was experiencing that immediately before I turned out the lights and I have not moved since." Here I know something, but by a discursive argument from a previous experience, rather than by virtue of currently experiencing it. It may be that the difference between God's knowing what I know and my knowing it is something like this difference. God is not having my experience of sitting at my computer or lying in my bed. He does, however, know that because I am at a certain place, in a certain position, and with my eyes open and my head turned toward the window that looks out at a lake, I am seeing the lake. But he does not see it through my eyes.

The difference, then, between God's knowledge and mine may not be so much in the content of our knowledge—in what each of us knows— as it is in how that knowledge is known, or more correctly, how the information that constitutes it is obtained. It may be like knowing that the circumference of this circle, which is 10 inches in diameter, is approximately 31.416 inches, because of measuring it, and knowing it because of computing it mathematically, using the value of π. The knowledge has the same content, but it is arrived at differently. So it is possible for God to know what I know while still remaining a separate being from me, but to know it in a different way than I do, that is, to know it in third-person, rather than first-person, fashion.

3. Omniscience and moral perfection. The final point of incompatibility appears between God's omniscience and his perfection, especially his sinlessness. The ancient Greeks wondered if God knew all things. They were especially concerned about his relationship to certain distasteful things, like dirt, filth, mud, and so on. Some perfect being theo-

11. Thomas Morris, *Our Idea of God: An Introduction to Philosophical Theology* (Downers Grove: InterVarsity, 1991), p. 79.

logians, to be sure, considered this not to be a problem, since these are such insignificant things that the absence of knowledge of them is not a genuine lack on the part of God. Thomas Morris sees this as a rather fastidious God. On the contrary, he finds that the Bible pictures God as the Creator of everything that exists, and therefore, as having a universal scope to his knowledge of all that is within the world, including these supposedly distasteful items.[12]

Of more significant concern is the question of God's knowledge of sin. While God is the object of sin and the recipient of its consequences, he is never the *subject* of sin. He knows what is like to be sinned against, but not to sin. Not only that, but he apparently cannot sin, and in fact, cannot even be tempted to sin, according to James 1:13: "When he is tempted, no one should say, 'God is tempting me.' For God cannot be tempted by evil, nor does he tempt anyone." Thus if what I know is, "I am now committing a sin," and if God cannot know what I am knowing because he is a distinct person from me and cannot commit sin himself, he cannot know sin. Either, therefore, God knows sin and is omniscient but not morally perfect; or he is morally perfect but does not know sin, and so is not omniscient.

Here again it appears that we must appeal to the distinction between knowledge in general, and experience, or between knowing something firsthand and knowing it secondhand. God knows what sin is, for it is a deviation from his moral and spiritual law. He also has experienced being sinned against. What he lacks is the *personal* experience of committing sin himself. Is this, however, really a lack? Consider a mathematician who has never arrived at a wrong answer to any problem she has computed, or an athlete who has never failed at the particular event in which he competes, has never lost a game. They do not know the experience of erring, in the first case, and of defeat, in the second. But are they really lacking anything? Our emotional response may be "yes," but reflection tells us that they do not really lack anything that is a positive experience of knowledge. So it is with God. His failure or even inability to sin does not constitute a lacuna in his knowledge.

God's Knowledge and the Future

One particularly persistent and difficult issue concerns God's knowledge of the future. Traditionally, omniscience was understood as involving knowledge of all objects of knowledge, including future events. There have from time to time been challenges to this. In many cases,

---

12. Ibid., pp. 85–86.

these redefined omniscience in a fashion parallel to the redefinition of omnipotence that we examined in the preceding chapter. There, it will be recalled, we noted that many, indeed most, theologians and philosophers contend that God's ability to do is not simply completely unlimited. There are locutions that describe actions which are not really actions at all, including doing the self-contradictory. These are really not objects of power, so that inability to perform them is not a threat to God's omnipotence. Similarly, says this argument, there are locutions that describe what purport to be objects of knowledge, which are not really that. Most prominent of these are propositions about the future, especially, the actions of free agents in the future. "Johnny will go to town on Wednesday," or even, "It will rain on Wednesday," are grammatical statements that purport to give information but do not actually do so. For, on this theory, the future is not knowable. So God's inability to know the future is not an actual threat to his omniscience, any more than his inability to make square circles undermines his omnipotence. There are basically three types or classes of objections: that the future does not exist; that the future is of such nature as to be unknowable; that complete, divine foreknowledge would be incompatible with the freedom of human agents within that future. These are, respectively, metaphysical, epistemological, and volitional objections to divine foreknowledge.

Before proceeding to examine these objections, we should note the importance of understanding how God knows anything. William Craig correctly points out that many if not all of the contemporary denials of divine foreknowledge rest on the perceptual model of foreknowledge.[13] If there is nothing yet occurring in the space–time universe, there is nothing to perceive or observe. Yet, because God does not have organs of sense perception, his "seeing" the future must be considered metaphorical. He knows these things by direct intuition, or, Craig would say, this knowledge of God is innate.

Anti-Realism about the Future

The first of these objections, from P. T. Geach, is the claim that apparent knowledge of the future is only apparent, not real, by which he means not that it is not really knowledge, but that it is not really about the future. It is not apparent knowledge about the future; it is knowledge of what is apparently the future.[14]

---

13. William Lane Craig, *The Only Wise God: The Compatibility of Divine Foreknowledge and Human Freedom* (Grand Rapids: Baker, 1987), pp. 119–25.
    14. Kvanvig, *All-knowing God*, p. 5.

Basically, Geach's contention is that what we are knowing when we claim to be knowing the future is actually present tendencies of things. His objection is a metaphysical one:

> Future-land is a region of fairytale. 'The future' consists of certain actual trends and tendencies in the present that have not yet been fulfilled. What the Moving Finger has once writ cannot be erased: either by tears of repentance, or by the wit of man inventing a time machine, or by the very dubious piety of praying that something may or may not *have* happened (I have written about the last matter elsewhere). But ahead of where the Moving Finger has writ there is only blank paper; no X-ray vision can reveal what is going to stand there, any more than some scientific treatment of the paper on my desk can show what words I am going to inscribe on it.[15]

Geach holds an antideterministic view of the future. We can change the future. We can bring it about that an event that would have been the case before our action does not turn out to be the case. For example, speaking of a situation in which Johnny has been seriously injured, he says before the operation it was right to say, "Johnny is going to bleed to death from the injury." After the operation, however, this was no longer the case.[16]

Kvanvig has presented an extensive discussion and refutation of this position, which, because of its technical nature, would require treatment exceeding the scope of this chapter. He does, however, offer a response that he believes is more telling and more easily handled here. He suggests the following premise: (8) The present tends toward p's being true, but p will in fact be false even though no one prevents p from being true. He illustrates this with instances where this is true, such as a die loaded so as to come up a 6, but which can nonetheless come up a 2. This statement is therefore not a contradiction, for that would require that it be impossible for it to be true, which simply is not the case. But if it is consistent, then either of two premises that he believes are essential to Geach's argument must be false:

(1) Propositions apparently about the future are propositions about what is going to be the case.
(2) Propositions about what is going to be the case obviously refer to the present, not the future.

15. P. T. Geach, *Providence and Evil* (Cambridge: Cambridge University Press, 1977), pp. 52–53.

16. Ibid., p. 50.

For these two statements to be true, however, requires translating (8) into a different sentence, in each case. He believes that (1) requires that (8) be equivalent to:

(8') The present tends toward p's being true, but p is going to be false even though no one prevents it from being true.

In addition, (2) requires that talk of what is going to be the case in the future is just talk about the present tendencies of things. Thus, (8') is equivalent to:

(8") The present tends toward p's being true, but the present does not tend toward p's being true even though no one prevents it from being true.

This, however, is clearly a contradiction, even though it purports to be a translation of (8) and (8) is not a contradiction. Thus, either the move required by (1) or that required by (2) must be defective. Geach's argument for the unreality of the future must therefore contain a false premise.

Conflict of Foreknowledge with Human Freedom

A more common objection to divine foreknowledge is that fore-knowledge, if genuine, would conflict with the free actions of human agents.

The structure of the argument is as follows. If God is omniscient, he knows all things, including knowing the future exhaustively. This knowledge also includes all human actions. If, then, God knows that at t A will do x, then it must be certain that A will do x. If, however, it is certain that A will do x, then it must be necessary as well that he do x. If not, if he did y instead, for example, then God would turn out to be mistaken. But if it is the case that A must do x, will inevitably do x, then A must not be free to do otherwise. At this point, the argument becomes a disjunctive syllogism. Either humans are not free or God is not omniscient. As human beings we know, intuitively and indubitably, that we are free (or not unfree). Therefore, God must not know all things.

This particular objection, in all of the many forms in which it has been expressed, has evoked a large number of responses. In fact, this is perhaps the largest source of problems and of discussion of the general issue of divine knowledge at the present time. The position taken on this issue affects and is affected by, one's position on other aspects of the doctrine of God or other attributes of God.

Atemporalism

One ancient solution is to contend that, in effect, God's foreknowledge is really not *fore*knowledge at all. It is, rather, the knowledge by God, who is outside time, of all history in one great glance, such that nothing is seen as future or past. Boethius, who perhaps gave the first real formulation of this view, used timelessness in this fashion, as did Aquinas, but neither Anselm nor Augustine did. Boethius stated his understanding of the matter as follows:

> Since the state of God is ever that of eternal presence, His knowledge, too, transcends all temporal change and abides in the immediacy of His presence. It embraces all the infinite recesses of past and future and views them in the immediacy of its knowing as though they are happening in the present. If you wish to consider, then, the foreknowledge or prevision by which He discovers all things, it will be more correct to think of it not as a kind of foreknowledge of the future, but as the knowledge of a never ending presence. So that it is better called providence or 'looking forth' than prevision or 'seeing beforehand.' For it is far removed from matters below and looks forth at all things as though from a lofty peak above them.[17]

Norman Kretzmann and Eleanor Stump wrestled with this issue in their article entitled, "Eternity." Their major contribution was the development of the concept of ET simultaneity. This involves the idea of T-simultaneity, which is "existence or occurrence at one and the same time," and E-simultaneity, "existence or occurrence at one and the same eternal present."[18] This combination of factors means that ET simultaneity exists when a party or an observer is timelessly eternal, and an event occurs within time. They state their view as follows: "Thus the entire life of any eternal entity is coexistent with any temporal entity at any time at which that temporal entity exists. From a temporal standpoint, the present is ET-simultaneous with the whole infinite extent of an eternal entity's life. From the standpoint of eternity, every time is present, co-occurrent with the whole of infinite atemporal duration."[19]

Ockhamism

This approach utilizes a distinction between the certainty that each person *will* act in a particular way, and the necessity that he or she *must* act. Ockham contends that "every true proposition about the present has [corresponding to it] a necessary one about the past—e.g., 'Socrates

---

17. Boethius, *Consolation of Philosophy*, v. 6.

18. Eleanore Stump and Norman Kretzmann, "Eternity," in *The Concept of God*, ed. Thomas V. Morris (New York: Oxford University Press, 1987), p. 226.

19. Ibid., pp. 232–33.

is seated,' 'Socrates is just,' and the like. Other propositions are about the present as regards their wording only and are equivalently about the future, since their truth depends on the truth of propositions about the future. Where such are concerned, the rule that every true proposition about the present has a necessary one about the past is not true."[20] The statement, "Socrates is seated," once that time becomes past, is now a necessary statement about the past, but is a case of accidental necessity, since Socrates might not have been seated. In the case of God's knowledge about future events, however, the statement, "God knows that A will do x," depends upon a contingent action, namely, A actually doing x. Therefore the statement, "God has known that A will do x," is not accidentally necessary.

Ockham believed that this interpretation solved the seeming contradiction between foreknowledge and free will. He contended that God does know future contingent events. Yet he was unable to explain how this occurred. He said, "I maintain that it is impossible to express clearly the way in which God knows future contingents. Nevertheless it must be held that He does so, but contingently."[21]

More recent philosophers have adapted this solution. God is omniscient. He has always known what will occur, including the fact that I will get up from my chair and get a drink of water at 1:30 P.M. on Thursday, May 2, 1996. Yet, if he is omniscient, he cannot be wrong. This does not, however, mean that I must do this at this time and in this way. It only requires that I will. Could I, however, have acted differently at this point than I did? The answer is, "Yes." Would God then have been mistaken in his belief? No, for if that were the case, he would then have always held a different belief about this matter than he did.[22]

Molinism

Luis de Molina, a sixteenth-century philosopher and theologian, sought a new way of reconciling these two apparently contradictory factors by distinguishing three kinds of knowledge. Aquinas had referred to two kinds of knowledge. "Vision" is knowledge of that which exists, has existed, or will exist. It is, in other words, knowledge of the actual. There also is "simple understanding," a knowledge of the purely possible, of things and events that do not exist, have not existed, and will not exist. Molina referred to these two types of knowledge as "free

20. William of Ockham, *Predestination, God's Foreknowledge, and Future Contingents*, trans. Marilyn McCord Adams and Norman Kretzmann (New York: Appleton-Century-Crofts, 1969), pp. 46–47.

21. Ibid., p. 50.

22. Thomas V. Morris, *Our Idea of God* (Downers Grove: InterVarsity, 1991), pp. 94–95.

knowledge" and "natural knowledge," respectively. Between these two, however, said Molina, we must think of a "middle knowledge," God's knowledge of contingent events: "Finally, the third type is *middle* knowledge, by which, in virtue of the most profound and inscrutable comprehension of each free will, He saw in His own essence what each such will would do with its innate freedom were it to be placed in this or in that or, indeed, infinitely many orders of things—even though it would really be able, if it so willed, to do the opposite."[23] Thus, God foreknows the realm of possibilities and that certain individuals will respond to certain influences in a certain way. Thus, his decision to create the world and bring certain individuals into existence, within certain circumstances, is a form of foreordination. It brings about certain actions of these persons, although they are free actions—in the sense that they could have done otherwise.

Limited Omniscience

The final solution to the problem comes from those who maintain that omniscience does not require knowledge of everything whatsoever. Just as omnipotence must be limited to ability to do those things that are proper objects of knowledge, that is, the logically possible, so omniscience is ability to know that which is knowable. And the future, being contingent and even nonexistent, is not knowable. Because it depends on the free choices of free moral agents, the future will be uncertain or unreal until such time as those persons make their choices and actions. Whereas some of the views we have been examining seem to regard the future as being like a rug that exists and is being unrolled as the future becomes present, this view says that the rug has not yet been woven, and consequently cannot be known until it is. Human beings are doing this by their free choices and actions.

No one knows the future—not even God. He knows the past perfectly, as he does the present. He also knows the possibilities that there can be for the future, and knows his own plans and intentions for the future.[24] It is appropriate to call him omniscient because he knows everything that can be known, everything that is an object of knowledge.[25]

God could have decided to make humans in such a way as to be controllable, and thus made the future sure and knowable. His decision to make humans free agents involved a decision to limit his own power. It

23. Luis de Molina, *On Divine Foreknowledge (Part IV of the Concordia)*, trans. Alfred J. Freddoso (Ithaca, N.Y.: Cornell University Press, 1988), disputation 52, par. 9.

24. William Hasker, *God, Time and Knowledge* (Ithaca, N.Y.: Cornell University Press, 1989), p. 192.

25. Ibid., p. 187.

also, concomitantly, involved a similar limitation of his knowledge. If we can accept God's self-limitation in the former area, why can we not also accept his self-limitation in the latter?[26]

One who has advocated such a view is William Hasker, in a number of journal articles, especially in his book, *God, Time, and Knowledge*. After posing the problem of human freedom and divine knowledge, he considers each of the alternatives we have discussed, and finds flaws in each of them. He then proposes the idea of an open future, along the lines that we have described. He cites the work of Clark Pinnock, who makes much of the biblical passages about God repenting or changing his mind.[27] Surely this must suggest that there are events and considerations God did not previously know, which is why he then changes his mind when these occur.

Hasker recognizes that one problem facing his view is the phenomenon of biblical prophecy, in which God declares what is to come to pass, presumably because he knows the future. God has a certain degree of knowledge of the future, based on three factors. He has knowledge of possibilities of what persons will do, and what he will do depending on those actions. Consequently, many of God's prophecies are conditional in nature. They are what God will do, unless the people (such as those of Nineveh) repent. Second, he knows fully present trends and tendencies, and on that basis is able to make certain predictions. Finally, he knows what he purposes to do and thus can predict those things.[28] But he does not know in advance the contingent actions of free persons in any detail. Swinburne, however, holds that if God is truly free, then he cannot even know what actions he is going to take in advance of making those decisions, or the results of those actions.[29]

Let us explore for a moment this contention of Swinburne's. We can note the argument used by Hasker against divine omniscience:

(C1) It is now true that Clarence will have a cheese omelet for breakfast tomorrow. (Premise)

(C2) It is impossible that God should at any time believe what is false, or fail to believe any true proposition such that his knowing that proposition at that time is logically possible. (Premise: divine omniscience)

(C3) God has always believed that Clarence will have a cheese omelet tomorrow. (Assumption for indirect proof)

26. Clark Pinnock, "God Limits His Knowledge," in *Predestination and Free Will: Four Views of Divine Sovereignty and Human Freedom*, ed. David Basinger and Randall Basinger (Downers Grove: InterVarsity, 1986), pp. 145–54.

27. Ibid., pp. 190–91.

28. Ibid., pp. 194–95.

29. Swinburne, *Coherence of Theism*, p. 176.

(C4) If God has always believed a certain thing, it is not in anyone's power to bring it about that God has not always believed that thing. (Premise: the unalterability of the past)

(C5) Therefore, it is not in Clarence's power to bring it about that God has not always believed that he would have a cheese omelet for breakfast. (From 3,4)

(C6) It is not possible for it to be true both that God has always believed that Clarence would have a cheese omelet for breakfast, and that he does not in fact have one. (From 2)

(C7) Therefore, it is not in Clarence's power to refrain from having a cheese omelet for breakfast tomorrow. (From 5,6) So Clarence's eating the omelet tomorrow is not an act of free choice.

(C8) Clarence will act freely when he eats the omelet for breakfast tomorrow. (Premise)

(C9) Therefore, it is not the case that God has always believed that Clarence will have a cheese omelet for breakfast tomorrow. (From 3-8, indirect proof)[30]

For C3 to be true, it would be necessary for C8 to be false.

As we noted in Hasker's discussion of biblical prophecy, however, God can predict certain things about the future, if they are his declarations of his intention to do those things. Suppose, then, that we reinterpret Hasker's argument to apply to such cases. To avoid entering the discussion about whether God's action is eternal, let us simply refer to a time t, when the prophecy of Jesus being raised from the dead is to be fulfilled:

(D1) It is now true that God will at time t raise Jesus from the dead. (This statement is assumed to be made at t-x.) (Premise and *God, Time, and Knowledge*, p. 195)

(D2) It is impossible that God should at any time believe what is false, or fail to believe any true proposition such that his knowing that proposition at that time is logically possible. (Premise: divine omniscience)

(D3) God has always believed that he will at t raise Jesus from the dead. (Assumption for indirect proof)

(D4) If God has believed a certain thing, it is not in anyone's power to bring it about that God has not believed that thing. (Premise: the unalterability of the past)

(D5) Therefore, it is not in God's power to bring it about that God has not always believed that he would at t raise Jesus from the dead. (From 3,4)

(D6) It is not possible for it to be true both that God has always believed at that he would at t raise Jesus from the dead, and that he does not in fact raise him. (From 2)

30. Hasker, *God, Time, and Knowledge*, pp. 73–74.

(D7) Therefore, it is not in God's power to refrain from raising Jesus from the dead at *t* . (From 5, 6). So God's raising Jesus from the dead at *t* is not an act of free choice.

(D8) God will act freely when he raises Jesus from the dead at *t* . (Premise)

(D9) Therefore, it is not the case that God has always believed that he will at *t* raise Jesus from the dead . (From 3-8, indirect proof).

We must now extend the argument a bit:

(D10) But God has always fully intended that he will at *t* raise Jesus from the dead. (From *God, Time, and Knowledge*, p. 195).

(D11) What God fully intends to do he believes.

(D12) Therefore God has always believed that he will at *t* raise Jesus from the dead. (From 10–11).

(D13) Therefore it is not the case that God will act freely when he raises Jesus from the dead at *t*.

If this argumentation is correct, then Swinburne would appear to be right, and Hasker has proved more than he intended. He has succeeded in explaining a certain class of prophecy, but has done so at the expense of denying God's (libertarian) freedom. There would appear to be two ways in which Hasker could evade this conclusion. One would be to reject D11, thus denying the connection between divine intention and divine knowledge, or denying that what God fully intends to do he will actually do. That would seem to require either a rejection of God's truthfulness, in declaring that he will do something, and then not doing it, or of his omnipotence, in being unable to do what he declares he will do. The alternative would be to say that one's freedom to do or not do is not incompatible with one's knowing what one is going to do, only with someone else knowing that. Such an approach, however, would require a major revision of D6.

Probably the objection that Hasker would make is that this is indeed a case of God's not being free, but that he has limited himself in this fashion. Note, however, that if God has *always* known what he was going to do, then it was *always* the case that he has not been free to do otherwise.

Foreknowledge and Freedom: An Alternative Solution

There is another approach that has not received a great deal of attention of late, but nonetheless has real promise for this solution. It is a frankly Calvinistic approach.

On this view, God knows the future in its entirety because he has rendered it certain. He knows what free human beings are going to do because he has foreordained their actions. This scheme involves several components: an eternal knowledge of all possibilities within all possible worlds, an omnipotent God, and a compatibilistic view of human freedom. Compatibilism is the understanding of freedom as not being inconsistent with the decisions and actions of the person having been rendered certain.[31] It is also sometimes referred to as "soft determinism." This conception is not popular currently, even among Christian philosophers. Clearly this idea conflicts with the mood of contemporary culture, especially in the individualistic West. William Hasker acknowledges that on such a view of freedom, most of the problems connected with foreknowledge and human freedom disappear, although a whole new set of problems takes their place. He simply declines to deal with that view, since that would have made his book twice its current length.[32] In his treatment of Calvinism in *The Openness of God*, however, as we have already observed, he assumes the incompatibilist or libertarian view of free will, and criticizes Calvinism from that perspective.[33] A number of other theologians and philosophers simply assume the libertarian view and proceed from there. The clue to this assumption is often revealed by identifying foreordination with fatalism and depicting any sort of compatibilist view of the human as being a "robot," "puppet," or something of the sort.[34] D. A. Carson explicitly repudiates this puppet imagery of the biblical view of human free will, which he interprets compatibilistically.[35]

There is a considerable amount of biblical data that seems to affirm both that God renders certain all that occurs and that humans are responsible for their actions. Among these are Psalm 115:3; Proverbs 16:9, 33; Daniel 4:33–35; Acts 2:23; 4:27–28; Ephesians 1:11; Philippians 2:12–13; and Hebrews 13:21. This understanding of human free will also enables the Christian to deal with those puzzling passages of Scripture that speak, for example, of Pharaoh hardening his heart, but also of God hardening Pharaoh's heart. D. A. Carson has documented at some length the juxtaposition of divine foreordination and human responsibility, especially in the Old Testament and the Gospel of John.

31. Some compatibilists speak of God "determining" these choices and actions. Because that language tends to evoke the conceptions of coercion and constraint, I am here using the terminology of rendering *certain*, rather than *necessary*.

32. William Hasker, *God, Time, and Knowledge* (Ithaca, N.Y.: Cornell University Press, 1989), p. x.

33. *The Openness of God*, pp. 141–43.

34. Ibid.; Craig, *Only Wise God*, pp. 44–47.

35. D. A. Carson, *Divine Sovereignty and Human Responsibility: Biblical Perspectives in Tension* (Atlanta: John Knox, 1978), pp. 10, 167.

The usual definition of freedom given by the noncompatibilist is something like, "has it in her power to choose to perform A or choose not to perform A. *Both A and not A could actually occur;* which *will* actually occur has *not yet been determined.* "[36] Actually, the concept of having it in one's power or being able to do something is a rather ambiguous concept. I would prefer to speak of the person being able to do either A or not-A but it being certain that the person will choose, and will do, one or the other.[37]

Among the possible meanings of "can do *x*," Thomas Morris lists ability to do *x*, which includes power, skill, opportunity, and practical knowledge; determination, or "will power"; and capability. The last element means being morally capable, or being the sort of person who could bring himself or herself to do such a thing.[38] Feinberg lists no fewer than seven possible meanings of "can":[39]

1. It can be defined in the contra-causal sense that "no cause or set of causes is sufficient to produce any particular choice on the agent's part."
2. It can be interpreted conditionally. Thus, the meaning of the agent could not have done otherwise is "she would have done otherwise if she had so chosen."
3. Someone lacking this ability cannot do something, even if he or she wills to do so. A paraplegic may will to run a mile, but lacks the ability to do so.
4. In the opportunity sense of *can*, one both has the ability and the opportunity to do the action in question.
5. The "rule consistent" sense of *can* means that there is some rule that either permits or prohibits the action in question.
6. An agent cannot do something because of the negative consequences that would follow, and that therefore serve as a deterrent.
7. *Can* means that it is something reasonable to do, *cannot* that it is something unreasonable to do.

36. David Basinger, "Middle Knowledge and Classical Christian Thought," *Religious Studies* 22 (1986): 416.

37. William Lane Craig, a libertarian on free will, also draws a similar distinction: "from Smith's and God's foreknowledge it follows only that Jones *will* act in a certain way, not that he *must* act in that way." *The Only Wise God: The Compatibility of Divine Foreknowledge and Human Freedom* (Grand Rapids: Baker, 1987), p. 71.

38. Thomas V. Morris, *Our Idea of God: An Introduction to Philosophical Theology* (Downers Grove: InterVarsity, 1991), pp. 69–81, esp. p. 72.

39. John S. Feinberg, "God Ordains All Things," in *Predestination and Free Will: Four Views of Divine Sovereignty and Human Freedom*, ed. David Basinger and Randall Basinger (Downers Grove: InterVarsity, 1986), pp. 27–28.

Feinberg says of this list: "The point is that a soft determinist may interpret *can* in any way except the first and agree with the indeterminist about the agent doing otherwise. If being able to do otherwise is the criterion for being free, then a determinist can legitimately speak of freedom. The determinist has removed freedom from the universe only if arbitrarily limited to the first sense of *can*."[40]

Freedom is not to be understood as spontaneity or random choice. The usual version given of freedom is quite imprecise. The will is understood almost as if one just randomly chose and acted, arbitrarily and without any pattern. The usual reason given for holding this view is also quite imprecise. It is often understood as an intuition: we just know that we are free. In practice, however, it appears that the human will is not quite so random or chance in nature. There is considerable evidence that each individual adult human being has a "nature," consisting of patterns of behavior, conditioned responses, or something of the like. There also is a growing body of evidence that much of our behavior is affected by heredity. The studies done on identical twins, for example, reveal some remarkable similarities even between twins who have been separated for most of their lives: their personal tastes in many areas, the type of person they marry, even the names they give their children.

Further, there is considerable predictability about much human behavior. We have all learned that we can anticipate with a fairly high degree of certainty how our close friend or our spouse will act or react in a given situation. Anyone who has worked professionally in the management of human beings knows that, in the final analysis, the best predictor of future behavior is past behavior.

It appears, therefore, that there are limitations, or at least circumscriptions, on the absolutely spontaneous freedom that we sometimes believe we possess. This may seem contrary to our common sense or our intuitions. Many things in this world and life are, however: the rotation of the earth versus the movement of the sun, the relativity of space and time. These seem counterintuitive.

Freedom, on this conception, is freedom from constraint or external compulsion. It is freedom from unwilling action. This is freedom to act consistently with who one is. It is freedom to act as one chooses, and to choose as one wishes. But it does not necessarily mean pure spontaneity, nor does it mean freedom to choose contrary to one's nature or character. Just as we saw that God is not truly free to act contrary to his nature, to lie, be cruel, or break his covenant word, so humans are not necessarily free either to act in ways that presuppose that they are

40. Ibid., p. 28.

someone other than themselves. We may be free to do as we please, but we are not necessarily free to please as we please.

On this model, God knows completely every conceivable possibility, both of possible beings who could be brought into existence, and of every event that might ever occur. He knows how each of these individuals would react in each possible situation. This is the truth behind the theory of middle knowledge, which can be incorporated into this view.[41] Thus, God chooses to bring a certain being into existence, rather than one very much like him. Even such a seemingly chance factor as which sperm successfully unites with an ovum makes a major difference in who and what a given person is.

Beyond that, however, God works in numerous ways to bring about his will by rendering it certain that I and each other individual will freely choose what he foreordained. He does this through placing circumstances such that I will want to act in a certain way. Where I was born and the parents to whom I was born, the people who come into my life in significant ways, the countless experiences that I have make me to be the person that I am, and bring it about that of my own free will I choose and respond as God wills for me to do. Further, he utilizes direct influence on my mind and my entire psyche. God is the supreme salesperson, who also knows completely and perfectly the psychology of the person whom he wishes to influence. And he presents his persuasion in nonmanipulative but powerful ways. He has control over all sorts of circumstances that most humans could not control or even influence. And out of this, he does not coerce but renders his will certain. There may be various ways in which he brings this about in different situations. In some cases, he provides the means or the strength to accomplish something. In others, he simply refrains from intervening to prevent a particular action.

It is essential to recognize that on this view God does not foreordain the ends without also foreordaining the means to them. What is clearly being rejected by this view is fatalism, or the idea that what is going to happen will happen, regardless of what we do, and that therefore we

41. There are some major differences between this understanding of middle knowledge and that of Molina. One is that the possible person that God envisions is not simply a possible person existing as a free entity, but a possible person who would be what he would be because of God's activity. In other words, the "essence" of the person, as it were, includes all that will come to be in the personality as a result of God's foreordaining of certain circumstances and experiences. Thus, this position is closer to that of Suarez than that of Molina. For a more complete exposition of the differences between those two versions of middle knowledge, see William Lane Craig, *The Problem of Divine Foreknowledge and Future Contingents from Aristotle to Suarez* (Leiden: Brill, 1988), chapters seven and eight, especially the synopsis on p. 228. The view of compatibilistic foreordination can utilize, but does not require, the doctrine of middle knowledge.

need not exert any effort in connection with those ends.[42] This misunderstanding of the compatibilist or soft determinist view is widespread. Indeed, even such a skilled philosopher as Bruce Reichenbach says of this view, "Finally, there is no need for divine persuasion, for all attitudes and desires cannot but be in accord with the divine decrees if everything is as decreed by God."[43]

To some the view here proposed seems far too complex. Think of all the circumstances God must know, initiate, and control. This, however, may not be nearly as difficult a matter as we sometimes make it out to be. For in a cybernetic age, in which computers may take into account huge numbers of variables in making their computations, it should not be hard to realize that an infinite God can work with immense numbers of variables. God knows all things, even all future matters, because he has rendered certain all things that come to pass, including the free actions of human beings. And it should not even be so difficult for us to conceive of God understanding contingent events. Although we must not think of God as merely a very powerful computer, he should not be thought of as having less capability than a computer. On a spreadsheet, numerous scenarios can be set up and their consequences observed, even without taking the action simulated in the model. The same thing can be done with various types of mechanical or electrical design. Virtual reality allows exploration of possibilities without actualizing these in the real world.

This persuasive action of God, unfortunately, is often depicted as coercion when it is nothing of the sort. John Feinberg uses the illustration of wanting a particular student to leave the classroom. He notes that there are at least three ways in which he could accomplish this. The first is, if he is physically strong enough, to bodily pick up the student and remove him. The second would be to point a loaded gun at him and threaten to shoot him if he does not leave. The third would be to persuade him, by showing him that it would be in his best interest to leave the room. The first two options would not be instances of free action by the student. The third would, however, understanding freedom as compatibilistic freedom.

In the final analysis, the choice of solutions to the problem of omniscience and human freedom will largely come down to a choice between two sets of presuppositions regarding the nature of freedom. While the solution proposed by no means resolves entirely the apparent tension between divine omniscience and human freedom, I would con-

---

42. Feinberg, "God Ordains All Things," pp. 23–24.
43. Bruce Reichenbach, "Bruce Reichenbach's Response [to John Feinberg's statement]" in *Predestination and Free Will*, p. 51.

tend that it does a better job, not only of reconciling these two, but of accounting for a larger sweep of the biblical data, with less distortion of those data.

To be sure, this position on human freedom needs considerable elaboration and defense, since in today's intellectual environment it is controversial. To do the task adequately would require a major treatise on the nature of human freedom, something that would go well beyond the bounds of a book such as this, which is a survey of certain of the attributes of God. Numerous competent presentations of this view have been made. Among them, D. A. Carson's *Divine Sovereignty and Human Responsibility* surveys very competently the biblical material, John Feinberg's chapter in *Predestination and Free Will* states ably the philosophical case, and *The Grace of God, the Bondage of the Will*, edited by Thomas Schreiner and Bruce Ware deals with a number of the issues.[44] For our purposes here, it is sufficient to note that, even by the admission of a free will theist such as Hasker, this view resolves many of the problems with the doctrine of omniscience and freedom. The issues that it may create in other areas of doctrine, such as anthropology, will require treatment elsewhere.

---

44. *The Grace of God, the Bondage of the Will*, 2 vols., ed. Thomas R. Schreiner and Bruce A. Ware (Grand Rapids: Baker, 1995).

10

God's Being and Simplicity

The discussion of specific attributes of God raises the question of the re-lationships among them. In some cases, there seem at points to be some tension between certain of them, at least in the judgment of some theologians. This raises the question of God's being or essence or nature. Does God have a being or nature in addition to which he has certain attributes? Is there a complexity of a unity to the divine nature? These and other questions have traditionally been discussed in terms of the somewhat puzzling doctrine of divine simplicity.

Divine Simplicity

When we come to the issues connected with the being of God, especially the question of divine simplicity, we are entering a relatively less well known area. William Hasker says that "the doctrine of divine simplicity has probably been the least appreciated aspect of classical theism."[1] Ronald Nash puts it more strongly: "The doctrine of divine simplicity has a public relations problem. Few people have even heard that God supposedly has the property of simplicity. Fewer still have any idea what the doctrine entails or why theologians have thought it necessary to ascribe the property to God."[2] Many, if indeed not most, recent systematic theologies do not even discuss this doctrine. Its popularity and discussion peaked during the medieval period. Yet in recent years, several significant philosophers have picked up this doctrine and submitted it to intense scrutiny.

1. William Hasker, *God, Time, and Knowledge* (Ithaca, N.Y.: Cornell University Press, 1989), p. 183, n. 20.
2. Ronald Nash, *The Concept of God: An Exploration of Contemporary Difficulties with the Attributes of God* (Grand Rapids: Zondervan, 1983), p. 85.

Reasons for This Disregard

Why has this doctrine, which once enjoyed such a high degree of attention in theological circles, fallen into such disdain? Basically, the reasons seem to be two. Either theologians believe that this doctrine does not make sense, that is, it cannot be explicated using categories available to us today. Or they think it is intelligible but irrelevant. Even if it is true, it makes no real difference, and therefore may be ignored at no cost to the believer or the theologian.

If we can establish that this is an important or significant doctrine, then the problem would seem to be that it cannot be understood or accepted. But if this is the case, then we are faced with three possible ways of proceeding, corresponding to three ways of dealing with the attempt to maintain any doctrine in our time.

The first is simply to conclude that the doctrine is obsolete. It may have played an important part in doing theology in the past, but the problem that it deals with was internal to a particular system of philosophy. With the passing of that school of thought, it is no longer a real problem. Consequently, we may discard it. A second approach is to consider it indispensable. It must be maintained, and in its classical or traditional form. If necessary, we must be prepared to preserve the thought forms or philosophical frameworks of the past. The third approach says that the values and principles represented by this doctrine must be preserved, but we must be prepared to alter the form of expression of it.

Conceptions of God

One method of finding our way into the issues is to note several different conceptions of the relationship of God to his attributes. These can be put in popular form by noting several models.

1. The pincushion model. This is the view that God has an essence or being, which is unknown to us, and several attributes that attach to it, like pins stuck into a pincushion. They are not the essence of God. They are logically distinguishable from God's nature and from his other attributes.

2. The bundle or building model. This says that God is a composite of his attributes. They are like a bundle of sticks bound together, or perhaps, like the bricks that make up a wall. They are all distinct from one another, but together they form the entirety, the bundle or the wall. God is his attributes, but he is not those individually, but collectively.

3. The facets of the diamond model. On this model, the essence of God is not something hidden beneath the attributes. The essence or being of God is unitary. The attributes are not really separate from one

another either. They are simply different facets, different ways of viewing his nature in relation to different perspectives.

The problem can be seen in terms of the question, "Does God possess his attributes?" On the first model he does, but on the second, he does not. He simply is his attributes, or at least, the sum of them.

Adopting one or the other of these models creates a dilemma. On the first model, God possesses his attributes, but in theory they are separable from him. He could be, without being merciful, for example, or patient, for these are not part of his essence or essential attributes of him. On the second model, God is not independent of the attributes. Since they are of his very nature, he cannot exist without them. He is therefore not fully self-caused or fully self-sufficient. He is dependent on the existence of something else, such as the properties of love or righteousness.

Another way of viewing this dilemma is to ask who is responsible for these properties being what they are. To take the example of kindness, did God decide that kindness is good, and that cruelty is bad, so that in theory he could have decided the reverse? This is in effect the implication of the second view. Or, on the other hand, does he act kindly because it is good, and being good, that is how he must act, rather than acting cruelly? If this is the case, however, then there is something external to God to which he is subject, and he is not ultimately sovereign.

The third model represents an attempt to slip between the horns of the dilemma. On this model, kindness is good and cruelty is evil, objectively. It could not have been otherwise. But, this standard is not something external to God himself. It is his very nature. These values are internal to God himself. It is not something he chose to be, nor something he is compelled from without to be. It is simply the way he is. This is the most ultimate frame of reference for value. On this model, God does not *have* these qualities of love and righteousness. He *is* them. We do not say that God has the attribute of love, or that he is loving, or that he acts in a loving fashion. He is love. He also is righteousness, power, knowledge, and so on.

Immediately, however, some problems arise. On the one hand, this seems to make love, justice, and omnipotence, as well as the other attributes or properties of God, the same thing. If he is love and justice, then since things equal to the same thing are equal to each other, love must be the same as justice. Second, this seems to make a God an attribute, a thing, and that in turn makes him impersonal. Third, this seems to lend support to the view of someone like Paul Tillich, who maintained that all statements about God are symbolic, except the statement that God is being-itself, or Edward Scribner Ames, who said that God is like Uncle Sam. He is a set of values.

This third view is basically the doctrine of simplicity. It has come into being to provide a solution to the problems we have described. And it carries with it the problems we said attach to such a view.

Varieties of Simplicity

Thomas Morris links the idea of divine simplicity especially with the doctrine of aseity, or the idea that God is ontologically independent. This means that he draws his very existence only from himself, not from any cause or force outside himself. If he were dependent on anything other than himself, he would not be able to be the cause of everything else. This idea of aseity, however, led many theologians and philosophers to the conclusion that God must not have any complexity involving composition. Wholes composed of parts are dependent on their parts for what they are. If God had such a composition, he would possess his attributes in the same way humans do, able to gain or lose such qualities.[3]

These considerations have therefore led many theists to affirm the doctrine of divine simplicity. This means that God's being does not involve any sort of metaphysical complexity whatsoever. This, according to Morris, usually has meant a threefold denial:

- spatial simplicity: God is without any spatial parts.
- temporal simplicity: God is without any temporal parts.
- property simplicity: God does not have the sort of metaphysical complexity "involved in his exemplifying numerous different properties ontologically distinct from himself."[4]

The first of these, spatial simplicity, is the most widely held and least controversial aspect of the doctrine of simplicity. Since virtually all theists would hold that God is not a physical object, they conclude that he does not have physical, or spatially located, parts.

The second aspect, temporal simplicity, is quite controversial. It holds that God's existence is not divisible into temporal segments the way our lives are. God's existence is simply one great present moment, so there is no past, present, and future in him. There are no moments of coming to be and passing away. This is associated with the idea of eternity as atemporal duration, rather than extension within and throughout time.

---

3. Thomas V. Morris, *Our Idea of God* (Downers Grove: InterVarsity, 1991), p. 113.
4. Ibid., p. 114.

Nature of the Issues

The idea of property simplicity is the most interesting and unusual, and the area usually referred to when divine simplicity is being discussed. It stems from the contrast between God and all created beings. All God's creatures have properties that are distinct from themselves. All these properties exist distinct from us and are logically separable from us. They do not depend on us in order for them to be and to be what they are. We, however, depend on our properties for what we are. We could not be what we are apart from them. God, however, in light of his aseity, cannot depend on anything other than himself. Consequently, he must not have properties distinct from himself.[5]

Many commentators believe that the question of divine simplicity arises out of concern for two major attributes or characteristics of God: his aseity and his sovereignty. The former, which literally means his self-being, and suggests that he is the cause of his own existence, is usually explained rather as the view that he is uncaused. This means he is totally independent of anything other than himself. His sovereignty means that he has created everything, that all continues to depend on him, and that he is directing everything to the goals that he has in mind for these things.

Augustine was one of the first theologians to state the doctrine of divine simplicity. He says

> There is accordingly a good which alone is simple and for that reason is alone unchangeable, and that is God. All good things are created by this good, but not simple and for that reason changeable. . . . For this reason, then, a nature is called simple in which it is not the case either that it has something that it could lose, or is different from that which it has; as a vessel is different from that which it has; as a vessel is different from some liquid, or a body from its colour, or air from heat or light, or a soul from wisdom. . . . Therefore, according to this those things are called simple which are pre-eminently and truly divine, in which a quality is not one thing, the substance another, nor are they divine or wise or blessed by participation in other things.[6]

There are, as William Mann has pointed out, at least three elements in this classic definition of simplicity: (1) A simple being is immutable. There seems to be an inseparable link between these two qualities of God. The order of precedence, however, seems to belong to simplicity. God is unchangeable because he is simple, whereas other things are changeable because they are not simple. (2) Simplicity is not acciden-

5. Ibid., pp. 114–15.
6. Augustine, *The City of God* 11.10.

tal. If something is simple it does not have anything that it could lose. This presumably means that simplicity itself is one of those things included in this specification. This seems to mean that a simple being has no accidental qualities. (3) A simple being is the same as the qualities or attributes it has. Unlike other things, which have a substance and qualities or attributes, a simple being does not have such a separation and does not participate in something other than itself. This interpretation is supported by Augustine's statement in *The Trinity*: "But he [God] is the same as his greatness, which is wisdom—for he is not great by means of bulk, but by means of power—and the same as goodness, which is wisdom and greatness, and the same as truth, which is all these. And in him it is not one thing to be blessed and another to be great, or wise, or true, or to be good, or to be altogether himself."[7] This reveals another characteristic of the simplicity of God: he is not only identical with each of his qualities, but, as a logical inference, each of the attributes of God is identical with each of the others. Anselm says as much: "Therefore life, wisdom, and the like are not parts of You, but all of them are one, and each one of them is entirely what You are and what all the others are."[8]

It appears that the discussion took on urgency during the Middle Ages because of something called the universals controversy, in which attempts were made to avoid two extremes that were considered threats to Christian theology: extreme realism and nominalism. Interestingly, because these same movements related to Islam and Judaism, we find the doctrine of divine simplicity playing a major role in those religions as well. The extreme realist view went back to Plato. According to him, every particular exists because it is an instantiation of a universal, called a Form or Idea. Thus, every particular white object is white because it participates in the Idea of whiteness. Every horse exists because it participates in the Idea of horseness. The Idea does not exemplify the quality which it is; it is not an instantiation of itself. Thus, the idea of whiteness is not white; indeed, it is not colored at all. Color is not something that applies to forms. The Idea of horseness is not a horse. These are really, more nearly, formulas for the objects that instantiate them.

Extreme realism, then, insisted on the independent existence of these qualities, apart from any individual instance of them. They were themselves uncreated. Nominalism was an extreme example in the other direction, and was found in the thought of persons such as William of Ockham. According to this view, qualities have no real existence

7. *On the Trinity* 6.7.8.
8. Anselm, *Proslogion* 18.

at all. They are simply names that we assign to things.[9] Ronald Nash contends that the doctrine of simplicity was an attempt to avoid falling into either extreme.[10] This is certainly a plausible explanation of the medieval discussion in terms of the thought of Aquinas and others who built their theology on the philosophy of Aristotle. Aristotle's view, often referred to as moderate realism, was that the Ideas or Universals have real objective existence, but that such existence is only in combination with particulars. They do not exist as pure form without matter. Nash's contention is not, strictly speaking, correct in the case of Augustine, Anselm, and others whose thought was essentially Platonic. For Augustine was, in a certain sense, an extreme realist, believing in the ideas as independent of any concrete instantiation of them. For Augustine, however, unlike Plato, these Forms or Ideas did not exist in some realm of their own, but reside in the mind of God. Thus, it was a modification of the theory of extreme realism rather than a rejection of it.

How does this bear on the question of God's aseity and sovereignty, however? With respect to the created objects, there is no problem. All of these have been created by him and exist by his continued permission and enablement. They are therefore dependent on him. He, however, is not dependent on them, for either his existence or his nature. To be sure, he may grant some members of his creation the power of free will, and they may choose to use this independently of him and even against him, but anything they do is done by the life and strength derived from him who created them.

More serious, however, are the abstract objects, or what Alvin Plantinga calls the whole Platonic pantheon: universals, properties, kinds, propositions, numbers, sets, states of affairs, and possible worlds. These can be thought of as everlasting, as having neither beginning nor end. And, as Plantinga points out, whereas there was a time when there were no human beings, there was no time when there was no such thing as the property of being human or the proposition, "there are human beings." These abstract objects are necessary features of reality; their nonexistence is impossible: "There could have been no mountains or planets; but could there have been no such thing as the property of being a mountain or the proposition *there are nine planets?* That proposition could have been *false,* obviously, but could it have been *non-existent?* It is hard to see how."[11]

---

9. S. J. Curtis, *A Short History of Western Philosophy in the Middle Ages* (Westminister, Md.: Newman, 1950), pp. 49–50.

10. *The Concept of God*, pp. 90–91.

11. Alvin Plantinga, *Does God Have a Nature?* (Milwaukee: Marquette University Press, 1980), p. 4.

This then poses, however, the question of how these abstract objects are related to God. If everything is created by God, as Augustine maintains, did he create these? Presumably not, since they have no beginning. Nor does it appear that they depend on God, since their nonexistence is impossible. What about the characteristics they display? Does God simply find them that way and have to put up with their being the way they are? This seems to put them outside his control, thus challenging his sovereignty.

The problem is more serious than this, however. What about God's own properties, such as omnipotence, justice, and wisdom? Did he create them? If so, then he existed before they did, and there was a time when God was not just or wise. Yet it seems that he must always have had these characteristics. He seems, then, to be dependent on and limited by these characteristics. If God did not have these characteristics, then he would not be wise or just. Thus he is dependent on them, not for his existing, but for his being the type of being that he is. So, in at least one sense, they seem to threaten the doctrine of divine aseity.

Plantinga puts the issue in terms of the question, "Does God have a nature?" By a nature he means a property he has essentially that includes each property essential to him. Perhaps, for example, God is essentially omniscient, that is, he is incapable of *not* being omniscient. If that is the case, then he has no choice in the matter. He is just that way. Thus there would seem to be a conflict between his having a nature and his being sovereign.[12]

The Traditional Statement

The traditional doctrine of simplicity has a long history. It finds its philosophical background in pre-Christian times in the thought of Parmenides, who understood reality as one great undifferentiated whole, within which no distinctions can be made.[13] As already mentioned, it was promulgated by Augustine and Anselm. It has persisted down to the present time. Not only the ancient creeds of the church but also such a recent creed as the Belgic Confession includes it. A Reformed theologian of the previous generation, Louis Berkhof, maintained it,[14] and it is also found in the contemporary evangelical systematic theology of Wayne Grudem.[15] But here, as in the case of so

---

12. Ibid., pp. 7–9.

13. Parmenides, in G. S. Kirk, J. E. Raven, and M. Schofield, The *Presocratic Philosophers: A Critical History with a Selection of Texts*, 2nd ed. (New York : Cambridge University Press, 1983), fragment 8:53–54.

14. L. Berkhof, *Systematic Theology* (Grand Rapids: Eerdmans, 1941), p. 62.

15. Wayne Grudem, *Systematic Theology* (Grand Rapids: Zondervan, 1994), pp. 117–80.

many other doctrines, the classic formulation and expression have been given by Aquinas.

Criticisms of the Traditional View

This formulation has come under considerable criticism of late, none more vigorous than that of Alvin Plantinga. After expounding Aquinas's view, he states his two major objections:

> There are two difficulties, one substantial and the other truly monumental. In the first place if God is identical with each of his properties, then each of his properties is identical with each of his properties, so that God has but one property. This seems flatly incompatible with the obvious fact that God has several properties; he has both power and mercifulness, say, neither of which is identical with the other. In the second place, if God is identical with each of his properties, then, since each of his properties is a property, he is a property—a self-exemplifying property. Accordingly, God has just one property: himself. This view is subject to a difficulty both obvious and overwhelming. No property could have created the world; no property could be omniscient or know anything at all. If God is a property, then he isn't a person but a mere abstract object; he has no knowledge, awareness, power, love, or life. So taken, the simplicity doctrine seems an utter mistake.[16]

This pair of criticisms is not atypical. An even more comprehensive set of objections to the doctrine has been offered by Thomas Morris. He considers both the need for and tenability of the doctrine of simplicity. He notes that it has been propounded as a necessary protection for the doctrine of aseity. Given the necessary goodness of God, if goodness is a property distinct from God, then it is true that, if the property of goodness did not exist, God would not exist. But on Morris's view, the existence of God is necessary, that is, he must exist in every possible world. If this is the case, however, then it can also be said of the property of goodness that it is essentially such as to be possessed by God. Thus, if God did not exist, goodness would not exist. If, however, the former statement, that without the property of goodness God would not exist proves his dependence on goodness, then this latter statement must also prove goodness's dependence on God. But it is not possible for ontological dependence to flow in both directions. We must therefore recognize that these sentences do not demonstrate ontological dependence. "Their truth merely reflects the logical relation which holds between propositions about necessarily existent entities, and alone im-

16. Plantinga, *Does God Have a Nature?* p. 47.

plies nothing about the ontological dependence or independence of those entities."[17]

Further, on the view of creation that Morris propounds, "any necessarily existent entities distinct from God can be viewed as ontologically dependent on God as the divine, ontologically independent source of all else."[18] But, if this is the case, then the doctrine of divine simplicity is not necessary to protect divine aseity. And in view of his earlier argument for the necessity of the divine attributes, any other motivation for the doctrine does not seem plausible either. There is no question of their coming to be or ceasing to be, so the instability often attributed to complexity does not really apply here.[19] God's status as the greatest possible being is secure without introducing the controversial doctrine of divine simplicity.

Finally, Morris contends that the doctrine in its various aspects is radically counterintuitive. There are two dimensions to this. The first is that if God is a property, then either he is an abstract object or some property is a concrete object. Either alternative, however, is quite counterintuitive, violating standard distinctions between abstract and concrete. Further, if God has only one property, himself, then it seems difficult to speak of the various distinctions that we seem to make with respect to God. There seem to be both necessary and contingent aspects of God. His knowledge may be a necessary characteristic, but having the specific knowledge that he does is contingent on the states of affairs that obtain.[20]

Morris makes clear that although the doctrine of property simplicity does not make sense, it may still be the case that what it is trying to express, namely, the metaphysical unity of God, is valid. Further, the idea of spatial simplicity is widely recognized, and temporal simplicity, although quite controversial nowadays, is accepted by a number of significant theologians and philosophers.[21]

A Contemporary Reformulation

Most theologians and philosophers recognize the cogency of the criticisms as stated above. Nonetheless, the doctrine of simplicity has not been abandoned. In the 1980s, a new version was propounded by William Mann. He modifies the Thomistic version of the doctrine by the introduction of four crucial concepts, for at least one of which he finds

17. Morris, *Our Idea of God*, p. 116.
18. Ibid.
19. Ibid., pp. 116–17.
20. Ibid., p. 117.
21. Ibid., p. 118.

justification in Aquinas's own thought, as distinguished from Anselm's version of the argument.

The first concept is introduced by noticing a slight adjustment Aquinas makes in Anselm's statement. Whereas Anselm stated that God is identical with goodness, wisdom, power, and so on, Aquinas says that God is *his* goodness, *his* wisdom, and the like. Mann observes that Aquinas's statements typically come in one of two forms: what Mann calls *Deity-instance identities*, such as "God is his *F*-ness"; and *instance-instance identities*, such as "the *F*-ness of God is the *G*-ness of God." He believes that this enables Aquinas to sidestep Plantinga's first criticism, because he does not claim that wisdom = power, but that the wisdom of God = the power of God. Yet, Plantinga would no doubt contend, this does not solve the problem. What kind of thing is the wisdom of God? Plantinga construes this as a state of affairs. If this is the case, then the state of affairs of being wise and the state of affairs of being powerful are the same state of affairs, which appears to be absurd, because then, for any individual, the state of affairs of having any property essential to him is the same state of affairs as having any other property essential to him. Further, it is still the case that God has properties that are distinct from him. Finally, God would then be a state of affairs, which Plantinga contends would be as outrageous as the claim that he is a property.[22] Mann, however, contends that this is not the case. Why, he asks, should we reconstrue Aquinas's view in terms of states of affairs? He proposes that, instead, we should think in terms of "property instances." A person characterized by a particular property is not to be thought of as being in the state of affairs of possessing that property, but of being an instance of that property.

Working from Aquinas's view, Mann agrees that in our present state, short of a beatific vision, a mystical experience, or special revelation, we cannot know God's essence. All our natural knowledge begins with our senses. Hence, our conceptual repertoire, as he terms it, is derived from sense experience. We can experience in some creatures, certain great-making qualities, and infer that these must also be found in God, the greatest of all beings. Examples of these are goodness, knowledge, and power. We realize, however, that these do not apply to God in exactly the same way as they apply to humans. While the word "good" calls to mind the goodness of creatures, it would be inadequate to use human goodness as a model for understanding the goodness of God. It is true of him literally and completely, but not so of any creature.

This leads to Mann's second important distinction: degreed and non-degreed properties. Many of the crucially important great-making qual-

---

22. Plantinga, *Does God Have a Nature?* p. 50.

ities are also degreed qualities. Knowledge is an example. Jones and Smith may both be knowledgeable, but Jones may be more knowledgeable than Smith. Further, within the class of degreed properties we can distinguish between those that have maxima and those that do not. Mann says, "Degreed property F has an intrinsic maximum if and only if there is some individual (actual or only possible), x, such that x is F, and for any other individual (actual or only possible), y, it is not the case that y is more F than x."[23]

This distinction will be used in a crucial turn of Mann's argument. He believes, with Aquinas, that the concepts of goodness, knowledgeability, and power are not only degreed properties, but degreed properties with intrinsic maxima. Thus, he says, "the intrinsic maximum of *being knowledgeable* is *omniscience*, and the intrinsic maximum of *being powerful* is *omnipotence*. Now what I offer on Aquinas's behalf is this. Although the properties of *being knowledgeable* and *being powerful* are distinct properties, the properties of *being omniscient* and *being omnipotent* are not. If this is so, then we have excellent grounds for asserting that the omniscience of God = the omnipotence of God."[24] Thus, he would contend, while the degreed properties being knowledgeable and being powerful vary somewhat independently throughout the range of their less than maximal cases, when we come to their intrinsic maxima they converge or, more correctly, coalesce.[25]

Mann then considers the thesis that if two properties are co-extensive, they are identical. He now introduces a third distinction, between two theories of property identity. The predicate synonymy view holds that "for every well-formed predicate expression there is a property, which is the meaning of that predicate, and that any two nonsynonymous predicate expressions *ipso facto* pick out distinct properties."[26] Thus, two properties can be co-extensive but distinct. It could be the case that every instance of one is the instance of the other, but unless the predicate expressions used to designate them are synonymous, they are distinct properties. This is what Mann calls a fine-grained view of the distinctness of properties.

The other view he describes is at the opposite end of the continuum from this view, being a very coarse-grained view of property distinctness. He calls this the set-extensional view. According to this view, properties are identified with groups of actual objects that embody them. Thus, he says, "the property of *being green* just is the set of all and only

23. Mann, "Divine Simplicity," *Religious Studies* 18 (1982): 459–60.
24. Ibid.
25. Ibid., p. 461.
26. Ibid., pp. 462–63.

green things; the property of *being a marsupial* just is the set of all and only marsupials."[27] If, then, every green thing were a marsupial and every marsupial were green, these would be the same property.

Consider, then, the properties of being an equilateral (Euclidean) triangle and being an equiangular (Euclidean) triangle. Certainly these properties are not synonymous. The first means having three angles, each of which is equal to each of the others. The second means having three sides, each of which is equal to each of the others. But every equiangular triangle is an equilateral triangle and vice versa. They are, therefore, co-extensive. They are two different concepts, but it does not follow, Mann insists, that they are two different properties. Rather, he says, "there is one structural property of certain triangles in virtue of which they are both equilateral and equiangular, or to put it another way, the structural property which is a particular triangle's being equilateral = the structural property which is that triangle's being equiangular."[28] It shall remain to be seen whether this is saying the same thing in two ways, or whether it is saying two different things.

On the basis of the foregoing arguments, Mann believes he has reconstructed the doctrine of simplicity in a way that avoids the usual difficulties and criticisms. There remains, however, he recognizes, another difficulty to be dealt with. This attaches to the Deity-instance concept, which expresses identities of the nature of "God is his F-ness." According to such a principle, God is omniscient, which means that God is an instance of the property of being omniscient, which therefore means that God is a property. But this offends a deeply held tenet of all theisms, namely, that God is a person, and since property instances are not persons, God is not a property instance.[29] In Plantinga's statement of it, the rationale for this conclusion is in the form, "No property is alive, knowledgeable, capable of action, powerful or good."[30] Although Mann says that this does not really apply to the form of the doctrine of divine simplicity that he is presenting, it can probably be treated as equivalent to "No property instance is alive, knowledgeable, capable of action, powerful or good."[31]

Is it the case that no property instance is a person, however? Mann believes that the argument rests on the tenet "Persons are concrete, property instances are abstract. Thus they are of different ontological sorts." He contends that this is simply not so. What does it mean to say

27. Ibid., p. 463.
28. Ibid., p. 464.
29. Ibid., p. 465.
30. Plantinga, *Does God Have a Nature?* p. 57.
31. Mann, "Divine Simplicity," p. 465.

that a person is concrete? This means being in space and time, or at least in time. But while properties may not be concrete, especially if identified as sets, meanings, or the like, property instances most certainly can have spatial and temporal location.[32]

A further objection that Mann anticipates is that property instances are ontologically inferior to persons, because persons are substances and thus are independent entities, whereas property instances are dependent, parasitical entities. They are always instances attaching to some substance. They cannot exist without the substance, but the substance could exist without them. This, Mann concedes, may well be true of accidental property instances, but not of essential property instances. So, for example, Smith may survive the loss of his wisdom but not the loss of his personhood. So, if God were to lose his omniscience, he would cease to be God. There is a relationship of mutual dependence between God and his omniscience. If one should cease to exist, the other would also.[33]

At this point, Mann introduces his final special concept, that of the rich property. Think, he says, of Giles, who is green and oblate. This means that he instantiates a conjunctive property that of *being green and oblate*. If, in addition, Giles is also slimy, he instantiates the further conjunctive property, of *being green and oblate and slimy*. Now if Giles has some temporal duration, some of the properties he instantiates may have temporal indices. If this is the case, then he may exemplify a conjunctive property of the form of *being-green-at-t_0 and red-at-t_1*. Now if we consider all the properties Giles instantiates throughout his entire career, we find a very complicated conjunctive property indeed. Mann calls this property a *rich property*. What then is Giles? He is an instantiation of the appropriate rich property. Giles is a property instance, albeit a very complicated one.[34]

Mann then proceeds to generalize: "For anything whatsover, there is an appropriate rich property. Therefore, everything is a property instance of some rich property or other. Therefore, every person is a property instance, and since there is at least one person, (P*) ["No property instance is a person."] is false."[35] There is also a rich property of which God is an instance: "the rich property associated with God has but one element—*being a Godhead*, which is the same property as *being omniscient, being omnipotent*, and all the rest."[36] Although this approach is

32. Ibid., p. 566.
33. Ibid.
34. Ibid., pp. 466–67.
35. Ibid., p. 467.
36. Ibid.

not found in Aquinas, Mann believes that it meshes with some of Thomas Aquinas's doctrines.

Morris's Critical Response to Mann

Thomas Morris has formulated a major response to Mann's attempted rehabilitation of the simplicity doctrine in a lengthy article entitled "On God and Mann: A View of Divine Simplicity." He has criticized a number of the key concepts in Mann's argument.

One of these is the idea of a rich property. A number of difficulties attach to such a concept, in Morris's judgment. Each of us is an instance of his or her rich property. But if my rich property includes all the properties I will ever have, then presumably next year I will exemplify properties that I do not now have. If the existence of a rich property requires the instantiation of its conjunct properties, then no instance of my rich property yet exists, and if I am an instance of it, I do not yet exist. Indeed, no temporal being ever can exist. One way of resisting this implication applying to God would be to restrict it merely to temporal beings. But if this is the case, then we seem led to the conclusion that we can only identify an individual with the exemplification of its rich property only if we hold all its properties to be essential. If, however, we want to acknowledge individuals as having accidental as well as essential properties, then we must include as conjuncts in the rich property only properties we independently and intuitively recognize as essential to them.[37]

A further question Morris raises regarding Mann's view pertains to the identity of property instances. Mann's answer to the question as to under what conditions an instance of a property F will be identical with an instance of G is a principle he labels C.

> Property instances *the F-ness of x* and *the G-ness of y* are identical if and only if (1) the property *being F* is necessarily coextensive with the property *being G* and (2) $x=y$.[38]

Is this principle, C, true, however? Morris states that it may well be that this necessary coextensiveness of properties is *necessary* for the identity of property instances, but to claim that it is *sufficient* is quite a different matter. He contends that while being coextensive, triangularity and trilaterality are different features of objects. And if, as Mann responds, F and G are actually one and the same property, then we must ask about the implications this principle and its supporting claim have

37. Thomas V. Morris, "On God and Mann: A View of Divine Simplicity," *Religious Studies* 21.3 (September 1985): 303–5.
38. Mann, "Divine Simplicity," p. 465.

when applied to the case of God. Here the consequence is that there can only be one divine property instance, one with which God is identical, only if there is only one divine property.[39]

Morris contends that all the distinctions and principles that Mann introduces have a number of consequences worth examining. First, for all the differences between the property view and the property instance view, they have one factor in common: in the case of God, only one property is involved. This is problematic in several ways. One is the problem of modal uniformity. If God has only one property, then it is not possible for him to have properties that are essential and others that are accidental. Yet certainly we would want to maintain that God is essentially omniscient, omnipotent, and good, but only contingently or accidentally such that he created the world and did the other actions he is described as doing. On Mann's account, however, such discriminations are not possible, and this is certainly unacceptable.[40]

The second problem is that of supervenience. Supervenience means that one property supervenes another if an instance of the former essentially depends on there being an instance of the latter on which it depends for its existence. It is often thought that some of the divine attributes supervene certain other distinct properties. So, for example, God's omniscience is thought to supervene his knowing this, that, and so forth. So also, God's omnipotence would be thought to supervene the property of being able to do various things. But if this is the case, then Mann's view cannot be right, for at least one property of God must supervene upon numerically distinct properties he would need to have as well.[41]

At this point, Morris engages in a series of highly refined discussions of how Mann could avoid the difficulties resulting from his view and how those responses, in turn, produce various difficulties. As interesting as they may be, they take us beyond the extent of discussion that can be given in a work of this type. In effect, they end up saying that, in the final analysis, the standard objections to the simplicity doctrine apply even to the highly nuanced view that Mann has formulated.

Do these criticisms of Mann's view by Morris eliminate Mann's approach as a viable understanding of simplicity? It would appear that while there is much here that should help produce a sharpening of the issues, at some points the criticisms miss the target.

One of these is Morris's criticism of the idea of a rich concept. Morris contends that since one's rich concept includes all the properties he or

39. Morris, "On God and Mann," pp. 306–7.
40. Ibid., p. 307.
41. Ibid., p. 308.

she will ever have, and there are some properties that I will have next year but do not have now, I do not yet exist, because my rich concept does not exist. Morris, however, overlooks Mann's full specification of the rich concept. The concept includes such considerations as *"being-green-at-t_0 and red-at-t_1."* If it is not yet t_1, Giles is not yet red, but that does not vitiate the idea of his rich concept. The rich concept is not *"being-green and being-red,"* but rather, *"being-green-at-t_0 and red-at-t_1."* So my rich concept does exist, but some of the elements within it are indexical in nature.

There is, however, a more serious and extensive problem with Morris's criticism. It would appear that part of the difference between Mann and Morris is presuppositional. The theory with which Mann is working seems to be Platonic in nature, where an instance of a property is just that, an instantiation of a quality or form, rather than a substance or subject possessing an attribute of this type. Morris's critique seems to presuppose the latter way of conceiving of properties. This is why the property-instance view seems in Morris's judgment to be susceptible to some of the same problems as the property view. The question of the validity of these two different approaches goes beyond the scope of our discussion here. That is the issue which needs to be discussed, however, for this debate is not taking place in a metaphysically neutral context. It does appear, however, that on the basically Platonic orientation that characterizes Mann's view, his understanding of simplicity is correct, whereas on a more Aristotelian approach it would not be.[42]

This is not to say that there are not problems with the property-instance view, for it has the same difficulties that Platonism has always encountered. One of these is the identification of the exact extent and complexity of the rich ideas. Platonists have always had a problem deciding whether a white stallion participates in the Forms or Ideas of whiteness, horseness, and maleness, and if so, how this complexity of participation occurs, or whether there was one form that embodied all

---

42. Nicholas Wolterstorff recognizes this difference, but indicates that contemporary relation ontology denies "the Platonic thesis that properties are ideal examples of themselves—that justice is the ideally just entity, etc. We hold that, in general, properties are not self-exemplifying. Essential in Plantinga's argument is the assumption that knowledge does not know, that love does not love, that potency does not do anything, etc." "Divine Simplicity," in *Philosophical Perspective, 5: Philosophy of Religon, 1991*, ed. James E. Tomberlin (Atascadero, Calif.: Ridgeview, 1991), p. 548. This, however, seems to repeat the common misunderstanding of the Platonic forms as being self-exemplifying, that the "third man" in the "Third Man Argument" is a man, albeit a perfect man. For an examination and critique of this interpretation, see my *Platonic Forms and Self-Predication: A Critical Examination of Gregory Vlastos' Interpretation of the Third Man Argument in the* Parmenides (unpublished M.A. thesis, Department of Philosophy, University of Chicago, 1958).

of these and other qualities, in which this animal participates. Those issues do need to be addressed.

The Values in the Doctrine

It is perhaps worthwhile, as we seek to assess the fundamental reasoning and motivation behind the advocacy of the simplicity doctrine, to ask just what its advocates see as the benefits of this doctrine. This may lead us to ask if there is some other way those benefits can be retained, perhaps with a view of God that parallels but differs from the standard simplicity doctrine.

In a later article, Mann especially develops the concern for the value of the immutability doctrine. He notes that we ordinarily attach great value to steadfastness in persons. So it is especially important that we know that such indications of fickleness do not apply to God. Mann notes that one of the objections raised to this doctrine is that an immutable being could not be a personal being, because he would be a completely impassive God. Further, change is not a bad thing, and on close inspection, it becomes apparent that the biblical God changes in all sorts of ways that are to his credit. He changes his mind, which results in good effects.[43]

Mann wonders, however, whether the dispute between the medievals and moderns has really been joined. For far from maintaining that God is passive and inactive, the medieval theologians actually argued that God was supremely active, with no trace of passivity. How can this be? How can a being be both immutable and active? Mann responds, "I suggest that the answer lies in a relatively neglected doctrine which the medievals thought entailed both characteristics, and which illuminates the present issues."[44] This is the doctrine of divine simplicity, which includes the idea that God has no parts or components whatsoever, that he has no properties, either accidental or essential, that he has no spatial or temporal extension. Its motivation stems from the idea that God is a perfect being, and consequently cannot be dependent on anything, and must be sovereign over everything. Strictly speaking, omnipotence is not an attribute of God on this view of simplicity. He is his omnipotence.[45]

A simple being will have no successive stages to his existence, because there is no division of his life temporally. Consequently, a perfect being

43. William E. Mann, "Simplicity and Immutability in God," *International Philosophical Quarterly* 23.3 (September 1983): 267–68.
44. Ibid., p. 268.
45. Ibid.

will also be immutable, for if there are no time periods within the life of the person, it is not possible for him to have a predicate at one moment and then not have it at a successive moment, or vice versa. "Thus," says Mann, "the DDS [doctrine of divine simplicity] implies that God is eternal, which in turn implies the DDI [doctrine of divine immutability]."[46]

The question still remains, however, whether an eternal, immutable being can be a person. In effect Mann says that really depends on the definition of person. He proposes that six criteria of personality have been given by philosophers, and that each of these is considered a necessary if not a sufficient reason. On these criteria, A is a person only if:

(1) A is a rational being.
(2) A is a being to which states of consciousness can be attributed.
(3) Others regard or can regard A as a being to which states of consciousness can be attributed.
(4) A is capable of regarding others as beings to which states of consciousness can be attributed.
(5) A is capable of verbal communications.
(6) A is self-conscious; that is, A is capable of regarding him/her/itself as a subject of states of consciousness.

Even if we take the position that A must satisfy all six of these in order to be a person, Mann argues that an eternal, immutable God does satisfy all of these.[47]

Eleanor Stump and Norman Kretzmann also published an article on "Absolute Simplicity" in 1985, in which they argued for a renewed case for the ancient doctrine. Most of their attention was directed to resolving problems that are frequently raised against the doctrine of simplicity. The three that they especially examine are the apparent incompatibilities between: (1) God's simplicity and his free choice; (2) essential omnipotence and essential goodness; and (3) perfect goodness and moral goodness.[48] Because all these are associated with certain features of God's will, the authors find the resolution of the three incompatibilities in an account of will in general and of God's will in particular. These considerations will be examined in other chapters. For our purposes here, the major feature of interest is the concluding portion of the article, in which the authors present certain benefits they believe derive from the doctrine of divine simplicity.

46. Ibid., p. 269.
47. Ibid., pp. 269–71.
48. Eleanor Stump and Norman Kretzmann, "Absolute Simplicity," *Faith and Philosophy* 2.4 (October 1985): 355–74.

The first is in resolving problems of religious morality. The question frequently posed is, "What is the relationship of God to morality?" One answer commonly given is that God's will creates morality in the sense that what he wills is good just because he wills it. The opposite theory is that God approves of right actions because they are right and disapproves of wrong actions because they are wrong. There are problems with each of these theories, however. The former view constitutes theological subjectivism. Anything could be established as morally good by divine fiat. Consequently, nothing can be ruled out as immoral. The difficulty with the latter view is that while it gives an objective basis for morality, it is really not a religious morality because there is no essential connection between God and the moral standards. In addition, because of the apparent independence and priority of these standards, God's sovereignty seems to be impugned.[49]

The doctrine of divine simplicity resolves this problem by preserving the strengths and advantages of each of these theories without retaining their attendant weaknesses. Being simple, God is identical with his goodness. The divine nature itself is perfect goodness. This preserves both the objective nature of the standards, and God's freedom, independence, and sovereignty.[50]

The other area where the doctrine is helpful is with respect to the cosmological argument. Since this argues back from contingent existents to God, an important question frequently asked is, "Why does God exist?" The answer to this is that he cannot *not* exist, and the reason is that because he is absolutely simple he is identical with his nature. Further, a simple being, whose existence is necessary, provides a simpler stopping point for universal explanation than does the universe itself.[51]

It appears that theologians who have espoused this doctrine were trying to preserve certain basic values that still are important today. It is helpful to restate and summarize these:

1. God is not to be thought of as having a being or essence that is unknown to us. On such a way of thinking, what we know is the attributes; God's essence remains unknowable. Rather, we must assert, God is his essence, he is his attributes, the predicates that attach to him. When we know the attributes of God, we are truly knowing him. It is not as if what he truly is in his essence might be somehow different from what we know of him and what he has revealed of himself. There is certainly a dimension of the unknowability of God, but this is a mat-

49. Ibid., p. 375.
50. Ibid., p. 376.
51. Ibid, pp. 376–78.

ter of depths of understanding of the attributes to which we are unable to penetrate, rather than an unknown substrate in which the attributes inhere.

2. This means that God's attributes are not something external to him, or added to him, as if he could exist and could be God without possessing these attributes. God is his attributes, and without them he would not be God. The idea that God "has" omniscience, freedom, goodness, omnipotence, and so on, is misleading. He is God because he is all these things. Sometimes theologians identify the love of God, not as an attribute, but as his very nature. There is truth in this concept, but the nature of God is not limited to that one characteristic. He is inseparably good, wise, powerful, and the like.

3. God's attributes are distinguishable, but not separable. God is not powerful and also wise, loving, and holy. He is what he is, and these are facets of his nature. Sometimes tension is seen between two or more of these attributes. So, for example, the love of God and the holiness of God may be thought to conflict or compete with one another. Actually, however, the love of God must be seen as holy love and the holiness of God as loving holiness. The apparent conflict comes from attempting to define such qualities in an abstract fashion, and then, upon combining them, finding that they are incompatible with one another.

There are two other major considerations involved in this point. One is the unity of the God who is depicted and acts throughout Scripture. At times the love of God and the holiness of God are described in such a way that they are seen to be in contrast, conflict, or competition with one another. Some have even questioned whether they might belong to different Gods. An extreme form of this was the teaching of Marcion. Although his teaching must be reconstructed from others' writings about him, he may well have taught that the Bible actually reveals two gods, one good and one evil.[52]

The other concern this doctrine addresses is the unity of the persons in the Trinity. The three persons are ultimately one. Thus, none of the various qualities that characterize God can be assigned as properties to one or the other of the members of the Trinity. Each person possesses all of these perfections.

4. The ultimate values of our universe, such as love, justice, and the like, are objective. They are not merely arbitrary, in the sense in which William of Ockham thought of them, as if God could have chosen to make cruelty or deception good, rather than kindness and honesty. Yet they are not independent of God. He is not dependent on them, or re-

52. Irenaeus, *Against Heresies* 3.25.3; Tertullian, *Against Marcion* 5.18.12; 5.13.15.

quired somehow to conform himself to them. They are the very way he is and has always been. Thus, they are eternal, just as God is. He could not have chosen to make something else good, for to do so would have been to choose something foreign and contrary to his nature, and he is the highest object and value in the entire universe.

5. The final "screen," the final measure or context of value in the universe, is God. There is nothing more basic, no broader or more ultimate frame of reference to which to appeal or look. Everything must have some fixed point of reference. This, in the case of moral values, as well as ontological values, is found in the nature of God.

6. God is a unitary being. Sometimes one gets the conception that the nature of God is a bundle of attributes, somewhat loosely tied together. God, however, is not an attribute or a predicate. He is a living person, a subject. Perhaps what we need is a new metaphysic of persons. Much of the discussion has been carried on in terms of a substance metaphysic, in which reality is a substance possessing certain attributes. A better way of thinking may be to conceive of reality as fundamentally personal rather than impersonal. Thus, God is a subject, a person—and a very complex person at that. He is what he is, and is unique. If he did not possess the essential attributes we have discussed in this volume, he would not be the person he is. The attributes, then, are not qualities added to this nature. They are facets of his complex and rich nature.

It does not seem necessary, in order to preserve these values, to follow the full traditional meaning of simplicity with its attendant problems, such as God having but one attribute and being equivalent to that attribute, with the paradoxical conclusion that each attribute of God is the same as each of the others.

The doctrine of divine simplicity need not involve all of the details it has sometimes borne. Carl F. H. Henry has summarized succinctly what evangelicals mean by the doctrine, and this is found in the thought of many who do not necessarily use the term:

> Evangelical theology insists on the simplicity of God. By this it means that God is not compounded of parts; he is not a collection of perfections, but rather a living center of activity pervasively characterized by all his distinctive perfections. The divine attributes are neither additions to the divine essence nor qualities pieced together to make a compound . . . God's variety of attributes does not conflict with God's simplicity because his simplicity is what comprises the fullness of divine life. Augustine wrote of God's 'simple multiplicity' or 'multifold simplicity.'[53]

53. Carl F. H. Henry, *God, Revelation and Authority* (Waco, Tex.: Word, 1982), vol. 5, p. 131.

As foreign as the concept of divine simplicity seems to modern persons, it was formulated to express an important truth about God: the unity of his nature, the harmony of his attributes, and the fact that his actions involve the whole of what he is. Whether we choose to use this doctrine as the means, we will want to preserve these values.

11

God's Goodness

The goodness of God would seem to be among the highest of God's qualities. For although we may respect and even fear a God who can do all things and knows all things, presumably if we are to admire and love God, it must be because he is good. Indeed, this was a very prominent, if not the most prominent, reason given when the people of Israel praised God or when they were commanded to praise him. And since some theologians contend that divine love is not only the supreme attribute of God, but actually his very nature, this would seem to be a further contention of the importance of his goodness.

Yet, in spite of the widespread recognition of the goodness of God and the importance of the topic, there are considerable differences among Christians when we begin to reflect on just what this means. At times it appears that the goodness of God, if genuine, is in tension with some of the other qualities which we generally attribute to God, such as his power or his freedom. And God's goodness seems to be in tension with what we see going on in the world.

Biblical Evidences

The Bible is replete with testimony to the goodness of God, both directly predicating this goodness of him and ascribing goodness to his actions. Basically, these evidences can be classified into three groups.

Direct Predications of Goodness of God

A very common basis given when exhorting the people of Israel to give thanks to God was, "Give thanks to the LORD, for he is good; his love endures forever" (1 Chron. 16:34). This expression can be found in virtually identical form in 2 Chronicles 5:13; 7:3; Ezra 3:11; Psalms 106:1; 107:1; 118:1, 29; 136:1; Jeremiah 33:11. The uniformity of the expression indicates that this was a formula of praise or a liturgy practiced by the people of Israel. Other direct attributions of goodness to God are found in the Psalms: "Good and upright is the LORD; therefore he instructs sinners in his ways" (25:8); "Taste and see that the LORD is good; blessed is the man who takes refuge in him" (34:8); "You are forgiving and good, O LORD, abounding in love to all who call to you" (86:5); "For the LORD is good and his love endures forever; his faithfulness continues through all generations" (100:5); "You are good, and what you do is good; teach me your decrees" (119:68); "Praise the LORD, for the LORD is good; sing praise to his name, for that is pleasant" (135:3). These descriptions of God as good are not restricted to the Book of Psalms. Nahum wrote, "The LORD is good, a refuge in times of trouble. He cares for those who trust in him" (1:7). When a ruler asked Jesus, "Good teacher, what must I do to inherit eternal life?" Jesus replied, "Why do you call me good? No one is good—except God alone" (Luke 18:18–19 and parallels).

Descriptions of God as Doing Good

There also are many references in the Scriptures to God as doing good works. Joshua reminds the Israelites that God has done good, and will do good to them in the future: "Now I am about to go the way of all the earth. You know with all your heart and soul that not one of all the good promises the LORD your God gave you has failed. Every promise has been fulfilled; not one has failed. But just as every good promise of the LORD your God has come true, so the LORD will bring on you all the evil he has threatened, until he has destroyed you from this good land he has given you" (23:14, 15). The psalmist wrote, " For the LORD God is a sun and shield; the LORD bestows favor and honor; no good thing does he withhold from those whose walk is blameless. O LORD Almighty, blessed is the man who trusts in you" (84:11–12). In other psalms we read, "The LORD will indeed give what is good, and our land will yield its harvest" (85:12); "You are forgiving and good, O Lord, abounding in love to all who call to you" (86:5); "who satisfies your desires with good things so that your youth is renewed like the eagle's" (103:5); "When you give it to them, they gather it up; when you open your hand, they are satisfied with good things" (104:28); "You are good, and what you do is good; teach me your decrees" (119:68); "The LORD is good to all; he has compassion on all he has made" (145:9). Lamentations 3:25 says, "The LORD is good to those whose hope is in him, to the one who seeks him." Jesus taught his disciples, "If you, then, though you are evil, know how to give good gifts to your children, how much more will your Father in heaven give good gifts to those who ask him!" (Matt. 7:11). Paul wrote, "And we know that in all things God works for the good of those who love him, who have been called according to his purpose" (Rom. 8:28). James assured us, "Every good and perfect gift is from above, coming down from the Father of the heavenly lights, who does not change like shifting shadows" (1:17).

Appeals to Believers to be Good Because of the Nature of God

Finally, there are numerous appeals to believers to live in a certain way, to do good, with the basis being either explicitly or implicitly that God himself is good. The psalmist prayed, "Teach me knowledge and good judgment, for I believe in your commands. . . . You are good, and what you do is good; teach me your decrees" (119:66, 68); "Teach me to do your will, for you are my God; may your good Spirit lead me on level ground" (143:10). Jesus said, "In the same way, let your light shine before men, that they may see your good deeds and praise your Father in heaven" (Matt. 5:16). Paul wrote, "For we are God's workmanship, created in Christ Jesus to do good works, which God prepared in advance for us to do" (Eph. 2:10); "being confident of this, that he who began a good work in you will carry it on to completion until the day of Christ Jesus" (Phil. 1:6); "For everything God created is good, and nothing is to be rejected if it is received with thanksgiving" (1 Tim. 4:4). Probably the clearest of all the commands of this type is 3 John 11: "Dear friend, do not imitate what is evil but what is good. Anyone who does what is good is from God. Anyone who does what is evil has not seen God."

Objections to the Goodness of God

A number of persons, however, have questioned whether in fact God really is good, at least as we understand this word. The objections are of two kinds. One is certain biblical materials that seem to describe God in ways that appear morally reprehensible. The second, usually referred to as the problem of evil, consists of certain empirical data in the world in which we live, which suggest that if God is truly in control, then he must not be a good God.

Biblical Pictures of God

Critics sometimes appeal to certain passages, especially in the Old Testament, to support their contention that God is really not a good God. For example, there are numerous biblical passages in which Jehovah commands the people of Israel to slaughter indigenous tribes surrounding them and occupying lands that he has promised to them. He demands worship and indicates that he is a jealous God (Exod. 20:5). He allows Job to be tortured and his family killed, just to prove a point. The prophets even report that God is responsible for evil as well as for good (Isa. 45:7; Jer. 44:27; Ezek. 5:16, 17).

These passages and incidents must be seen in context to be properly evaluated, however. This involves both the biblical and theological and the social contexts. Since God is not simply a human being, he has the right to expect complete and undivided worship and loyalty. Thus when he speaks of being "jealous" he is simply exercising the right which is properly his. What spouse would be thought improperly jealous if he or she insisted that the vows taken by his or her spouse at the wedding ceremony be fulfilled? A husband or wife has certain rights of exclusivity that would be considered improper by a mere friend. If God is the only true God, then he not only is right to insist on this exclusiveness, but would be wrong *not* to.

Further, the commands to kill must be seen in the context of what were essentially situations of warfare. In such a context, somewhat different rules apply than are ordinarily in effect. God's great purpose was to preserve his people as a covenant nation, his servant in carrying out his plan on the earth. It was essential, to that end, that the Israelites keep their faith and worship of him pure, but their constant temptation was to be eclectic, to absorb the religion of the neighboring nations and to assimilate their gods into Israel's faith. Radical measures were therefore necessary to preserve the purity of their religion. One measure was the forbidding of intermarriage with these other tribes. An even more radical measure was expunging these other nations. As serious as this action was, it was a lesser evil than would have been the case if Israel's faith and practice had been corrupted. This was a form of spiritual sterilization.

The idea of God being responsible for evil must be seen in the context of the general nature of God's will. The view that we have been developing here is that everything that happens is part of God's will and working. That does not mean, however, that he directly causes everything. Rather, he *wills* everything, some of it by direct causation, some of it by indirect causation, some of it by deciding to permit, or not to intervene to prevent, what will happen. His is not the primary impetus given to these actions in the latter type of situation. But although he has willed (passively or permissively) for this to happen, he does not bear primary responsibility for these actions. He has been known to accomplish his good will even through the evil actions of humans. A prominent example would be his use of the crucifixion that evil persons inflicted on Jesus, to accomplish his good end, as seen in Peter's speech in Acts 2:23.

In all of these matters, a primary principle of hermeneutics must be borne in mind. There are two basic types of passages in Scripture: narrative and didactic. We can choose to rely primarily on the narrative passages and conform the didactic or explanatory passages to them. This is what is being done in this objection. On the other hand, we can interpret the narrative passages in light of the teaching of didactic passages. This is usually the preferred hermeneutical principle, since teachings are generally less susceptible to ambiguity and consequent interpretation than are actions. In this case, this means that the clear teachings that we have already examined regarding God's goodness should motivate us to seek an understanding of the narratives that cohere with them.

Empirical Materials

The problem of evil occurs because of the co-existence of three contradictory factors: the goodness of God, the power of God, and the existence of evil in the world. By evil is meant both natural evil, such as cancer and earthquakes, and moral evil, such as crime, war, and abuse. The problem emerges in the following fashion. If God is all-powerful, he will be able to prevent evil. If he is completely loving, he will desire to prevent evil. Yet there is still evil in the world.

This is probably the most difficult intellectual problem for the Christian faith, and the greatest minds of Christian theology have wrestled with it without being able to formulate a final and satisfactory solution. Space will not permit a very adequate treatment here, but we may be able to indicate at least some general directions from which the solution could be expected to emerge.

For the most part, proposed solutions have attempted to modify, reduce, or redefine one or more of the components of the problem—either the goodness or the greatness of God, or the apparent evil. One of the most common solutions is the free will argument: that God has created in such a way as to allow human beings a measure of freedom, which they have then exercised in such a way as to bring evil into the world and to expand it. This expedient, at least as usually stated, is not available to us, however, given the position taken on human will and divine providence. Further, it really does not dispel the problem, for there is still the difficulty of why God created in that way, rather than choosing not to create at all or to create humans without that type and degree of freedom. There are, however, several motifs that may help reduce some of the tension, most of which attempt to reinterpret the apparent evil.

1. Evil must be judged in a long-range context. Some of what is unpleasant in the short term turns out to be the means to a greater good. This is the teaching of passages such as "because you know that the test-

ing of your faith develops steadfastness" (James 1:3), and of Joseph's testimony to his brothers, "You intended to harm me; but God intended it for good to accomplish what is now being done, the saving of many lives" (Gen. 50:20).

2. Good and evil must not be judged on too individualistic a basis. Often evil is thought of simply in terms of the pain or distress that comes to us as isolated individuals. God, however, is concerned with the welfare of the entire creation and with the fulfillment of his plans.

3. Good must be defined in light of God's inclusive purposes. Often by good we mean what is pleasant to us, and by evil, what is unpleasant to us. In the much-quoted verse, Romans 8:28, "And we know that in all things God works for the good of those who love him, who have been called according to his purpose," we often proceed as if we can determine the good by how the events of life please us. It must be seen as defined in the next verse: "For those God foreknew he also predestined to be conformed to the likeness of his Son, that he might be the firstborn among many brothers." The good is not our health, wealth, and happiness, as some think of these, but that we might bear the spiritual likeness of God's son.

4. This world is not as God created it or in the final form that it will take. Evil in general is the result of sin in general. The Bible teaches that because of the fall of humanity, the creation was affected in ways that now often cause pain and distress: "For the creation was subjected to frustration, not by its own choice, but by the will of the one who subjected it, in hope that the creation itself will be liberated from its bondage to decay and brought into the glorious freedom of the children of God. We know that the whole creation has been groaning as in the pains of childbirth right up to the present time. Not only so, but we ourselves, who have the firstfruits of the Spirit, groan inwardly as we wait eagerly for our adoption as sons, the redemption of our bodies" (Rom. 8:20–23; see also the curse passage in Gen. 3:14–19).

5. Some specific evils are the result of particular sins. God has so structured the spiritual universe that it obeys certain spiritual laws, just as the physical universe follows physical laws. This means that the warnings against sin mean that disobedience to God has unfortunate results. So Paul wrote, "The one who sows to please his sinful nature, from that nature will reap destruction; the one who sows to please the Spirit, from the Spirit will reap eternal life" (Gal. 6:8). Just as one who chooses to defy the law of gravity and tries to break it will suffer uncomfortable results, so some of the evil we experience is the result of our own or others' violation of divine moral and spiritual law. Although this principle needs to be used carefully and sparingly, it is a valid insight.

6. God has involved himself in bearing the pain of this world. God is not simply an aloof, indifferent spectator to the suffering of the creation. As we pointed out in the chapter on impassibility, God himself experiences something of the pain. Whether one says that God is culpable for not preventing the evils that have come into the world, we must recognize that he did so, fully realizing that the second person of the Trinity would come to die and bear the direct consequences of human sin. When we say that in God's judgment it must have been better overall for the creation to be as it is than some of the alternatives, that his judgment includes his foreknowledge that he himself would be the major object of the evil that would come.

7. This life is not all there is. If life consisted only of birth, death, and the intervening period, there could be little satisfactory relaxation of the tensions, given the way the world is presently constituted. There does not seem to be perfect justice within this life. The Bible teaches, however, that this is not all there is. There is a life beyond this world, with a time of judgment and justice. While we cannot now see the administration of final good within this lifetime, and do not know all of the details of the life to come, we can understand God as good in terms of the final disposition of creation and of the human race.

The Necessary Goodness of God

One of the stronger claims made about God is that he is necessarily good. That is to say, he does not simply always do what is good. Rather, he *must* do what is good; he cannot possibly do that which is not good. For some theologians, this stems from a perfect being theology approach. According to that view, a being that is incapable of doing what is bad is superior to a being that could sin but never does. Beyond that, however, there is biblical support for the idea that it is impossible for God to sin. James 1:13 states, "When tempted, no one should say, 'God is tempting me.' For God cannot be tempted by evil, nor does he tempt anyone." If God cannot even be tempted, then he most surely cannot possibly sin. He must be not only good, but necessarily good. The issue is whether God is free to do evil, or whether this is impossible to him, and this approach takes the latter conclusion. It appears as if God's power is limited by his moral nature.

Anselm

Several arguments have been offered in support of this idea. One, which goes back to Anselm, wrestles with the apparent compromise of God's omnipotence if he is unable to sin. Anselm's method of handling the problem, however, is to say that the ability to sin is not actually a power.

To be capable of these things is not power, but impotence. For, he who is capable of these things is capable of what is not for his own good, and of what he ought not to do; and the more capable of them he is, the more power have adversity and perversity against him; and the less has he himself against these.[1]

The argument appears to be that these things are not for a person's own good, but that the more one engages in them, the more control they gain over him. An omnipotent being, however, who cannot be enslaved by anything external to him therefore cannot do evil. Stephen Davis, however, believes that this argument does not succeed, for two reasons. First, the argument could be applied as well to the doing of good acts, which then presumably would also have control over a being. On these grounds, then, the argument would also establish that God cannot do good. Second, although evil certainly seems to have the power to enslave human beings, why should we conclude that it can also do this to an omnipotent being?[2] One response that could be made to Davis's criticism is, of course, that good is not alien to the nature of God, in the sense in which evil is.

Thomas Aquinas

Thomas advanced a similar but somewhat different argument: "The will never aims at evil without some error existing in the reason, at least with respect to a particular object of choice. For, since the object of the will is the apprehended good, the will cannot aim at evil unless in some way it is proposed to it as a good; and this cannot take place without error."[3]

A number of philosophers have analyzed Thomas's argument in basically similar ways. Morris's is as follows:[4]

(1) Agents can only do what they see as good.
(2) To see evil as a good is to be in error.
(3) God cannot be in error.

So

(4) God cannot see evil as a good (2, 3)

---

1. Anselm, *Proslogion*, chap. 7.
2. Stephen T. Davis, *Logic and the Nature of God* (Grand Rapids: Eerdmans, 1983), p. 87.
3. Thomas Aquinas, *Summa contra Gentiles* 1.95.3.
4. Thomas V. Morris, *Our Idea of God* (Downers Grove: InterVarsity, 1991), p. 51.

And thus

> (5) God cannot do evil. (1, 4)

Is this a sound argument? To be such, it must be valid, that is, its conclusion must follow logically from the premises and the premises must be true. It is apparent that this is a valid argument. The question then to be settled is, Are the premises true? Since line (5) is inferred from lines (1) and (4), and since line (4) follows from lines (2) and (3), it can be seen that lines (1), (2), and (3) are the basic premises of the argument.

Lines (2) and (3) are generally accepted by most theists, at least by most of those who still do not accept Aquinas's argument. The debatable premise therefore appears to be (1). This is an instance of a theory of morality going back to Plato which maintains that wrongdoing is basically a matter of ignorance. One who saw the good would immediately recognize it and would therefore do the good. This is basically an intellectualist view of morality. But, as numerous critics have pointed out, this involves a confusion of two senses of good: good for me, that is, desirable or expedient, and good in a moral sense.[5] These are not necessarily the same, and in fact, might turn out to be diametrically opposed in some cases. Beyond that, however, this assumes too narrow a view of morality to square with the realities of life. To do good seems to require three factors: knowing and recognizing the good; willing to do the good; being able to do what one wills. Now it may be the case that God, being God, always knows the good and being omnipotent, is always able to do what he wills. But what about the second point, always willing the good? Does God always will the good, or does he will the good necessarily? Would he be able to will otherwise? We seem to have the same problem, except that it is now more precisely focused.

Richard Swinburne

Recognizing this problem, Richard Swinburne has expanded the treatment somewhat. He contends that there are two grounds from which one may do evil: both ignorance and impulse. However, since God is completely free, that is, subject to no irrational forces, he cannot possibly do evil:

> An omniscient person who is also perfectly free will necessarily do right actions and avoid wrong ones—since . . . being perfectly free, he will necessarily do those actions which he believes wrong, and . . . being omniscient, he will hold true beliefs in this field. A man may fail to do his duty

5. Davis, *Logic and the Nature of God*, p. 89; Morris, *Our Idea of God*, p. 53.

because he does not recognize what his duty is or because he yields to non-rational influences outside his control. But neither of these possibilities is a possibility for a perfectly free and omniscient person. It is logically necessary that a perfectly free and omniscient person be perfectly good.[6]

When analyzed closely, this argument seems to parallel closely that of Aquinas, the major difference being that "right" is substituted for "good." It participates, however, in the same difficulties as Aquinas's argument, since "right" has the same ambiguity as "good," namely, that which is right or suitable for me, and that which is morally right. Morris thinks that truly free agents are free to choose arbitrarily and even perversely, and that there is no reason to believe that God would not be also.[7]

William of Ockham

A rather different approach was taken by William of Ockham. He contends that there is only one moral obligation on human beings: to obey God. There is nothing more basic to justify the rightness or goodness of an action. Thus, good is defined by the will of God. Whatever God wills is good. Ockham says, "A thing becomes right solely for the reason that God wants it to be so."[8] Therefore, God must be necessarily good. This means that if God had willed something different than what he did, that would have been good, just as this is good by virtue of his having willed it. Whatever God does is by definition good. Thus, again, God cannot will or do evil. He can will or do what we would otherwise have termed evil, but if he wills it, it is not evil.

Divine Goodness and Human Goodness

In a way this solves the problem, but in the process it creates another problem. We may know the truth of the statement, "God is necessarily good," but we have lost control of its meaning. What do we mean when we say, "God is good"? We are not able to explain this statement by reference to any sort of common human experience. We cannot point out what humans call love, loyalty, honesty, or something of the type, and then show how God fulfills those qualities. Thus, what we seem to be saying is, "whatever God is, is good." But the question becomes one of

6. Richard Swinburne, *The Coherence of Theism* (Oxford: Oxford University Press, 1977), p. 202.

7. Morris, *Our Idea of God*, p. 53.

8. Stephen C. Tornay, ed., *Ockham: Studies and Selections* (LaSalle, Ill.: Open Court, 1938), p. 180.

whether there is a correspondence between what goodness means in God and what it means in humans. Those who adopt this approach are attempting to avoid the idea that something independent of or external to God defines standards, something to which he must be subject. But if this is the case, says this way of thinking, is he really still God? Settling the matter by definition does not help if we do not know what the definition really means. Being good could be compatible with God willing and acting in a very untruthful or very cruel fashion.

P. T. Geach

This raises, then, the important question of the correspondence between divine moral values and human moral values. P. T. Geach argues that we cannot apply human standards of morality to God. He says, "Ought we to expect God the Creator of the world to have virtues like those of men? And ought we to admire and love him above all things even if he has not the character that would be deemed morally good in man? I shall argue that many human virtues cannot possibly be ascribed to God, and that all the same there can be nothing more worthy of love and admiration than God is."[9]

Geach concedes that certain human virtues must be ascribed to God in a fashion appropriate to his divine life, such as his being provident, wise, truthful, and faithful to his promises. But there are other virtues that cannot be ascribed to him, such as chastity, courage, honesty, and gratitude. To attribute these to God would be absurd, he contends. Even justice raises some serious problems. Commutative justice is not a possibility, for what can God be given that results in his owing something in return? Distributive justice similarly creates problems. Since everything that a creature has and is ultimately is a gift from God, how can the question be raised whether God has been equitable in his treatment of these creatures?[10]

Geach recognizes that some will take strong exception to his position, saying that "if God is not like a virtuous man then we ought not to admire and love him, or at least not as much as we admire and love virtuous men." He contends that this reaction is perverse, because "what is being asked is that God should be admired and loved for his great glory, for being God, for being utterly unlike man in nature . . . God is to be loved and admired above all things because he is all truth and all beauty: the truth and beauty that in the universe is scattered in separate pages, to us Dante's figure, is in God bound up orderly into one vol-

9. P. T. Geach, *Providence and Evil* (Cambridge: Cambridge University Press, 1977), p. 78.
10. Ibid.

ume."[11] But it is natural for us to love truth and beauty. Consequently only vice and folly prevent us from loving God above all things. "The protest that we ought not so to love and admire him if he does not share the moral perfections proper to his creatures is a mere impertinence."[12]

Geach considers the objection that as men "we can only judge God by human standards" to be sophistical. The term "human standards" is equivocal. It may be taken in several senses:

1. As humans, we can only judge God by standards that humans (as contrasted, presumably, with God) judge by. If this is the case, then we have an uninteresting tautology.

2. The standards we use in deciding whether God is lovable and admirable must be the same we use in deciding whether these qualities are true of humans. Geach simply denies that this is the case, however. They need not and should not be the same.

3. Our standards must be those that humans have invented for themselves. Geach rejects this concept also. The spiritual man is more and more taught by God to judge by God's standards, and will someday judge both humans and angels.[13]

A Response to Geach

How do we respond to this position that Geach has taken? In what sense, and to what degree, can we say that the standards of good in God are different from those for human goodness? While the transcendence of God means that the relationship between the things of God as we discuss them and the moral qualities of humans must be analogical in some sense, yet there must be some degree of commonality, since God repeatedly urges certain qualities and practices upon believers on the grounds that he is that way and they are to seek to resemble him. The passages cited above (e.g., Ps. 119:66, 68; Matt. 7:11; Phil. 1:6; 3 John 11) seem to imply that what is good when referring to God and what is good when referring to humans are generically the same, even if these qualities in God greatly exceed what they are when found in humans.

As we noted earlier, here also in the case of Geach the concern seems to be to protect the doctrine of God from the idea of any sort of external standard being imposed on him, any independently existing criteria of good and right. This seems to Geach and others to be the implication of there being common standards of the good for God and for humans. They also want to avoid the apparently arbitrary nature of right and

11. Ibid., p. 79.
12. Ibid.
13. Ibid., pp. 80–81.

wrong, as expressed by William of Ockham. There is another option, however: that there is an objective, universal set of values that define moral good and bad, right and wrong, but these are not external to or independent of God. There are objective criteria, but they are inherent in God's very being and nature. God is what he is, not by choice, but by his very constitution. Whatever he does and wills is the good, and in this sense Ockham was right. But he could not have willed to be some other way (cruel or promise-breaking, for example). The morality that he prescribes for his human creatures is what it is because that is what he wills, and he wills in accordance with his perfect nature.

There is one specific area or quality where there seems to be conflict or at least incompatibility between God's commands to humans and his own practice. One of the qualities most commended in humans is unselfishness, or to put it in a more positive way, concern for the welfare of others rather than for oneself. This is found in Paul's exhortation which is the application of the great incarnation passage in Philippians 2:1–11: "Do nothing out of selfish ambition or vain conceit, but in humility consider others better than yourselves. Each of you should look not only to your own interests, but also to the interests of others" (vv. 3–4). It is seen in Jesus' command and example to his disciples to wash one another's feet: "Now that I, your Lord and Teacher, have washed your feet, you also should wash one another's feet" (John 13:14) It is also found in Jesus' teaching that the one who would be the master must be the servant: "Jesus called them together and said, 'You know that those who are regarded as rulers of the Gentiles lord it over them, and their high officials exercise authority over them. Not so with you. Instead, whoever wants to become great among you must be your servant, and whoever wants to be first must be slave of all'" (Mark 10:42–44). It also was present in Jesus' attitude and practice, relative to the Father: "My food is to do the will of him who sent me and to finish his work" (John 4:34). Even the nature of love is depicted in this fashion of unselfishness: "Greater love has no one than this, that he lay down his life for his friends" (John 15:13).

In contrast to this seems to be the concern and action of God, for whom his own glory is often enunciated as the supreme value. The people of Israel are commanded to glorify God: "Ascribe to the LORD, O families of nations, ascribe to the LORD glory and strength, ascribe to the LORD the glory due his name. Bring an offering and come before him; worship the LORD in the splendor of his holiness" (1 Chron. 16:28–29; cf. Pss. 29:1–2; 96:3, 7–8). The psalmist appeals to God on this basis: "Help us, O God our Savior, for the glory of your name; deliver us and forgive our sins for your name's sake" (Ps. 79:9). The appeal to God is on the basis of preserving his reputation rather than the welfare of the people. God even indicates that this is the reason for his creating: "everyone who is called by my name, whom I created for my glory, whom I formed and made" (Isa. 43:7). The ultimate expression of this seeming divine egocentricity is found in Paul's statement in Romans 9 of God's having mercy on whomever he wills and hardening the heart of whomever he wills. "Does not the potter have the right to make out of the same lump of clay some pottery for noble purposes and some for common use? What if God, choosing to show his wrath and make his power known, bore with great patience the objects of his wrath—prepared for destruction? What if he did this to make the riches of his glory known to the objects of his mercy, whom he prepared in advance for glory— even us, whom he also called, not only from the Jews but also from the Gentiles?" (vv. 21–24).

Is there a conflict here? Does God, who commands his believers to be humble, to be less concerned about themselves and more concerned about others, and to desire to serve him, then reveal that his own glory and his own arbitrary will are more important to him than is the welfare of his creatures? On the surface of it, this might seem to be the case, but a closer examination of the matter reveals something quite different. The difference comes in the fact that God is God and that he is unique. He is the Creator, the self-existent, infinite One, and we are his creatures. In the final analysis, he is the supreme object and source of value in the universe. His relationship to us is not that of one person to an equal, as is the case of us and other humans, or to a superior, as is the case of us and God. For us to put any finite object, whether ourselves or some other human, ahead of God would be wrong, for it would be a denial of the very structure of reality. It is even possible to sin unselfishly, by preferring, not ourselves, but some other human, over God. Similarly, if God were to make some created object the ultimate value, over even himself, that would be wrong. Not merely selfish concern for himself, but concern for the preservation of "the nature of things" requires that he seek his own glory. This is why he displays what sounds like jealousy: "I am the Lord; that is my name! I will not give my glory to another or my praise to idols" (Isa. 42:8). So we see that there are certain differences in what is good in the case of God and of humans, stemming from the fact that they are different types of persons. Just as God cannot commit adultery or gluttony, so humans cannot genuinely be worshiped; failure to do so in either case, then, is not a wrong. God, however, is the Lord, and he must preserve the proper relationship—for the sake of the whole creation as well as himself. Yet this concern for his own glory does not prevent him from showing the kind of loving, compassionate concern that is so often referred to as "steadfast love" or "lovingkindness" in the Old Testament.

Divine Praiseworthiness and Freedom

The problem that arises is that if God is free to do evil, he is only accidentally, not necessarily, good (bearing in mind the special meaning of that term in this context). But if he is necessarily good, if he cannot do evil, then he seems not to be free. This has resulted in what is sometimes called the problem of praiseworthiness. How can God be deserving of our praise and worship if he really has no choice in the matter of being good? We do not praise inanimate objects or events for the good that they do us. We do not praise the wind for cooling us on a hot day, or the sun for warming us on a cold day. We do not say "thank you" to automatic doors or escalators when they provide assistance to us. We simply take it for granted that this is what they are doing, necessarily. So, similarly, if God is good necessarily, how and why should we praise him? It is apparent, even on a casual reading of the Book of Psalms, that God is deemed praiseworthy. An example is Psalm 48:1: "Great is the Lord, and most worthy of praise." Does this not require that God be free to do evil as well as good?

Analysis of the Problem

Thomas Morris has analyzed the argument and dilemma in syllogistic fashion:

(1) A person is praiseworthy for an action only if he could have refrained from doing it.
(2) A necessarily good being cannot refrain from performing good actions.

So

(3) A necessarily good being is not praiseworthy for any of his good actions.

If

(4) God is necessarily good,

then

(5) God is not praiseworthy for any of his good actions

But, surely,

(6) God is praiseworthy for his good actions.

So

(7) It is not the case that God is necessarily good.

The argument is valid, but is it sound? The controlling premises here are (1), (2), and (6). The last of these, praiseworthiness, seems to be admitted by virtually all theologians, if not, indeed, all Christians in general. Thus, our attention needs to focus on the thrust of lines (1) and (2).

Morris distinguishes among different models of divine goodness. The plenitude of being model defines goodness metaphysically. This model says that "God is metaphysically or ontologically complete, without flaw or defect or lack with respect to his *being*."[14] This involves both the Anselmian perfect being concept and the idea that he is the cause of the being and goodness of all that is. The duty model means that God acts in perfect accordance with every principle that specifies moral duties. God does perfectly anything that ought to be done by a moral agent in God's relevant circumstances. The benevolence model says that God not only does what would be morally required of an agent in his situation, but goes beyond those requirements, doing acts of supererogation.[15]

Using this third definition of goodness, Morris believes he resolves the problem. He holds that a necessarily good being is incapable of performing any evil. "But," he says, "it is compatible with being necessarily good that a being have the option to perform or refrain from performing any number of good actions which are not required of him, but which rather fall into the category of the *supererogatory*."[16] He believes that God freely does many things that are not required of him. This is, indeed, the meaning of grace, that God does and gives that which on the one hand is not deserved by the recipients, and on the other is not required of him.

Stephen Davis

Stephen Davis takes a different approach. He is convinced that the arguments to the effect that God is necessarily good all fail. He therefore examines the idea that God is free to do evil. He considers briefly the argument of Jonathan Harrison, that there is a sense in which even if doing evil is within God's power we can still say that doing evil is not logically possible for him. It is, according to Harrison, within the power

14. Morris, *Our Idea of God*, p. 50.
15. Ibid., pp. 50–51.
16. Ibid., p. 58.

of the being whom we now think of as God to do evil. It is just that if he were to do so, he could no longer be called God.[17]

Davis sees this approach as involving a distinction between two senses of the word "God"—namely, as a proper name for a specific being such as Yahweh and as a title for any divine being. He does not think the solution works, however, because on his understanding, perfect goodness is not an *essential* property of God in either of these two senses, although he believes that perfect goodness is a property of God in either of these senses (italics mine). He says, "I do hold that Yahweh will never exercise his power to do evil: but that is not the same as saying that Yahweh does not have such power or has the power but would no longer be God if he exercised it."[18]

This, then, is the distinction Davis follows: God is perfectly good, meaning he does no evil, but he is not *necessarily* perfectly good, meaning it is possible for him to do evil but he will not. This is an important distinction that is frequently overlooked in the discussions of human free will and of such matters as the eternal security of the believer. Davis asks whether since doing evil is both logically possible and within God's power, there is any probability that he will ever actually do any evil, and replies, "Not at all. I believe that we can be quite sure God will never do evil. Doing evil is in his power but he will not do evil . . . Nelson Pike's phrase is apt: God 'cannot bring himself to do evil' because doing evil would contradict a 'firm and stable feature of his nature', i.e. his moral strength and goodness."[19] This approach has the virtue of making it appropriate to praise God for his goodness, a phenomenon that is found repeatedly in Scripture, especially in the psalms. And it makes God a genuine moral agent, as contrasted with the opposite situation of necessary perfect goodness: "If God's nature causes or determines him to do good in such a way that doing evil is not in his power, I would conclude that he is not a free and responsible moral agent and thus is not a fit object of the praise and thanks of his people."[20]

Thomas Morris

Let us now revisit the approach of Morris. Expanding on the issue of praiseworthiness, he also raises the issue of freedom. He apparently holds to libertarianism, according to which morally significant freedom is the freedom to have done morally otherwise than one has actually

---

17. Jonathan Harrison, "Geach on God's Alleged Ability to Do Evil," *Philosophy* 51.196 (April 1976): 213.
18. Davis, *Logic and the Nature of God*, p. 94.
19. Ibid.
20. Ibid., p. 95.

done. If, then, God is necessarily good, he does not have such alternatives, so he is not significantly morally free. If he is not morally free, he is not really a moral agent and his goodness is not moral goodness. Morris says, "The problem can be summed up like this: 'necessary moral goodness' is a contradiction in terms. If something is necessitated, it can't be morally good; and if something is morally good, it can't be necessitated. Thus, holding that God's goodness is necessary prevents us from holding that God is morally good. . . . I believe that this version of the problem of moral freedom has caused many people to give up, for no good reason, the belief that God's goodness is necessary, in order to save the view that his goodness is moral."[21]

Morris examines the problem using two models of divine goodness that he has earlier expounded. With respect to the duty model, he says, "Because of his distinctive nature, God does not share our ontological status. Specifically, he does not share our relation to moral principles—that of being bound by some of these principles as duties. Nevertheless, God acts perfectly in accordance with those principles which would express duties for a moral agent in his relevant circumstances. And he does so necessarily. . . . We understand and anticipate God's activity by analogy with the behavior of a completely good moral agent."[22]

Is, then, God's moral goodness only analogous to moral goodness but not itself actually an instance of moral goodness? Morris believes that this can be satisfactorily dealt with on the basis of the benevolence model, with its concept of supererogation. Part of what God's goodness means is the idea of his doing more than he is required to do in his acts of gracious kindness. He uses the instance of God's promise to Moses that he will lead the people of Israel out of Egypt. When the time comes for the actual deliverance, is God free *not* to help his people? Morris's answer is "no." But did he have to make that promise in the first place? Here Morris maintains that God was at that point free to make such a promise or not to make it. His conclusion, then, is: "Surely there are cases where the good engaged in by God is purely a result of his grace. And any particular such good is one God could have refrained from bringing about. In supererogation, God does exercise the freedom of alternatives sufficient, I think, to render that action properly moral action."[23]

Yet, Morris observes, some philosophers maintain that if God lacks any component of literal moral goodness, then he is not the greatest

21. Morris, *Our Idea of God*, p. 59.
22. Ibid., pp. 60–61.
23. Ibid., p. 61.

possible being. This objection seems to apply to this question of moral freedom. Morris concedes: "On the picture of divine goodness I am suggesting, there is not to be found within the distinctively divine life of God a hard-fought achievement of moral duty fulfillment. This component of moral goodness is absent. Nor is there full, morally significant freedom. On this view, God does not nobly refuse to avail himself of evil options open to him. He does not have that sort of choice."[24]

Does this yield us an unworthy conception of God? Morris cites Mark Twain's facetious claim of superiority to George Washington:

George Washington could not tell a lie.
I *can* tell a lie but won't.

This line of thinking, Morris believes, generates a line of criticism, that it is better to be triumphant in moral freedom than to be unable to do evil, or in other words, necessarily good. He believes that if the necessity is from an external cause that is one thing, but that if it is internal, a result of one's own nature, that is quite a different matter. Morris makes two responses to this criticism.

First, he concedes that having full morally significant freedom and consequent moral duties is a great-making property and one that God does not have. He insists, however, that this does not mean that God is less than perfect. All that perfect being theology requires is that God possess the greatest array of *compossible* great-making qualities, not that he have all such qualities. Since moral freedom and being necessarily good are both great-making qualities but cannot be had together, they are not compossible. Thus, lacking one of these is not incompatible with being a greatest possible being.[25]

Second, Morris asks whether having a hard-won moral goodness, or having duties, is essential for a perfect being. He concludes that it is not. He appears to hold that it is not an intrinsically good thing: "Any such property is a good thing, but it may be a good for only a certain kind of being, the kind vulnerable to evil, the kind of being we humans are. And the property of having morally significant freedom—being able to go wrong as well as right—can plausibly be thought to be not an excellence of the highest order, but rather an imperfection, in contrast with the divine standard."[26] Morris believes this judgment to be at least as plausible as the contrary judgment.

24. Ibid., p. 63.
25. Ibid., pp. 63–64.
26. Ibid., p. 64.

Evaluation of Morris's and Davis's Approaches

How shall we evaluate these attempted responses to the problem of divine goodness and freedom? We may say first of Davis's view that it handles the problem quite well, but with a major difficulty. The biblical text from James about God's inability even to be tempted seems to commit us to a belief in the necessary goodness of God. Thus Davis's theory fails to account for a major biblical motif.

Morris's approach seems considerably more promising. It allows us to maintain that God is not only good but necessarily good. It also allows for his actions to be genuinely moral actions. Yet at some points the theory is not as strong as might be desired. Morris maintains that God's necessary goodness requires him not to commit evil, but that it does not require that he do the maximum amount of good. Does this really follow, however? A case could be made for saying that a perfect being ought to act in such a way as to maximize good. Morris does not seem to have supported his case adequately on this specific point.

He also seems to be committed to saying that the actions of God that are involved in abstaining from evil are not necessarily morally good actions, except in a qualified sense. This conclusion, however, appears to be required by his adoption of the libertarian or noncompatibilist view of will and freedom. Yet the compatibilist view seems to do even a better job of reconciling the problem of divine goodness and divine freedom, thus making all of God's acts morally good acts. With some adjustment of this view of freedom, the problem can be resolved more fully and with less strain.

An Alternative Approach

An article by Nelson Pike is especially helpful in this regard. After reviewing some of the classical treatments of the subject, he seeks to draw together several strands of thought. He believes that there are three major possible meanings of the statement "God cannot sin."

1. It could mean, "If a given individual sins, it follows logically that the individual does not bear the title 'God.'" This understands the "cannot" in the statement to express a logical impossibility. Pike says, "The meaning of the title term 'God' is such that it is a logically necessary condition of bearing this title that one be perfectly good and thus that one not perform actions that are morally reprehensible."[27]

2. "God cannot sin" might mean that "if a given individual is God, that individual does not have the ability to sin, i.e., he does not have the

27. Nelson Pike, "Omnipotence and God's Ability to Sin," in *Readings in the Philosophy of Religion*, ed. Baruch A. Brody (Englewood Cliffs, N.J.: Prentice-Hall, 1974), p. 361.

creative power to bring about states of affairs the production of which would be morally reprehensible."[28] Here the "cannot" does not express logical impossibility, but a material concept: the limitation of creative-power. Pike also maintains that in this case God is not perfectly good either. A person who does not have the creative-power sufficient to bring about evil states of affairs cannot be praised (morally) for not doing them. As an example, Pike says, if he lacks the physical strength to crush his nextdoor neighbor with his bare hands, it is no moral credit to him that he does not do so.[29]

3. "God cannot sin" might mean that although God has the creative power to bring about morally reprehensible states of affairs, "His nature or character is such as to provide material assurance that He will not act in this way." Here, the "cannot" does not mean logical impossibility or lack of creative power, but a moral restraint within, stemming from his moral character. It is the type of thing we mean when we say, "He just cannot do that;" or, "He cannot bring himself to do that." Pike says, "On this third analysis of "God cannot sin,' the claim conveyed in this form of words is that the individual that is God (Yahweh) is of such character that he cannot bring himself to act in a morally reprehensible way. God is strongly disposed to perform only morally acceptable actions."[30]

It is in this third sense that Pike sees the goodness of God. While he does not say so in so many words, the import of this position seems to be that God is necessarily good, but the necessity is neither logical nor material, but moral. God does not lack the ability (creative power) to do evil, but he does lack the capability (moral inclination). Although both Davis and Morris in their own way came close to this position, they did not draw this distinction, probably because of their commitment to a libertarian view of freedom.

But is God really free, on this model? I believe that it is appropriate to think of him as free. For freedom does not mean total indeterminacy. It does not require capability of doing the alternative, so long as the ability is there. Freedom is the absence of external constraints on one's choice and action. It is not necessarily freedom from internal factors. Freedom does not mean the ability to act in a way different than what one is. It means the ability to act consistent with one's nature and character. Thus, it really is not quite appropriate to say that God is not free to act cruelly. He has the ability to bring about situations that would count as such, but his moral character is such that he cannot be cruel.

28. Ibid.
29. Ibid., p. 362.
30. Ibid.

Freedom is not simply random action or unchanneled energy. In a very real sense, we are most free when actualizing fully our highest potential. Acting in that fashion enables us to have the greatest number of options at a later point, whereas succumbing to lesser courses of action introduces severe limitations on these possibilities.

Most golfers, when they begin to take professional instruction, find that instruction rather restrictive. They are told to keep their left arm straight (if right-handed), their head down, not to sway, to swing inside-out, and so on. All of the natural impulses seem to be resisted. What the teaching professional is after, however, is to develop a repeating swing, where the golfer will hit the ball correctly, not just once in a while, but consistently. That reduces the possibilities of where the ball will go. Rather than into the rough, the sand trap, or the water trap, the aim is to have the ball go straight and far down the center of the fairway and onto the green. Although those other possibilities are eliminated or restricted, the one possibility that is maximized is of a different value and importance than those others. The aim is to create a swing where hitting the ball incorrectly, with those other unfortunate results, becomes very unnatural. Then the golfer is most free to actualize his or her potential to become an accomplished golfer.

The analogy is applicable to the freedom of God. Although his goodness is not something that must be learned or acquired, it is his nature. His nature is such that doing evil would be utterly opposed to it, utterly unnatural and uncomfortable. His moral incapability for acting evilly is not a weakness. Rather, it is a strength, the greatest strength of all. And the action that flows from his nature is free moral action. Augustine once said, "Love God and do as you please." What he meant was that if we truly love God completely, then we can indeed do as we please, for our nature will please to do God's will. Is this lack of freedom? Similarly, God chooses and does as he pleases, but what he pleases is always what he has commanded to be the good and the right, and he does this completely freely.

Finally, we should note that much of the discussion of the goodness of God is based on his actions. On this basis, being good is defined in terms of doing good. This reflects the functional approach of our age, both in theology and in broader categories of various disciplines. In theology, it was first seen in the idea that the person of Christ is to be derived from the understanding of the work of Christ, rather than the reverse. Here, it is the idea that God's nature must be understood from his works. A good person is a person who acts in a good way.

Actually, the principle of being preceding doing is a helpful one and should be taken into account here. Jesus, for example, seemed to suggest that what we are is the most basic and determines the goodness or badness of human actions: "The good man brings good things out of the good stored up in his heart, and the evil man brings evil things out of the evil stored up in his heart. For out of the overflow of his heart his mouth speaks" (Luke 6:45; cf. Matt. 15:10–20). A person who is true is first of all a person of integrity, or is the truth, and then does the truth and speaks the truth.

If this suggestion is correct, then the objection that God must act freely to be morally good misses the mark. The goodness of God is first a matter of his moral character. What he does is a manifestation of what he is. He was good prior to any actions on his part. He is good because his character is so thoroughly good that he is morally incapable of doing evil. This can be noticed in connection with the issue of praise-worthiness as well. The Old Testament believers did not praise God simply because of what he did, but because of what he was. Exodus 20:2–3 says, "I am the LORD your God, who brought you out of Egypt, out of the land of slavery. You shall have no other gods before me." We misread this text if we interpret it as saying that because of what God had done in bringing them out of Egypt, they should be grateful and love and worship him. Rather they are to make him their only object of worship and service, because he is God, and the reference to his action of bringing them out of Egypt is merely a means of identifying who this God is. An examination of the psalms of praise (e.g., Ps. 90) will reveal that this is the case.

12

God's Immanence
and Transcendence

The paired concepts of immanence and transcendence underlie much of the discussion we have engaged in up to this point. By immanence, we mean that God is present and active within the created universe, history, and the human race. By transcendence, we mean that God is not limited to the creation. He is independent of and superior to it, and is morally superior to humans. These two aspects of God have rather far-reaching implications for any theology. Historically, alternations between these two positions on a scale have been involved in much of the shaping of theologies. In fact, Stanley Grenz and Roger Olson contend that this is the dominant issue of twentieth-century theology and have made this polarity the integrating motif for their treatment of twentieth-century theologies.[1] It also has significant implications for practical areas of Christian living. The two opposed concepts have a tendency to set definite "tones" to the nature of Christian experience and understanding. This affects the extent to which we emphasize prayer and communion with God rather than activity in his service. It affects the extent to which we seek his guidance and direction through reading the Bible and meditating on it, versus examining the coalescence of circumstances. It affects the understanding of ministry in terms of the extent to which we rely on God to work in more direct fashion, versus, for example, utilizing various marketing techniques formulated on the basis of empirical research. It affects our approach to evangelism, particularly in terms of whether we anticipate that there is within each

1. Stanley J. Grenz and Roger E. Olson, *20th-Century Theology* (Downers Grove: InterVarsity, 1992).

human some point of contact with the spiritual things of revealed divine truth, or whether persons may be utterly devoid of such sensitivity.

Since theology is an organic endeavor, the positions taken on this continuum considerably shape our understanding and formulation of several doctrines. Most certainly, this has a strong impact on the understanding of divine providence, in terms of whether this is seen as coming through gradual and more customary processes or through direct acts of divine intervention. It has considerable influence on the doctrine of the image of God in humans. It also has influence on the understanding of salvation. This appears at several points. Is the change often referred to as "new birth" a radically new occurrence, which comes in direct and unusual fashion, or is it the culmination of a process of education and nurture? And is sanctification something so supernatural that it cannot be assisted by our own efforts, or can we contribute to it by the use of some sort of spiritual exercises? Further, the church is very much a locus of the immanence–transcendence discussion. On a more transcendent model, it will be seen as a unique spiritual institution, whereas on a more immanent model it may be regarded as a social institution, capable of being studied and analyzed by the tools of social research as are other social institutions. In terms of eschatology, a more transcendent view of God and his working will see the final stage and state as being ushered in through a direct act of God, such as a visible bodily second coming of Christ, whereas a more immanent approach would see the kingdom of God as being brought in at least in part through human effort.

The doctrine of Scripture has also highlighted the issues of transcendence and immanence. The traditional view of the Bible included a rather transcendent view of God in his revelation and inspiration of Scripture. God communicated something that could not otherwise be known through any other channel. He then directed the Scripture writers' thinking and writing in such a way that the Bible is a record of God's mysterious truth.

In theological anthropology the dynamics of the immanence–transcendence tension also come into play. A more immanent understanding of God is correlated with a view of humans as basically like him, as thus fundamentally good and holy. A transcendent God, on the other hand, is seen as far apart from humans, radically different from humans as we now find them, and humans are seen as limited in their abilities and as falling far short of God's holiness.

Perhaps the doctrine where the issues have played the largest part is the doctrine of creation. The traditional view had been that God created by direct and immediate action, in what is sometimes termed "fiat creation." This was correlated with a view of God as primarily transcendent.

With the advent of evolutionary theory, however, God was seen as at least partly doing his creative work through processes within created nature.

Cultural Influences

Trends Contributing to Belief in Immanence

In general, the trend of approximately the past two hundred years has been toward a greater emphasis on the more immanent model of God. There are a number of reasons for this trend.

One factor contributing to this shift of emphasis has been the growing contact of different people from around the world with each other. In the past, different groups have been considerably isolated from one another, so that persons of different world religions seldom had contact with one another, and most people lived their entire lifetime without ever meeting someone of a different faith. Other religious beliefs and practices were something simply heard or read about. It was possible to think of non-Christians, although religious, as strange and different, and consequently, spiritually inferior. This isolation has greatly diminished in our time, however. Through world travel, immigration, and vastly improved means of communication such as television, many Christians have been able to observe firsthand the religious life of those of radically different faiths. The quality of these people's spiritual and moral life has surprised many Christians. It has also resulted in the revision of some theological ideas. Previously God was thought of as far off, separate from and removed from the lives of those who had never had access to his special revelation, as recorded in the Bible. The phenomenon of religious pluralism has contributed to a revision of such thinking. Perhaps, the reasoning goes, God is present in the life of every human to a greater extent than we have previously thought.

Another factor contributing to this stronger belief in divine immanence has been the growth in the positive thinking movement. According to this perspective, humans are not as sinful as formerly thought. God's transcendence has traditionally been thought of as both ontological and spiritual. God is much higher, a greater being metaphysically, than is the human. Beyond that, however, the nature of his moral and spiritual life is such that he is far "above" humans morally. Human sin is actually ungodliness, so that it separates us even further from God. The emphasis on the worth and goodness of each human being, and the idea that we are not necessarily held responsible for conformity to some standard of goodness external to us, necessarily reduces the distance between God and us. Hence the greater sense of closeness, or of divine immanence.

A further impetus for the doctrine of immanence has been the revolution in astronomy and physics. The Copernican revolution, of course, took place many centuries ago. Prior to that time, it was convenient and seemed appropriate to think of God as "up there," with heaven being thought of as high above the earth. The implications of the heliocentric view, however, gradually trickled down to where it was seen that "up" and "down" were not really considered appropriate. This led to a shift in thinking about God "out there." On this model, God was not elevated above the earth but was still spatially removed. Eventually, however, modern physics removed even further the concepts of "out there." Up and down were seen to be relative terms, and to be related to gravitational pull. Thus, if one were placed in a container attached to a large cable and the container swung by the cable in a large circle, one would experience "down" as being in the direction of the centrifugal force, which would not be distinguishable from gravity. Indeed, the measure of this force is expressed in gs, the multiple of the force of gravity that is being experienced. Further, space itself was seen to be relative, as was time. In fact, matter and energy are seen as not so distinct from one another. At the speed of light, matter is converted into energy. The realization that there can be alternate universes occupying the same space was an interesting revelation. Finally, space travel seemed to bring persons no closer to God than they were on the earth. The Russian cosmonaut, Yuri Gagarin, the first human actually to experience orbital flight, reported, "I didn't see God out there." All of this contributed logically and even more, psychologically, to making the doctrine of divine transcendence problematic. If God is other than our world, in what way can he be other?

Other cultural factors contributed to a belief in the immanence of God, or at least to a breakdown in belief in the transcendence of God. One of these is the increased presence of Eastern religions within countries where Christianity has traditionally been strongest and in which Christian theology has especially been done. These are basically pantheistic. Elements of this thought have been absorbed by popular American religion, especially in what is often referred to as "New Age" religion. Even among those who have not officially espoused this type of religion, there has been some "spillover effect" into more conventional Christianity.

A further influence of a more psychological than logical nature has been the trend toward a more classless society. By this I do not mean particularly economic classes, and most certainly I am not referring to what Marxism meant by the classless society, but rather to the growing sense of informality in social relationships, and the decline of social hierarchies. One indication is the rapid disappearance of any honorific status for the elder or senior members of society, occasioned in part perhaps by the sheer population bulge and consequent influence of the "baby boomer" generation. The nonutilization of titles denoting rank is another of these. "Sir" and "the Honorable" are not so frequently used as in the past. I recall being somewhat surprised when, as a seminary dean I received a call from a twenty-year-old student recruiter at the college affiliated with our school, with whom I had never spoken, and who began our conversation by addressing me by my first name. The president of the United States at the time of this writing is frequently referred to in the media not as "President Clinton" but simply as "Bill Clinton." All of this is symptomatic of a general leveling of social classes in the thinking of the general populace. In countries that have not had royalty within the lifetimes of most of the populace, this leveling is accentuated even further. There is, experientially, really no place for the concept of a lofty, high, and far removed or transcendent God to fit.

Finally, much of the popular piety of our day militates against a conception of the loftiness of God and contributes to the idea of immanence. Popular reference to God in movies and songs frequently refers to him as "the man upstairs" or something similar. This extends to popular Christian music where the emphasis is frequently on the dynamic transcendence of God, the fact that his working far exceeds anything humans can do. Yet there is little focus on God's ontological transcendence, the fact that what he is far transcends human being, and even less on the moral and spiritual transcendence, the fact that his holiness and goodness far surpass ours.

Trends Contributing to Belief in Transcendence

One such trend has been the growing secularity of the twentieth century. A major part of this is the rise of the scientific method and of specific scientific disciplines. When there were wide areas of mystery in our understanding of the universe, it was more common to fill these gaps with the idea of God, who was the explanation for the mysteries and the solution to the problems—the "god of the gaps." This was actually a transcendent view of God, in which his working tended to be regarded as miraculous rather than through processes of nature. When, however, he was no longer necessary to fill these needs, either explanatory or causative, some abandoned belief in God entirely, but for those who did not, God was made even more transcendent, even more removed from any real involvement in human life and history.

Some of the dark and tragic events of our century have also contributed to the belief in transcendence. An event like the holocaust, for example, has raised in a new way the question of God's relationship to the flow of history. If God was at work in all of history, how could this happen? This issue is far from being resolved at the present time. It was very difficult to hold to the idea of God working within these events. If there is a God at all, he must certainly be very far removed from, or indifferent to, the needs and problems of his people.

It is interesting to note that the philosophers of religion who in our time have given so much attention to the problems of God, his nature and attributes, and have contributed so much to our thinking, both in terms of sharpening the questions and of offering insights, have had little to say on this subject directly. Yet underlying the issues that we have examined is this polarity of immanence and transcendence. For what often separates the different positions on one of these issues is actually the question of the extent to which God is involved with the creation, nature, history, and humans, and the extent to which he also participates in the same processes and categories as the rest of reality. Thus, for instance, the question of mutability and immutability is partly one of the extent of God's involvement in the seemingly obviously changing reality. Similarly, the question of passibility and impassibility is closely related to these two categories, for if God is within the world and its processes, then he is affected by and feels the force of what happens herein more than if he is far off. Similarly, temporality or atemporality are questions of the degree to which God is immanent within or transcendent to time, just as he is to space.

This also characterizes several theologies of the type we examined in part 2 of this book. For process theology, one of the key factors in understanding God is that he is so much a part of the rest of reality that he shares in the same categories as the other parts of it. Similarly, various liberation theologies are based on the idea that God is at work in the world, feels the hurt of people, and uses those who work for social, political, and economic change. Pluralistic theologies such as those of John Hick see God as related to all people, not through a special revelation accessible only to a limited group, but through a general revelation, available to all persons.

Immanence

Biblical Basis

The doctrine that God is present and active within the created physical world and within human activity and experience has considerable biblical support. Part of this is related to the image and likeness of God in which he created humans (Gen. 1:26–27). This likeness to God was not lost even in the fall of the human race, so that the prohibition of murder was based on the fact that the human has been made in the image of God (Gen. 9:6). Job gave expression in several speeches to the idea that God is within him and provides the breath of life: "as long as I have life within me, the breath of God in my nostrils" (27:3); "The Spirit of God has made me; the breath of the Almighty gives me life" (33:4); "If it were his intention and he withdrew his spirit and breath, all mankind would perish together and man would return to the dust" (34:14–15). This thought is also expressed by Paul in a somewhat different fashion in his famous Mars Hill message: "God did this so that men would seek him and perhaps reach out for him and find him, though he is not far from each one of us. 'For in him we live and move and have our being.' As some of your own poets have said, 'We are his offspring'" (Acts 17:27–28).

This presence of God is not restricted to his involvement with human beings, however. The whole doctrine of creation is such that God is responsible for the origin of nature and for what happens within it. In Genesis 1:2, the Spirit of God is described as brooding over or moving upon the face of the waters. The psalmists frequently refer to God's actions within nature. Just the references to God's action through and use of the wind are impressive: "So Moses stretched out his staff over Egypt, and the LORD made an east wind blow across the land all that day and all that night. By morning the wind had brought the locusts; . . . And the LORD changed the wind to a very strong west wind, which caught up the locusts and carried them into the Red Sea. Not a locust was left anywhere in Egypt" (Exod. 10:13, 19). "He makes clouds rise from the ends of the earth; he sends lightning with the rain and brings out the wind from his storehouses" (Ps. 135:7). The psalmist describes at length God's utilization of the forces of nature: "The waters saw you, O God, the waters saw you and writhed; the very depths were convulsed. The clouds poured down water, the skies resounded with thunder; your arrows flashed back and forth. Your thunder was heard in the whirlwind, your lightning lit up the world; the earth trembled and quaked. Your path led through the sea, your way through the mighty waters, though your footprints were not seen. You led your people like a flock by the hand of Moses and Aaron" (Ps. 77:16–20). Jesus expressed this idea as well. It is God who sends sunshine and rain: "He causes his sun to rise on the evil and the good, and sends rain on the righteous and the unrighteous" (Matt. 5:45). He cares and provides for his creatures through regular processes of his working: "Look at the birds of the air; they do not sow or reap or store away in barns, and yet your heavenly Father feeds them. Are you not much more valuable than they? Who of you by worrying can add a single hour to his life? And why do you worry about clothes? See how the lilies of the field grow. They do not labor or spin. Yet I tell you that not even Solomon in all his splendor was dressed like one of these. If that is how God clothes the grass of the field, which is here today and tomorrow is thrown into the fire, will he not much more clothe you, O you of little faith?" (Matt. 6:26–30). He also is present in all that occurs within his created world, and knows and controls those occurrences: "Are not two sparrows sold for a penny? Yet not one of them will fall to the ground apart from the will of your Father. And even the very hairs of your head are all numbered" (Matt. 10:29–30).

This, then, is not the picture of the deistic God who creates once and then abandons the universe, letting his implanted laws operate. Rather, it is one of a God who is so involved with all that happens that even the normal processes of nature are considered his doing. Just how this phenomenon is to be understood, however, has been the subject of considerable discussion.

Early History of Belief in Immanence

The doctrine of divine immanence was not prominent in much of the early history of Christian thought. In a world in which demons and angels were thought to be behind much of what occurred, and there was not a very great understanding of the phenomena of natural law, it is not surprising that this concept was not very fully developed. It was in the nineteenth century, with the development of modern science, especially the theory of biological evolution, that immanence began to receive strong attention. It became an essential part of the worldview of classical liberalism. God was seen, not as separated from the world in a realm of supernature, as had been popularized by Thomas Aquinas and many later theologians, but as present within, and active within, the processes of nature. This was what John Hick called a "bungaloid" view of the universe, with reality made up of just one level.

One of the first to express this immanentism was Friedrich Schleiermacher. Responding to Immanuel Kant's *Critique of Pure Reason*, in which Kant contended that we cannot have knowledge of that which lies outside our sense experience, Schleiermacher made feeling the proper domain of religion. Thus, God became an object of feeling, and consequently was not thought of as very far removed from that feeling. Schleiermacher wrote: "The usual conception of God as a single being outside of the world and behind the world is not essential to religion. . . . The true essence of religion is neither this idea nor any other, but the immediate consciousness of the Deity as we find him in ourselves as well as in the world."[2]

2. Friedrich Schleiermacher, *On Religion: Speeches to Its Cultured Despisers* (New York: Harper & Brothers, 1958), p. 101.

A more metaphysical understanding of immanence is found in the philosophy of Georg Hegel. As an absolute idealist, Hegel understood the fundamental character of reality as being mental or ideational in nature. Reality is one great thinking mind, the absolute. In a very real sense, everything that happens within this world is merely a thought in the mind of God. For that matter, we as humans are also thoughts in the mind of God, who thinks and acts through us. Thus, history is God daydreaming as it were. This is a very thoroughgoing immanence.

A Classic Formulation: Borden Parker Bowne

Bowne was for many years professor of philosophy at Boston University, and is generally considered the founder of the school of thought known as personal idealism, or simply, personalism. In his discussion of immanence, he was seeking to combat two opposed conceptions, both of which he believed were incorrect. One was the view of supernaturalism, that God is removed from nature and that his actions are independent of the processes of nature. The other, naturalism, maintains that nature is a sufficient explanatory principle, and since it can account for all that occurs, there is no need for recourse to the idea of purpose. This antithesis is incorrect, however, in Bowne's judgment. According to Bowne, two quite different questions must be asked: on the one hand, the uniformities of co-existence and sequence which constitute the order of nature and on the other, the question of the underlying cause and purpose of the order. Whereas science investigates the former, the latter is properly the domain of philosophy. The answers to both questions are necessary to satisfy the mind fully. Consequently, the relationship of these two domains is being reformulated. "In this new conception the supernatural is nothing foreign to nature and making occasional raids into nature in order to reveal itself, but, so far as nature as a whole is concerned, the supernatural is the ever-present ground and administrator of nature; and nature is simply the form under which the Supreme Reason and Will manifest themselves."[3] This view of divine immanence enables us at once to refer to an event as both natural and supernatural:

> And nature being but the fixed form of the divine causality, we must say that events in general are at once natural in the mode of their occurrence, in that they come about according to rule, and supernatural in their causation, in that they all alike abut on that Living Will by which all things stand and from which they forever proceed. The commonest event, say the fall of a leaf, is as supernatural in its causation as any miracle would be; for in both alike God would be equally implicated.[4]

3. Borden P. Bowne, *The Immanence of God* (Boston: Houghton Mifflin, 1905), p. 17.
4. Ibid., p. 18.

We have, then, two rather different explanations in the work of science and that of philosophy. In fact, the explanations given by evolution are really not exactly explanations. They simply give a description of an order without accounting for it. Rather, Bowne says, "For real insight we need to know what the power is which is at work, why it works as it does, why the arrivals and survivals are such that their net result is to produce an orderly and progressive system; and to these inquiries mechanical naturalism has no answer."[5] Similarly, religion's attempt to dictate the conclusions is also unprofitable. The sure result of mixing the question of scientific description and formulation with that of philosophic interpretation is conflict between science and religion, or something similar. The two false conceptions the instructed theist sets aside are those of the self-running nature and the absentee God.[6]

This view of God's presence and activity is extended by Bowne to include not only nature but also history. Edward Farley has observed that there is a cosmological immanence, in which God is identified with nature and a humanistic immanence, in which God is seen as inhabiting human ideals and causes. The former usually precedes the latter, in Farley's judgment.[7] In Bowne's thought, both come together.

In history, as in nature, there is a danger of our separating the description and the explanation. In his chapter on history, Bowne emphasizes that he is not attempting to find God in history or to illustrate it, but to explain what such a presence would mean, and where we should seek for it. He says, "A divine purpose, a moral development in humanity, is the essential meaning of God in history."[8] When we accept the fact of the divine immanence, any separation between the natural and supernatural disappears: "Then we come to a natural which roots in the supernatural, and a supernatural whose methods are natural; and to this neither science nor religion has any objections."[9] Such a view keeps us from thinking of God as only found in the very unusual and rare events. Bowne repeats a story told by Archbishop Whately to make his point. A person was once telling in Whately's hearing a story of a shipwreck in which he was the only survivor, and regarded this as a very special manifestation of God's presence and providence. Whately replied that he knew of an even more wonderful story, of a ship which arrived safely with all the passengers and crew safe and the vessel and its cargo

5. Ibid., p. 22.
6. Ibid., p. 24.
7. Edward Farley, *The Transcendence of God; A Study in Contemporary Philosophical Theology* (Philadelphia: Westminster, 1960), p. 16.
8. Bowne, *Immanence*, p. 52.
9. Ibid., p. 54.

intact. It is only if one has separated the natural and the supernatural that this would not be seen as a greater instance of God's working.[10]

Finally, the understanding of divine immanence must extend to our view of the Bible. On the one hand, there are those who hold that the Bible stories must be completely miraculous, or there is no real evidence of God's presence and working. On the other hand, there are unbelievers who either deny the miracles outright or reduce them to misunderstood natural events. But both of these make the same mistake: they believe that if there is a natural event, it must not be supernatural. Such reasoning is not correct, however, Bowne contends. "The song of the angels may have been an hallucination of the shepherds; but is the only time before or since that shepherds were so divinely hallucinated. St. Paul may have had a fit on his way to Damascus, but it is the only known fit that had such mighty consequences. The vision of the Risen One may have been an illusion, but when we see that it is the greatest event in all history, we begin to wonder whether illusions can be so potent."[11] Many of the biblical descriptions of supernatural events are written from the standpoint of causality. Representing the conviction that God was at work, they refer them directly to God, without recourse to explanation in terms of natural law. As such, however, they are really interpretations, rather than descriptions.[12]

One result of a view of immanence such as we have just described is that it does not distinguish sharply between divine activity and human activity. If God is really at work in everything that happens, then such distinctions need not be drawn. The difficulty of a strong immanentism, however, lies in its inability to judge between better and worse in terms of what happens within history. Thus, liberal theology, with its strongly immanentistic orientation, had difficulty with some of the historical developments of the twentieth century. One of the developments that shocked Karl Barth into a repudiation of the liberal, immanent view in which he had been raised was the inability of German Christians to distinguish divine action from the actions of their leaders. This occurred, not once, but twice, in the twentieth century. In 1914, a group of ninety-three German intellectuals signed a statement in which they endorsed Kaiser Wilhelm's war policy. When Karl Barth read the statement, he saw among the list of signers some of his theological teachers. It was, in many ways, the end of the nineteenth century, theologically, for Barth realized that the liberalism he had been taught had lost all ability to discriminate between the divine and the human, between the sacred and

10. Ibid., p. 55.
11. Ibid., p. 71.
12. Ibid., p. 76.

the secular. Imagine Barth's shock and disappointment when, two decades later, he saw the same mistake being made. The German Christians approved of Adolf Hitler, referring to him as God's good gift to the German people. In 1933, the church issued a statement that said, "To this turn of history [Hitler's taking power] we say a thankful *Yes*. God has given him to us. To Him be the glory. As bound to God's Word, we recognize in the great events of our day a new commission of God to His church."[13] A year later they followed this with an even more amazing statement: "We are full of thanks to God that He, as Lord of history, has given us Adolf Hitler, our leader and savior from our difficult lot. We acknowledge that we, with body and soul, are bound and dedicated to the German state and to its Führer. This bondage and duty contains for us, as evangelical Christians, its deepest and most holy significance in its obedience to the command of God."[14] Once again, it seemed to Barth, a group of confessing Christians had made God so immanent that whatever happened in history was to be understood as God at work, no matter how bizarre that might turn out to be. It is this which has proved to be the major weakness of extreme views of divine immanence, that they are unable to distinguish the work of God from the work of humans, to distinguish God's word from the human word.

Transcendence

The doctrine of transcendence has been held quite widely throughout much of the church's history. It has been the search for relevant contemporary models through which to express the doctrine that has occupied the attention of those who hold it in recent years.

Biblical Basis

Numerous passages in the Bible depict the separation of God from the world and from humans. God's transcendence is seen both as metaphysical and as moral/spiritual. One of the most powerful passages is in Isaiah 55:8–9, where God's thoughts and ways are depicted as transcending those of humans: "'For my thoughts are not your thoughts, neither are your ways my ways,' declares the LORD. 'As the heavens are higher than the earth, so are my ways higher than your ways and my thoughts than your thoughts.'" In Isaiah 6, we have the account of Isaiah's vision of God, in which he sees the Lord "seated on a throne, high and exalted" (v. 1). The seraphs call to one another, "Holy, holy, holy is

13. Quoted in Karl Barth, *Theologische Existenz Heute* (Munich: C. Kaiser, 1934), p. 10.
14. Quoted in G. C. Berkouwer, *The Providence of God* (Grand Rapids: Eerdmans, 1952), pp. 176–77.

the LORD Almighty; the whole earth is full of his glory" (v. 3). Isaiah's response is a confession of his own uncleanness and unworthiness. It is significant that this same sort of response is seen in some other encounters of believers with God. In Exodus 3, when Moses encounters God who reveals himself in the burning bush, he is instructed, "Take off your sandals, for the place where you are standing is holy ground" (v. 5). When Peter experiences the greatness of Jesus exhibited in the miraculous catch of fish, he falls on his knees and exclaims, "Go away from me, Lord; I am a sinful man!" (Luke 5:8). These responses indicate God's moral transcendence to humans.

God's ontological transcendence is also seen in a number of places. Isaiah expresses both God's transcendence and immanence in 57:15: "For this is what the high and lofty One says—he who lives forever, whose name is holy: 'I live in a high and holy place, but also with him who is contrite and lowly in spirit, to revive the spirit of the lowly and to revive the heart of the contrite.'" In Psalm 113:5–6, the psalmist writes, "Who is like the LORD our God, the One who sits enthroned on high, who stoops down to look on the heavens and the earth?" Paul contrasts God's wisdom and that of humans in an extended way in 1 Corinthians 1:18–31. He says, "For the foolishness of God is wiser than man's wisdom, and the weakness of God is stronger than man's strength" (v. 25). Jesus also contrasted himself with his hearers: "You are from below; I am from above. You are of this world; I am not of this world" (John 8:23).

The Traditional Spatial Model of Transcendence

The teaching of these passages is the transcendence of God: God is other than the world and other than humans. This could be conceived and expressed in any one of several ways. Because during much of the early history of the church there was a belief in a geocentric universe, it was common to think of God's transcendence in spatial terms. Indeed, passages such as Isaiah 55, if taken literally, seemed to many persons to entail something of the type. So God was thought of as being very high above the earth, and off in some far-distant place. Jesus' ascension, by the very use of that term, seemed to involve the same sort of spatial beyondness.

For various reasons, this view came gradually to be called into question. One was simply the developments in astronomy. It became apparent that the sun, not the earth, was the center of our system of the creation. This made it apparent, also, that the earth was not flat, so that designations such as "up" and "down" were misnomers. God's removal could not really be "up there." This, however, still left many persons with a basically spatial way of thinking of God. God may not be "up there," but he is certainly "out there." This seemed to be the best way to express the metaphysical transcendence of God.

Difficulties with this conception became apparent as theologians reflected more on it, however. For one thing, space certainly is not eternal. Since God created the universe at some finite point in the past, space presumably did not exist before that time. What was the nature of God's existence or "location" prior to that point? Further, however, God in his very essence is spirit. How, then, could he even have any location within space? All of this seemed to call for some other type of conception.

In many ways, the way was led by the Danish philosopher and theologian, Søren Kierkegaard. Partly because of his reaction against the immanent view of God inherent in Hegel's system, and partly because of his revulsion at the general religiosity of the Denmark of his day, in which everyone was a member of the Danish state church, he developed the idea of the "infinite qualitative distinction" between God and humanity.[15] This was first a matter of the fact that God is infinite and eternal, and humans are individual, finite, existing beings. Thus, there is a vast metaphysical gap between humans and God.[16] Beyond that, however, there is a great moral and spiritual gap. Sin has enlarged this gap so that it is not just a crack, but a great chasm.[17]

This emphasis on God's moral and spiritual otherness was picked up by Barth in his strong emphasis on transcendence. While this doctrine had many facets in his thinking, nowhere does it come out more emphatically than in his debate with Emil Brunner over natural theology. The chapters of his contribution to the volume consist of responses to points raised by Brunner in chapters he has written. Two major points in Barth's response especially indicate his view of the extreme transcendence of God.

One is God's transcendence to humans. This is traditionally related to the question of the image of God in the human. Must this not therefore involve some similarity or "point of contact" in the human, such that communication between God and human beings can take place? Brunner maintained that the material image of God, the original righteousness, has been completely lost.[18] Nevertheless, the formal image

---

15. Søren Kierkegaard, *The Sickness unto Death* (Princeton, N.J.: Princeton University Press, 1941), pp. 192, 199, 207, 209; *Training in Christianity and the Edifying Discourse Which "Accompanied" It* (Princeton, N.J.: Princeton University Press, 1944), pp. 67, 125.

16. Soren Kierkegaard, *Concluding Unscientific Postscript* (Princeton, N.J.: Princeton University Press, 1941), p. 195.

17. *Sickness unto Death*, p. 99.

18. Emil Brunner, "Nature and Grace," in Emil Brunner and Karl Barth, *Natural Theology* (London: Geoffrey Bles, 1946), p. 24.

of God still remains in the human, by which Brunner means that even though sinful, the human remains a subject and is responsible. He is rational, has a capacity for words, and therefore is responsive to the Word of God. This says nothing about his acceptance or rejection of that word. It is the purely formal possibility of his being addressed. There is, then, a definite point of contact for the divine grace of redemption.[19]

Barth's response to this point is an emphatic "no!" He certainly grants that the human, even in sin, is a human and not a tortoise. But what is the "capacity for being saved" of which Brunner speaks, unless it means something more than that. While Brunner's other statements seem to indicate that the human does not somehow contribute cooperatively to what God does, it is difficult to see what he could mean, more than the mere fact that a human is a human and not a cat, unless it is something of this type.[20] If, however, humans have some capacity within them, not to produce revelation, but to receive it, must there not be some original relation to God's revelation? Barth believes that Brunner has opened the door to natural knowledge of God and, in so doing, has started on a pathway that will lead him to Thomism. He has been unable to adhere to the principle of *sola scriptura—sola fide—sola gratia.*[21]

The other concern is for the nature of revelation. Brunner had insisted that there are two kinds of revelation, that in creation and that in Jesus Christ.[22] Barth, however, takes issue with this approach. If Brunner maintains that there is real knowledge of the true God through nature, imperfect though it may be, how can this not bring salvation? If we can really know the true God from his creation, without Christ and without the Holy Spirit, then how can we say that the human does nothing for his own salvation?[23] The import of Barth's view seems to be that God is so transcendent that he cannot in any sense be known through nature, and that the human has no capacity to receive, understand, or respond to God's special revelation when it comes.

In addition to this aspect of Kierkegaard's view of God's absolute transcendence, picked up by Barth, there is another aspect, the concept of dimensional beyondness. God's existence is a totally different set of dimensions from ours. He is not merely in this universe, but far off in the outer reaches of it. He is in an entirely different universe, in a different dimension of being, something like the other universe that scien-

19. Ibid., pp. 23–24, 31.
20. Karl Barth, "No!" in Emil Brunner and Karl Barth, *Natural Theology* (London: Geoffrey Bles, 1946), pp. 79–80, 88.
21. Ibid., pp. 89–90.
22. Brunner, "Nature and Grace," p. 26.
23. Barth, "No!" pp. 81–82.

tists tell us could occupy the same space occupied by ours, but without persons being able to pass from one to the other.

Immanence and Transcendence

It may be possible to understand God as immanent, and also to understand something of his transcendence, but what presents particular difficulty is the relationship of these to each other. How can God be both immanent and transcendent? Are not these two so opposed to one another that we must choose between them, rather than trying to combine them? This is a problem for all views of God that think of him as being nonspatial in nature. It is also a problem for those that consider him to be timeless, as well as views such as those of Padgett and Craig, which hold that God is not in cosmic time, but has a time of his own.

Space

Based on what we have seen of Kierkegaard's concepts, it appears that it is appropriate to think of God's spatial transcendence to the physical universe and to humans as being not primarily quantitative but qualitative. This means that God is not just of such immensity that he is extended over all space. Nor is it the case that he is very far removed within our space, even infinitely far away, but still in the same extension of space as ours, in the same spatial continuum. Rather, there is a very real sense in which he is not simply everywhere; he is rather, no *where*. "Where," in other words, simply does not apply to God. He does not have location in the sense that physical objects have location. He is of a different nature than physical objects, and therefore cannot be located.

Yet, having said that God is metaphysically or ontologically outside space, we still face the fact that God is present and active within this universe. How can this be? It is significant to note that the texts that we cited as evidence of God's immanence primarily refer to his action, his activity. Thus, it may be said that while God is ontologically distinct from the universe and the human race, he is influentially present. His actions take place within this universe.

Does it make any sense, however, to speak of God acting in and through that from which he is metaphysically distinct? Are there any analogies of this which might serve to help us grasp what is involved? I believe there are a number of these. Note that what we are talking about here is metaphysical difference, not just spatial difference.

The first of these are primarily spatially removed objects influencing others. We see in all sorts of electronic ways the ability to affect something far removed. Some of these are exotic, such as the control that the

Houston Space Center has over unmanned space vehicles millions of miles away, so that it can send a radio signal and alter the course of the rocket. More conventional are the illustrations of radio and television, where sound and light waves are converted into electrical vibrations, transmitted over vast distances, and then converted back, so that images are seen and heard many thousands of miles away.[24] Thus, there is a measure of change from one type of reality to another.

There are other examples, however, in which one person may influence another person who is metaphysically distinct and even spatially removed. One is the genetic factor. One man said to his wife after talking to their daughter on the telephone, "In some ways, she is more like me than I am like myself." Some of the same personality qualities he possessed were also present in her, certainly at least in part because of the genes he had transmitted to her. Their other daughter, on the other hand, was much more like her mother. There is a sense in which the parent is present within the child, because of that which has been transmitted genetically.

At this point the image of God is very helpful theologically. In Christian theology we have the doctrine of creation, not of emanation. Thus, God does not impart some of his nature to humans. But he does create them with a likeness, an affinity, to himself. The resemblance is like a replica (although only partially so) to an original. So there is a family resemblance between God and his human creatures.

There are other analogies. We have all seen cases where a teacher has been so effective and so influential with a student that the student has come to think, not only the same thoughts as the teacher, but in the same pattern of thinking. I have frequently used as an illustration of the possibility of verbal inspiration the phenomenologist, Edmund Husserl, and his student, Eugen Fink. Fink had written a phenomenological essay on a topic on which the teacher had never written or taught.[25] When the teacher saw the student's work, he exclaimed, "It is as if I had written it myself," and decreed that this essay should be included in *Husserliana*, the collection of his own writings.

Suppose that it were possible for someone to transmit thoughts across space, even across the barriers of different kinds of reality. While we do not hear much today about clairvoyance or extrasensory perception (ESP), the research done at Duke University in the 1950s showed

24. This is not intended as a technical explanation. Actually, these vibrations are not converted but are used to "modulate" a radio frequency vibration, either in terms of amplitude or frequency, and then the resultant signal is rectified by the receiver.

25. Eugen Fink, "Die phänomenologische Philosophie Edmund Husserls in der gegenwärtigen Kritik," *Kantstudien* 38 (1933): 319–83.

some statistically significant evidence of such unusual communication. We speak of how some persons are very empathetic and others are very suggestible. If it is possible for God to communicate across the metaphysical gap between himself and us, then he can work in and through human beings.

Are there ways of thinking of this divine and human cooperation, or of both divine/spiritual and natural/physical causation being both involved in the occurrence of some event? There are analogies where two forces of the same type work on an object, with the result being a compound of the actions of the two. One of these is simply vectoring. Here, for example, an aircraft flying at a heading of 360 degrees, but with a quartering headwind of 285 degrees, may actually follow a course of 15 degrees. Another example is where two persons work together to accomplish a task, with a simple addition of the force of their separate strengths. There are other cases where the application of force multiplies the force already present and acting. For example, power steering in an automobile applies additional leverage to the steering gear beyond that which the driver supplies mechanically.

There are also senses in which one event or one object has multiple causes. Take, for example, the construction of a building. Who is the cause of its coming into existence? One might well argue that the contractor is the one who builds the building, even though the owner or the manager of the construction company may not exert any actual effort at the construction site. More literal-minded persons would perhaps insist that it is the construction workers who actually are the cause, as they cut, nail, solder, string electrical wires, install insulation, and so on. Further, the building material suppliers are in a very real sense the cause, for without their contribution there would literally be no building. Or one might well contend that the architect, who designed the building, who quite clearly created the idea or the model or the form of the building, is the cause. On the other hand, the lending agencies who supply the funds for construction in the first case and the permanent financing without which someone could not purchase the building, are the cause of its being built. Yet, in the final analysis, the owner, who commissioned the construction of the building and who undertakes to pay for it, is the real cause.

These, however, are primarily physical actions. In theory, if God causes by supplementing the "natural forces" that are ordinarily at work in the event, then it ought to be possible to detect the presence of such activity by noting the difference between a purely natural event and one in which God is at work as well. But if God really is influentially present or immanent within *all* that occurs, such a method of difference is not possible, apart from technical difficulties of measurement. Are there other examples of multiple causation that come closer to depicting the causative spiritual working of God in addition to natural forces? I believe that there are some clear examples in which, in addition to natural forces of nature or human activity, another kind of causation, primarily of the nature of an idea, is operative.

Take, for example, the events of the holocaust, in which large numbers of Jews, perhaps 6 million or more, were exterminated by the Nazis. What killed the Jews? One might say that it was the actual means used, such as the guns or the poisonous gas. Beyond that, however, we have the persons who actually executed the deeds leading to these deaths, whether soldiers or their commanding officers. Yet, in another sense, it was the ideas of Nazism, the concept of the master race and the threat of the Jews, which captivated Adolf Hitler and many of his followers and were the reason these actions were carried out. Similarly, communism was once a very aggressive movement, reaching out imperialistically to capture and suppress numerous countries and peoples. The military force of the Communist Party was the means used. Yet, in a very real sense, dialectical materialism, the ideological basis of communism, was the cause of these actions, including some atrocities as horrible as those committed by Nazis.

Time

More problematic, in some ways, is the relationship of God to time. Actually, this should not be the case. In theory, the relationship of God to space should be as difficult a concept as that of God to time. Yet, for some reason, philosophers and theologians have not given nearly the attention to the former, or considered it nearly so severe a problem as the relationship of God to time.

In an earlier chapter we contended that space and time are inseparable, and consequently, what applies in terms of God's relationship to space must also be true of his relationship to time. We are here referring to time as it is usually defined, as cosmic time. We are, for the moment, not considering whether God may have sequence within his experience, whether or not that is coincident with cosmic time. Specifically, we have contended that God must be thought of both as immanent within space and as transcendent to it. This must therefore also be true then of his relationship to time. He must be active within it, but also be ontologically distinct from it. And if transcendent, this transcendence must be not merely quantitative but also qualitative. So the duration of God is not simply quantitative, so that he endures everlastingly through unending time, without beginning or end, but still the same type of time as humans experience. Rather, he is outside time, or timeless. Time does not apply to him, any more than does space. He is not merely everlasting, stretched out throughout all time, but is atemporal; in other words, ordinary earthly time does not apply to him at all. Just as he is really spaceless, so he must be not merely omnitemporal (to parallel the omnipresence of God), but must actually be in some sense, atemporal. We might speak of him as supratemporal, indicating that he is not inferior, but vastly superior, to time.

Is it possible for something in one place to affect something else that happens in another place? Obviously, this is the case. It is true not only of physical forces, but also of other kinds of forces. One of these is economic. What happens in the American stock market often is followed by similar reactions in the Asian and European stock markets. The decision of Japanese investors to buy or not buy U.S. Treasury securities has a strong effect on mortgage interest rates, and thus on home purchases, employment in the construction industry, and numerous other elements of the American economy. These, of course, are examples of something that is spatially transcendent in a quantitative transcendence.

But what about causation of something in a different time? Here again, we could cite numerous examples. Some of the effects of events in the past function independently of our conscious knowledge of them. The signing of the Magna Carta by King John at Runnymede on June 15, 1215, affects both British and American citizens today whether they have ever heard of that event or not. Other events in the past may affect us as we know of them. Who is not stirred and inspired by hearing the speeches that Winston Churchill made to the British people during World War II? Or the speech of Martin Luther at the Diet of Worms? Or Martin Luther King's "I Have a Dream" speech?

This sometimes happens in striking fashion. I once saw a throw made in a baseball game that not only won that game, but the game the following day as well. The New York Yankees were playing the Minnesota Twins in Minneapolis. I knew that Paul O'Neill, the Yankees' right fielder, was a fine hitter, who had hit almost .400 one year. I did not realize until that day what a strong throwing arm he had. Early in the game he almost threw out a runner going from first base to third base on a single. Then, with the tying run on third base in the person of Twins shortstop Pat Meares and one out, the batter hit a fly ball to rather deep right field. O'Neill caught the ball and fired a perfect throw to home plate, with the catcher tagging Meares out. The next day Meares was again on third base as the potential tying run with one out, and the batter hit another fly ball to right field, somewhat deeper than the one the previous day. O'Neill again fired a strong, accurate throw to home plate, but Meares never moved from third. There was strong public criticism of both Meares and the third base coach, but the throw the previous day had won that game as well.

Sometimes it is almost as if the past is brought into the present, and affects it. Through the use of audio and video recordings, even dead persons can be seen and heard again. In a sense, time has been collapsed. The event is replayed.

What about the future influencing the past? We have dealt with that in chapter 8, where we observed that there truly is such a thing as final causation or teleological effect. In a January course, I asked the seniors in the class whether the university commencement which was to take place in May had any influence on their doing the work of the course. They unanimously agreed that it did.

All these illustrations, however, whether spatially or temporally transcendent, are quantitative. They show the possible influence of something that is removed within space or time. Does this carry over to qualitative transcendence, that is, transcendence from outside space and time? Here we must note that, because we have experienced only that which is within space and time, we really cannot form any conception of spacelessness or timelessness.

If God is metaphysically outside of space–time, how does he influence what happens within it? It would appear that the direct working of God is simply by his thinking or willing something to be. In other words, his actions are in some sense acts of creation. If God in his mind thinks something to be the case, it is. This does not require him to exert physical influence on the physical universe. In this sense, his activity influencing the physical world is parallel to his nonperceptual knowledge of the creation. As problematic as is the body–soul problem, there may be something of an illustration or analogy here. When I move my hand, how do I do it? I simply will it to happen, and it occurs (assuming I do not have any neurological ailments). Unless we are prepared to accept a materialistic monistic view of human nature, there would appear to be some help here for understanding the action of God in and on a space–time universe.[26]

The incarnation is evidence that at one point in space–time, God (or at least the second member of the Trinity) entered our universe metaphysically. He became more than just influentially or causally immanent; he became *metaphysically* immanent. He took on a physical body. Whatever God is, he is capable of entering space–time metaphysically and certainly also causally.

Tentatively, we may then hold that prior to the creation, God was both absolutely timeless and spaceless. With the creation of the physical and temporal universe, however, he became related to that universe,

---

26. We are not suggesting that the universe should be thought of as God's body, which some process theologians would hold.

and thus became immanent within it. This, however, does not mean that he lost his transcendence. He himself still does not have location or extension, but is present and active everywhere within the universe. Nor does he have location or extension in time, although he is related to all of time. He knows what time it currently is at any point in the space–time universe. Does this mean that there is sequence and succession within him? The usual contention is that if he knows what time it is, there must be succession within his experience and he therefore is temporal. That, however, assumes that the existence and experience of God is of just the same nature as ours. That does not necessarily follow. This seems to extrapolate from the experience of time here, to a time that is on a different timeline, but nonetheless resembles physical time in requiring succession, though not measurable or demarcatable time. Whether there is such a time is something we cannot determine, but may simply have to confess that we are here in the presence of mystery. To argue otherwise requires the assumption of a rather univocal relationship between God and us.

We must be careful not to correlate our theological views too closely to or make them too dependent on any current scientific theory. Yet, having said that, it is significant that the shape of physics today supports the argument that space and time are inseparable, and came into being with the creation of the universe. Thus, God must have been timeless prior to creation. Further, if God is to be understood as both immanent within space and transcendent to it, then he must also be regarded as both immanent with and transcendent to time. While outside of time ontologically, he is able to act on objects within time, just as he can exert influence on objects located within space.

Part **4**

Conclusion

13

The Practical Implications of the Doctrine of God

Having surveyed these several facets of the doctrine of God, some of them quite obscure and esoteric, we must ask what the implications of our belief in this sort of a God really are. Do and should these matters affect the way we live?[1] Here is where our theology really is assessed by the ultimate standard. For since the goal of theology is not merely knowledge but life, more broadly, it must pass this test.[2]

1. That belief in God does indeed answer some of the deepest questions of the human heart is part of an apologetic for an age that believes in God in some form, but does not think it matters. I have developed some of the ideas in this chapter at greater length and in more popular form in *Does It Matter If God Exists?* (Grand Rapids: Baker, 1996).

2. A group of theological students in a discussion group at one of the schools where I taught this material in an intensive course expressed this insight in humorous form. Although some of these reflect illustrations internal to the class, and with due apologies to David Letterman, here is their list of "Top Ten Reasons for Taking Erickson's Doctrine of God Course:"

10. How to answer the question "Why should we pray?"
9. Applying the transcendence of God in my ministry makes for great funeral sermons.
8. How to apply God's relationship with the future to spiritual direction.
7. Possible worlds make great dreams.
6. God is a jealous God who desires and deserves our praise.
5. God's autobiography could be entitled *I Am Not Spock,* because God is both transcendent and immanent.
4. I am that I am . . . and God loves me.
3. Human freedom must begin with God (theocentric).
2. If God has a will, does he know it?
1. Theology opens up a big can of worms, but the doctrine of God attempts to catch those worms and tie them into knots. [See *Does It Matter If God Exists?* p. 105]

Alternate: A day is as a thousand years to God; and a day is as two weeks at Truett Seminary.

1. The first point we must make is that if there really is a God, then he really must be God. This seems rather obvious, but the point is that we should treat him as God, not as something less. If there is a God who is the supreme, all-powerful, all-wise, all-loving being, then he deserves worship, obedience, praise, love, adoration, and much more. In the final analysis, if God is the infinite one and we are his finite creatures, then it is his will that is to be done, his word that is true, his glory that is to be sought. And it is here that much current popular piety goes astray. Sometimes one gets the impression that God owes humans something, and must answer to them. His truth must make sense to them. His actions must be pleasant and pleasing to them. His will must not conflict with their freedom. He must not impose any duties on them. He must grant whatever they ask.

This, however, is a case of what I term "inverted theology." Instead of God being the superior one and our being his servants who owe him total commitment, we have made ourselves the masters, and him the servant. Surely, however, this is to make him less than God, and to make us, at least functionally, God ourselves. Samuel knew better than this (1 Sam. 3:10). When Eli told him that the voice that he was hearing in the night was that of Jehovah, Samuel could have said, "What a great opportunity. I have the ear of God. When he calls, I will say, 'Listen, Lord; your servant is speaking. I have lots of things to tell you, lots of requests to make of you.'" Samuel did not suffer from inverted theology, however. He knew that God was God, and he responded by saying, "Speak, for your servant is listening."

Suppose, however, we put God in the situation of having to answer to us, to do our will. What does that mean for us? For one thing, it means that we have to take responsibility for everything that God ordinarily does. We have to know everything, including all the details about the future and ourselves in it, if we are to decide what God should be asked (or told) to do. We have to keep track, not only of ourselves, but of all the other persons in the world, for what we do and what happens to us very definitely affects and is affected by, their actions and experiences. And we must be prepared to justify what we have done.

What appears to be needed here is a virtual Copernican revolution in theology. We must move from an anthropocentric to a theocentric understanding of reality. The original Copernican revolution met with considerable resistance. There is every reason to believe that the resistance to this change will be even stronger, for human egos and wills, not merely human beliefs, are involved in this case. Yet, it must come, if God is truly to be God.

2. If there really is an infinite God, as we have attempted to describe him, then we need to realize that all our attempts to grasp and describe

him must ultimately fall short of what he is. For he is infinite and transcendent, and we are finite. Although we are made in his image, so that there is a theological basis for expecting that we can understand something of him, we will never be able to feel that we know all there is to know of him and as he is in himself. This is to say that while our knowledge may be correct, it is always simply an approximation, and we seek to make that approximation closer and closer to God as he really is. There is an element of mystery about the nature of God.

Thus, we will seek to understand him on the analogy of a human person, for that is the closest analogue to his actual nature. Yet, while he is like humans (or, more correctly, humans are like him), he far exceeds the quality of even the greatest humans. Our language is ultimately filled with many anthropomorphisms, which must not be pressed to an extremely literal interpretation.

This also means that all other analogies are only faint reflections of what God is. We sometimes get the impression that God could not possibly know everything that is going on in the world because of its great complexity. Similarly, he strikes us perhaps as a frustrated, hyperactive, harried, type-A personality. We may begin to understand somewhat the way in which he far exceeds our capacities when we think of large, powerful computers, which are able to work with immense amounts of variables, and to process information at high speeds, even multi-tasking, thus performing many operations simultaneously. Yet God's intellectual capacities infinitely exceed the capability of the most powerful computer in existence.

3. The existence of God means that in a relativistic world there is some basis for truth and for right and wrong, good and bad. In our world, there are strong differences of opinion among persons who see the same set of data and set of issues from different perspectives. Because of the limitations of time and circumstance, no one is really able to survey the entire field. This means that opinions will conflict and settlements will be made on the basis of some sort of majority vote. God, however, stands outside the process, is able to know all truth and all considerations, and judges perfectly. Thus, there is some nonrelative point of reference by which everything can be measured. It is not, however, simply a matter of someone knowing what is right; there is a sufficient authority to make something right, to justify one value or set of values over another. The validity of that which guarantees a value is directly proportional to the stature, even ontologically, of that which offers this support. In this case, it is the highest being, the highest reality, in the entire universe, in the whole sweep of reality, that supports this.

4. The matter of prayer is one of the most important issues in terms of the practical significance, for this is considered one of the most im-

portant dimensions of the Christian life by most Christians. Whether it is in terms of the personal communion with the Lord or the presenting of petititions to God, this is at the very heart of where Christianity makes a real difference in life. It is this area where the openness of God theologians have raised a serious criticism of the classical or orthodox view of God. How, they contend, can a God who exercises "specific sovereignty" really answer prayer, since he has determined in advance everything that will occur in the world? Is not prayer somewhat illusory?

Here we must take a hard look at the issues, and when we do, we will notice that the difficulty is not entirely on the side of the classical view. Just what is involved in praying to a God such as that described by the free will theists? Suppose that we ask God to grant something in the future. Part of the difficulty that arises is that God does not know the future in its entirety, at least not to the extent that it involves free human choices. Traditionally, Christians have taken comfort in the idea that because God is omniscient, including knowing the future in all its detail, he could answer wisely, in terms of that which humans did not know. He, knowing all of that, would do what is best. If the free will theists are right, however, God is really not qualitatively better off then we are. He will not necessarily know how to answer, for he may not know what will be the best in the situation that will prevail.

Beyond that, however, the open God will not necessarily be able to answer some of the prayers of his people. The reason for this is that because he must respect the libertarian free will of all humans, such a God cannot and will not override anyone. He will and can only work by appealing to them, seeking to persuade them, but he cannot render it certain that they will respond in the way in which God and the person praying the prayer desire. Note that this is not simply true of prayers where the author of the prayer consciously prays that God will cause the other person to act in a certain way, but also prayers where such is not specifically requested, but nonetheless is a necessary means to the desired end. This means that the prayers of a free will theist will be uttered without a great sense of assurance, either that God will know what is best to do or will be able to accomplish that in every instance, even if he knows what should be done.

There is a further difficulty with the openness approach to this matter of prayer. What is it that we hope to accomplish by praying? On the openness model, prayer actually changes the mind of God. What, after all, is the point of prayer otherwise, David Basinger argues?[3] We must

3. David Basinger, "Practical Implications," in Clark Pinnock, Richard Rice, John Sanders, William Hasker, and David Basinger, *The Openness of God* (Downers Grove: InterVarsity, 1994) pp. 156–62.

ask, however, about the cogency of this concept. For on openness grounds, God does not know the future in entire detail, insofar as it involves human wills. On what basis, then, does he decide whether to change his mind? How does he know whether it would be better to grant our request or not?

On the other hand, the person who believes in the classical or traditional God can pray with great assurance. For this God knows everything, including the future with all of the free actions of humans. He is therefore supremely wise, able on the basis of this vast knowledge, to choose the best course of action. Further, this God is capable of doing what he wills to do, for his will includes the free actions of free persons.

But we must now ask more specifically about what is involved in this type of praying and prayer-answering. If whatever God has willed to do is determined, so that it will all come to pass, what effect does this praying have? Why does God even encourage persons to pray? Is not such activity superfluous?

This question ignores or misunderstands the full basis of how God works and wills. It assumes that he wills the ends, and that if so, means to those ends are unimportant. The end will come to pass, regardless. This seems to say that if God has willed the end, the means are unimportant. Since prayer is usually thought of as a means to the end of God doing certain things, it is actually unnecessary or even illusory. Note, however, that this is a very transcendental understanding of the relationship of God to the events of history. More correctly, however, we should think of God as willing the end as well as the means to that end. And in the case of many of these things that God has purposed to do, he has ordained that prayer should be the means to that end. Thus, God has chosen to do something, and made it possible for himself to do that, by willing and thus rendering it certain that a believer would pray for him to do that. When we pray, we are entering into a partnership with God to enable him to bring our prayers into reality.

But are we really freely praying these prayers, or are we simply automatically carrying out what is already programmed? Here we are facing a specific issue of the general problem of human freedom, and the answer is the same as the answer to other forms of this problem. On a compatibilist view of human freedom, there is no inconsistency involved in saying that God renders it certain that a particular person will freely choose to pray such a prayer. There are a number of ways in which this dilemma may be resolved. One is that God, out of the infinite possibilities he foresaw of the persons whom he could create, chose to bring into existence the one who at this point would freely choose to pray, rather than another possible person, identical to this one in every way, except that at this point in time he would not choose to pray this prayer. Thus, the believer can pray with a sense of satisfaction, knowing not only that God will know what is the good in the situation regarding which this prayer is uttered, and will be able to do what needs to be done, but also that he or she, the believer, is doing God's will, and is participating and partnering with God in the achievement of the end that is desired. Another is that God would use the influences in the person's life to develop a regular reliance on prayer, and would work on the person at this point in such a way as to lead him or her to pray about this matter.

5. What about knowing God's will? Here again we must ask about the picture that has been drawn by the free will theists, both of their own view and of the classical view of God. Throughout Basinger's presentation of the practical implications of the doctrine of God, he presupposes his own incompatibilist view of human freedom. Thus, when the classical view of these matters is presented, it is via incompatibilist categories, with distortion and contradiction naturally resulting. The bigger issue, however, is whether compatibilism or incompatibilism is correct. Or, to put it another way, whether the set of phenomena is better accounted for by the openness view, utilizing the incompatibilist understanding of free will, or by the classical view, utilizing the compatibilist understanding of free will. It is important to bear this in mind as we present varying approaches to this matter, as well as to the other matters, such as prayer.

The view that we have attempted to develop and defend in this book is that God does indeed have a specific will covering all of the situations of life and history. It is not to be assumed that this necessarily means that his will for each individual differs in all respects from his will for all other individuals. Many of the concerns God has for me he has for all other Christians, and even non-Christians.

What does it mean to seek to determine God's will, unless he indeed has such a will? It would seem that there are difficulties for process theology in the fact that although God has a will for us, referred to as the initial aim that he has for each actual occurrence, we do not discern it on a conscious level and thus cannot respond to it consciously. It is, for the most part, being communicated to us on an unconscious level.[4] Thus, we must simply rely on our efforts to determine the best course of action. God has a will for us, but it is difficult to see how this really affects our conscious decision-making.

On openness grounds, however, the problem is more difficult. For it is questionable just to what extent it is appropriate to speak of God as

4. John Cobb Jr., "Spiritual Discernment in a Whiteheadian Perspective," in *Religious Experience and Process Theology*, ed. Harry Cargas and Bernard Lee (New York: Paulist, 1976), pp. 360–61.

having a will for us. God has general intentions, to be sure, but he does not really know the future in detail, insofar as it involves free human choices. He has only what Basinger calls "present knowledge." He does not have middle knowledge. "To the extent that freedom of choice would be involved, God would not know beforehand exactly what would happen if a couple were to marry."[5] This is considered by the openness theologians to be an asset. Since God does not have a specific plan, it is not really possible to mistake something else for that plan or to stray from it.[6] Think, however, of the liabilities of this sort of stance. It is not possible to consult God for guidance to what would be the best course of action, for he may not really know.

On the model we are proposing, however, there is validity in such prayer for guidance. God does know all things, including what the future will be and what would be the results of all possibilities that might be realized. Thus, he can know what would be the best course of action, given the values that he has and applies to this situation. His will is not simply general, but specific.

This does not mean that God wills in every case to bring about what he would wish or prefer. He may indeed desire every person to come to repentance and to a saving knowledge of his Son, Jesus Christ (1 Tim. 2:4; 2 Peter 3:9), but that does not mean that everyone will actually be saved. There are situations in which God wills to allow something to happen that he does not really wish in general. An example is his decision to accede to Israel's demand for a king, in 1 Samuel 8:22, an action the consequences of which he had warned them against.

Can we miss God's will? In one sense, we cannot. What God wills certainly will come to pass. This, however, if we have correctly understood the nature of God's will and ours, does not mean that there is any justification for passivity or indifference on our parts. Our discerning that will and acting on it are means by which it comes to pass. God assists us to find his will and to do it.

The measure of assurance for the believer in the classical view of God is that God does indeed know everything that is to come to pass or could possibly come to pass and what would bring which scenario into being. And there is also the assurance that he will not leave us to our own efforts to work out such a plan ourselves.

Further, there can be assurance that God will not simply let us wander into danger or onto destructive paths of activity. If God did not know what we or other free humans are going to do, or if he had bound himself in such a way that he could not or would not now intervene to

---

5. Basinger, "Practical Implications," p. 163.
6. Ibid., p. 164.

assure that we would act so as to avoid those ways of acting, we would have no such assurance.

6. The problem of evil, of course, is a major, and indeed, perhaps the largest, problem for any theism. How can a powerful and loving God allow the evil and suffering that is extant within our world? This is seen as especially difficult for a strong theism of the classical type, particularly of a Calvinistic variety. For here God wills everything that comes to pass, and knows all that will happen, as well as everything that might or could happen. Note, however, that this dilemma is presented in a caricatured way by the free will theists: "Calvinism asserts that, unconstrained by any requirement other than his own will, God has deliberately chosen to cause all of the horrible evils that afflict our world."[7] This is hardly what most Calvinists would hold.[8] This gives the impression that God has chosen by preference these evils, as if this were something he really wished. Rather he has done so through choosing to allow the free choices of humans who commit many of them, rather than intervening to preclude them. He is not the perpetrator of them, as this quotation almost seems to suggest. Again, the imposition of incompatibilist presuppositions on Calvinism results in a distortion of that view.

Actually, classical theism has some significant advantages over either process theism or free will theism. Is it wrong for God to allow situations to come into existence (sin to occur, for example), which bring suffering to human beings, when he could have prevented those? The free will theist claims that God is not culpable, because not knowing what free human choices would be made, he could not foresee the full consequences of his decision and acts. But consequently, no virtue can be found in the fact that God suffers as the result of these acts, for that was not a fully informed conscious decision to allow such consequences. In the classical theistic view, however, it is usually said that God has chosen to allow evil because it is a necessary means or an inevitable accompaniment of a greater good. Yet he did this, fully knowing all that would happen, including the suffering that he would bring on himself. Actually, because every sin is ultimately against God, he also experiences the consequences of every sinful act that every human being feels. It must certainly be that evil, or at least the system of which evil is an inevitable part, will in the long run prove to be of greater good than the alternative would have been. For God, who knows all things and all possibilities, deemed even the conse-

7. William Hasker, "A Philosophical Perspective," in *The Openness of God*, p. 152.
8. See, however, Gordon Haddon Clark, *Religion, Reason, and Revelation* (Philadelphia: Presbyterian & Reformed, 1961), p. 221.

quences he would experience, including the death of his Son, to be worth the total benefit. The openness people, and for that matter, the process or neoclassical theists, have stressed the empathy of God. Yet this is only a choice to suffer as do humans, on the view that God is making an informed decision when he chooses to allow evil to enter the world.

We should note, also, that this is the view that really allows for the fullest empathy on the part of God. For a God who knows everything, including us completely, and who knows our futures in their entirety, must certainly suffer with us more fully than would a God who did not know these things in as great detail. The former type of God experiences the suffering of anticipation. Although he does not personally experience our experiences, he sees the results that in themselves will be painful.

There is one other major area of superiority of classical theism over the competitors with respect to the problem of evil. For even if we could explain the difficulties involved with the presence of evil, we would still have a difficulty, namely, that the evil, while understood, would still be present and would still occasion suffering. In other words, while the problem of evil would not now be a problem for third parties, those who observe the suffering but are not themselves undergoing it, it is still a problem for those who are. To put it another way, while the problem of evil may be solved, evil is not. What is required is removal of the evil, or some assurance that it will be removed at some point.

The difficulty for process theology is that there is no real assurance that this will come to pass, only hope that such will happen. Since God never works coercively, he does not cause free human actions, but only lures persons to commit them, or to make his initial aim for them their subjective aim. Since, however, most evil in the world, or at least the most egregious evils, are the result of human wills, this leaves a serious lacuna in God's plans and hopes. There is a hope, a trust, but no real assurance, that more people will use their free wills to confirm or forward God's good purposes than to reject and to frustrate them. Thus, although God perhaps cannot be blamed for the presence of evil in the world, he cannot be relied on to remove such evil either.

To a lesser degree, but nonetheless genuinely, free will theism has the same defect. For this God does not coerce or override free human will. Further, he does not even know what humans are freely going to choose and do. How, then, can he really know how best to go about eliminating evil? Although there is a strong confidence that this will happen, it is not at all clear that such confidence is really warranted. To be sure, God will ultimately overcome evil, according to this view. But to do so, he may have to make one of his last-resort coercive efforts. Basinger says, "God retains the power and moral prerogative to inhibit occasionally our ability to make voluntary choices to keep matters on track."[9]

7. What about the consequences of this view of God for the Christian's participation in evangelism and social action? Does it promote it, or does it militate against it? One objection raised by free will theists and others to the classical view of God is that it removes the incentive for genuine activity in these areas. After all, if the outcomes in these areas are already determined, why concern ourselves with the effort to bring them about? This is thought by some who otherwise would be sympathetic to this classical theology to be a major defect in it.

Actually, the exact reverse is the truth. The relationship between divine sovereignty and human freedom need not lead to this rather fatalistic conclusion, as we have argued above. To be sure, the view of divine foreordination has frequently been caricatured, by both its proponents and its opponents. It need not be so, however. There is common knowledge that confidence, within proper limits, is not a negative factor in performance of any kind of activity, but is a positive encouragement and even inspiration. The team that believes it will win a game, so long as it is not overconfident, is more likely to do so than is the team that has grave doubts about the outcome. It appears to me that for those who criticize the classical view for leading to inactivity the preferred motivation is the power of negative thinking. As so many books and motivational speakers emphasize, however, positive thinking is extremely helpful. What would be a more positive factor than the belief not that one can do it oneself, but that the almighty God has rendered victory in the spiritual battle certain, and that our actions, empowered by God, are necessary means to that end? And since the doctrine of sin teaches that the changes needed are not something within human ability to produce, this supernatural factor is all the more important.

8. One of the things that we need in our harried world is the certainty that someone is in control, not only of the world, but of himself. In the chapter on impassibility, we used the illustration of a hospital emergency room. There is pain, fear, perhaps desperation, even chaos. In this situation, the presence of a calm, self-assured doctor is of the greatest importance. The doctor understands, knows what to do, and goes about doing it. The desperate situations of some of the patients do not cause him to panic. He remains focused, feeling the needs of the patients but not being overcome by them.

What we are talking about here is stability. It is a matter of not overreacting, of controlling one's reactions to provoking situations, rather than being subject to wide mood swings. We have all known persons

9. Basinger, "Practical Implications," p. 159.

who experienced severe mood alterations. Sometimes they were ecstatic, the next time they may be morose. In one institution where I taught, one professor said of his colleague, "I can tell when I look at him in the morning whether I should even say, 'Good morning.'" God is not this type of person. The tragedies and victories of life in the world do not cause him to undulate. He is aware of what goes on in the world, is affected by it, but is not controlled by it. Because he has known and planned from all eternity what is to happen, he is prepared for these things.

9. God is an integrated person. A major point made in the discussion of simplicity is that God's nature is not characterized by inner tension. Whereas some have pictured him as torn by conflict between his love and his justice, this is not the way he is. His love is a just love, and his justice is a loving justice. It also means that we should be careful not to emphasize one at the expense of the other, or even to develop our conception of one of these qualities of God in abstraction from the others.

10. God's omniscience is the guarantee that he is someone who indeed loves us unconditionally. Much of the love that we receive from other humans is limited or conditional. This is because they do not know us completely. We may feel that they love us as they do because of that incomplete knowledge. Perhaps if they knew us more fully, the unattractive as well as the attractive parts, they would not love us. But in the case of God, he loves us completely, and even in light of the fact that he knows us completely. Actually, he knows us more completely than we know ourselves. Yet in spite of this, he still loves us. This must be unconditional love.

Part of this omniscience is his complete knowledge of the future, including everything we will ever do. This foreknowledge means that his love is even more intense. Surely this kind of love is not based on our merit, but on complete and unmerited grace.

This is an advantage that free will theists do not have. For their God knows the present and the past completely, but does not have complete knowledge of the future, at least as that future pertains to free human actions. Thus, he loves us in the absence of knowledge of some of our future actions, which may turn out to be quite distasteful. It is true that free will theists acknowledge that Jesus knew that Peter would deny him three times, although the cogency of their explanation is somewhat doubtful. It would seem that on their grounds this was quite difficult to account for. But if Jesus did not really understand all that would be involved, perhaps his love for Peter was not quite so unconditional and thus, so reassuring to us.

11. God's omniscience and omnipotence also work to provide us with an assurance that what God has promised he will fulfill. Thus, with hu-

mans we sometimes encounter the problem that for all of their good intentions to fulfill a promise, they are unable to do so. Perhaps they have failed to calculate the magnitude of the obstacles to fulfilling their commitment, and have made a commitment they probably should not have made, because it exceeds their ability. Or perhaps they simply cannot do what they have promised. This never happens with a God who is all-powerful and all-knowing. He therefore never fails to fulfill his promises because of any inability to do so.

12. There also can be confidence in God because of his constancy. With humans, there is always change. We may make our plans based on what we know about a given person, only to find that the person changes, and consequently, so must our plans. Many persons find that the person they are married to really is not the same person whom they originally married. Many disappointments in life come from this. A person gives his word, then fails to fulfill it. This is not true of God, however. He is unchanging, which means fundamentally that if he is good, truthful, and merciful now, he will also be so for all generations to come.

13. God's existence and his being the Creator of all gives a basis for truth and rationality. There has been, in recent years, a move toward an emphasis on the paradoxical and irrational. Simultaneously, there has been an emphasis on the emotional and volitional aspects of human nature, as contrasted with the more rational dimensions. This is often carried over into our understanding of God, since he is a person, as basically incomprehensible as well, or as exceeding the laws of logic. Sometimes one has the impression that the sign of divine activity is that it is unexpected or radically different from what precedes. Any orderly or patterned activity is thought not to indicate God's presence. He is unpredictable.

If God has created the world, however, then we should be able to gain some understanding of his nature from that world. Here we find considerable order and structure. There is predictability. There are logical patterns that we can discover and trace out. If God created this world, then it is strange that he made it so different from him, if indeed he is the sporadic, unpredictable being he is sometimes pictured as being.

14. There is also encouragement for us in understanding heaven. As we noted in the earlier discussion of foreknowledge, certainty, and freedom, some believe that if it is certain what I am going to do, then I am not free not to do it. Certainty seems to involve necessity. But what of heaven? To be free, must humans be capable of sinning, of doing what is wrong? If not, are they truly free? Is not the goodness of the occupants of heaven a constrained or caused goodness, and therefore, is it really heaven? But if they are free to sin, then can it really be heaven, if

sin is not excluded? The solution to the dilemma might well be to redefine freedom, so that it is not inconsistent with the certainty of persons always doing what is right and good. Indeed, to the extent that sin consists of rebellion, or the desire to be free from God and to be autonomous as an individual person, heaven might be expected to be the place that such exercise of "freedom" is most absent.

We have seen that God's existence and nature have consequences for our behavior. Although we do not base our judgment of the truth of a view primarily on its usefulness, the orthodox view of an eternal, all-powerful, all-knowing, and unchanging God is one on the basis of which the practices of the Christian life can be justified and make sense.

Scripture Index

Genesis
chaps. 1–3 154
1:2 262
1:26–27 72, 261
chap. 2 72
chap. 3 103
3:14–19 238
6:5–7 103
6:6 77, 148
9:6 262
12:2 166
17:1–18:15 166–67
21:33 114
22:12 108
28:3 167
chap. 35 167
43:14 167
45:5–8 86
48:3 167
49:25 167
50:20 86, 238

Exodus
chaps 1–3 154
3:5 268
3:15 167
6:3 167
10:13, 19 262
20:2–3 255
20:3 165
20:5 86, 236
32:12 102
34:6–7 104

Numbers
23:18–20 104
23:19 77, 106

Deuteronomy
5:9, 10 107
31:6, 8 70

Joshua
1:5 70
23:14, 15 234

Ruth
1:20–21 167

1 Samuel
3:10 282
8:22 287
15:11 77, 105, 107
15:28–29 104–5
15:29 77, 106, 107
15:35 77, 105, 107

1 Chronicles
16:28–29 245
16:34 233
29:11 106

2 Chronicles
5:13 234
7:3 234

Ezra
3:11 234

Job
9:10 186
27:3 262
28:12, 13, 23, 24 186
33:4 262
34:14–15 262
37:16 188
42:2 168

Psalms
25:8 234
29:1–2 245
34:8 234
51 26, 164
77:16–20 262
79:9 245–46

84:11–12 234
85:12 234
86:5 234
90 255
90:2, 4 115
93:2 115
96:3, 7–8 245
100:5 234
102 96
102:11, 12, 25–27 115
103:5 234
104:28 234
106:1 234
107:1 234
110:4 105
113:5–6 268
115:3 168, 204
118:1, 29 234
119:66 235, 244
119:68 234, 235, 244
135:3 234
135:6 168
135:7 262
136:1 234
139 186–87
139:6 186
143:10 235
145:9 234
147:4–5 187–88

Proverbs
16:9, 33 204

Isaiah
6:1 267–68
6:3 86, 267–68
9:6 114
26:4 114
42:8–9 188
42:8 246
43:1–2 70
43:7 246

45:7 236
46:9–10 186, 188
49:15–16 70
chap. 55 186, 268
55:8–9 267
57:15 268

Jeremiah
4:27, 28 105
10:10 114
26:2, 3 102
26:12, 13 102–3
32:17, 20–29, 37–44 168
33:11 234
44:27 236

Lamentations
3:25 234

Ezekiel
5:16, 17 236
24:14 105

Daniel
4:33–35 204
4:35 168–69

Joel
2:13 104

Jonah
3:4, 9 103
3:10 77, 103
4:3 104

Nahum
1:7 234

Malachi
1:2b–3 108
3:6 70, 96

Matthew
3:16–17 146
5:16 235
5:45 262
5:48 70
6:26–30 263
7:11 235, 244
10:29–30 263
10:30 187
11:19 59
11:21–23 188–89
15:10–20 255

19:26 170
26:21, 25 188
26:34 188

Mark
10:42–44 245
14:36 170

Luke
1:34–37 169
5:8 268
6:45 255
7:34 59
18:18–19 234
18:27 170

John
4:24 86
4:34 245
8:23 268
10:10 60
13:14 245
15:13 245

Acts
2:23 236
2:23 204
4:27–28 204
17:27–28 262

Romans
8:20–23 238
8:28 170, 235, 238
8:38–39 170
9:13 108
9:21–24 246
11:33–34 186

1 Corinthians
1:18–31 268
2:10–11 187
15:23–28 130

2 Corinthians
5:18–20 85
5:19 152
6:18 169

Galatians
6:8 238

Ephesians
1:11 204
1:19 170

2:10 235
3:21 115

Philippians
1:6 235, 244
2:1–11 245
2:12–13 204

1 Timothy
2:4 287
4:4 235

Hebrews
2:3 130
4:9 130
4:13 187
6:13, 18 176
7:20b–21 105
10:37 130
11:10, 16 130
13:5 70
13:8 70, 130
13:14 130
13:21 204

James
1:3 238
1:13 177, 194, 239
1:17 70, 96, 235

2 Peter
3:8 115
3:9 287

1 John
3:20 188
4:8 76, 155

3 John
11 235, 244

Revelation
1:4 115, 130
1:8 169
4:8 169
10:6 130
11:17 169
15:3 169
16:7 169
16:14 169
19:6 169
19:15 169
21:22 169

Subject Index

actual occasions
  and experience, 51–52
  and "freedom," 54–55
  and modern science, 52–54
administration. *See* leadership
aion, 129–30, 131
Alston, William, 22
Ames, Edward Scribner, 213
analogy, and understanding God, 283
annihilationism, 164
Anselm, 70, 117, 178, 198, 217, 239–40
anthropocentrism
  in administration, 27
  in evangelism, 25–26
  in pastoral care, 26
  in theological method, 27–28
  in worship, 26
anthropology, 257
anthropomorphisms, 161
Apostles' Creed, 14
Aquinas, Thomas, 37, 117, 127–28, 147–48,
  151, 174, 181, 198, 199, 216, 240–41,
  242, 263
Aristotle, 98–99, 144, 145, 182, 216
Aristotelianism, 61, 112
Arminianism, 67, 82
Arminius, Jacob, 79
aseity, 213, 214
atemporal eternality, 115
atemporalism, 198
Augustine, 117, 121, 146–47, 198, 214, 215,
  217, 231, 254
axial period, 40, 41

Baillie, Donald, 43
Baker, John Robert, 153, 159
Barr, James, 87, 130–31, 166
Barth, Karl, 266–67, 269–71
Basinger, David, 67, 80–81, 284, 286, 287,
  289–90
Belgic Confession, 217
Bergson, Henri-Louis, 121
Berkeley, George, 37, 53
Berkhof, Louis, 217

Biblical Theology Movement, 87, 128, 130
Biblical Words for Time, 130
Bloch, Ernest, 152
Boethius, 117, 118, 198
Bowne, Borden Parker, 264–67
Boyd, Gregory, 68
Brasnett, Bertrand, 159
Brunner, Emil, 269–71
Buddhism, 24, 47, 66

Calvin, John, 148–49
Calvinism, 89, 91–92
  on foreknowledge and freedom, 203–9
"Cambridge criterion," 109
Carson, D. A., 204, 209
Castañeda, Hector-Neri, 190–91
causation, 182–83
change, definitions of, 100–101
chess game analogy, 150–51
Childs, Brevard, 87
Christ, person of. *See* incarnation, the
Christ and Time, 128
Christianity, 46
  lack of mission outreach success, 40
church, the, 257
Cobb, John, 49, 50, 51, 53–54, 55, 56–57,
  59, 60, 63
Coburn, Robert, 125–26
communicatio idiomatum, 148
communism, 274
compatibilism, 82, 89, 91–92, 204, 252
compossible qualities, 251
Concept of God, The, 65
concretion, 56, 66
Cone, James, 154
cosmological argument, 229
Craig, William Lane, 132–34, 195
creation, 257–58, 276–77
  and the openness of God, 72–73
Creel, Richard, 15–16, 22, 142–43, 151,
  155–60, 163
Critique of Pure Reason, The, 19, 37, 52
Crucified God, 152
Cullmann, Oscar, 128–31

Davis, Stephen, 110, 240, 248–49
deconstruction, 50, 61
Demarest, Bruce, 154
Descartes, René, 37, 174, 175
Divine Sovereignty and Human Responsibility, 209
Douglas, Ann, 161
Dummett, Michael, 182

Eastern religion, 259
Einstein, Albert, 137–38. *See also* physics, Einsteinian; relativity, theory of
El Shaddai, 166–69
empiricism, 37
endless temporality, 115–16
epistemology, 21, 45
Erickson, Millard, 79, 88
ET simultaneity, 198
eternity
    Barr's position on, 130–31
    Craig's position on, 132–34
    Cullmann's position on, 128–30
    Padgett's position on, 132–34
    synthetic position on, 134–40
    See also God, and eternity
evangelism, 25–26, 290
evil, problem of, 91, 237–39, 288–90
existentialism, 82–83
"experiencing-as," 33–40

Fairbairn, A. M., 142
Farley, Edward, 265
fatalism, 207–8
Feinberg, John S., 205–6, 208, 209
feminism, 23
Feuerbach, Ludwig, 32
Fiddes, Paul, 68
foreknowledge, 124, 149
    and human freedom, 197, 203–9
foreordination, 200, 204
Frankl, Viktor, 66
Franklin, Stephen, 68
free will argument, 237
free will theism, 27, 112–13
    evaluation of, 84–92
    open view of God in, 69–76
    presuppositions, 81–84
    and process thought, 84
    support for, 76–81
freedom, human
    and divine foreknowledge, 197, 203–9
    and the openness of God, 73, 81–82
Freud, Sigmund, 32

Friesen, Gary, 68
future, the, and the openness of God, 73–74

Garrett, James Leo, 155
Geach, P. T., 22, 99–100, 109, 150, 181–82, 195–97243–44
genetic fallacy, 81
Gnosticism, 129
God
    attributes of. *See* God, and eternity; God, goodness of; God, and outside influences; immanence; immutability; omnipotence omniscience; transcendence
    doctrine of
    and anthropology, 22–23
    foundational character, 13–14
    and philosophy, 19–22
    practical implications, 281–93
    and the practical Christian life, 16–18
    and sociology, 23
    Eastern conception, 23
    and eternity
    the atemporalist view, 117–24
    biblical data, 114–15
    the issue, 115–17
    the temporalist view, 124–28
    as framework for theology, 14–16
    goodness of, 233–55
    and outside influences, historical background, 144–49
    simplicity of, 210–32
    Mann's position on, 219–24
    Morris's position on, 224–27
    traditional doctrine, 217–19
    varieties, 213
    Western conception, 23
God, Time, and Knowledge, 67
"god of the gaps," 260
God's Foreknowledge and Man's Free Will, 67
Grace of God, the Bondage of the Will, The, 209
Greek philosophy, 56, 79, 85, 112, 87, 97–99, 126, 144–45. *See also* Aristotle; Aristotelianism; Parmenides; Plato; Platonism; Plotinus; Stoicism
Grenz, Stanley, 27–28, 155, 256
Griffin, David Ray, 49–50, 56–57, 59, 60, 63
Grudem, Wayne, 88, 95, 154, 217
Gruenler, Royce, 62, 63–64

Harrison, Jonathan, 248–49
Hartshorne, Charles, 22, 50–51, 57, 58, 63–
    64, 65, 66, 141–42, 153, 159, 160
Hasker, William, 67, 80, 82, 89, 90, 91, 135,
    201–3, 204, 209, 210
Hawking, Stephen, 137
heaven, 292–93
Hegel, Georg, 82
Heidegger, Martin, 83
Heisenberg, Werner, 55
Helm, Paul, 22, 118, 119–20, 122–23, 136
Henry, Carl F. H., 79, 95, 155, 231
Hick, John, 23, 31–48, 150, 261, 263
Hinduism, 24, 47
Hippolytus, 145
Hodge, Charles, 79
humanism, 83
Hume, David, 37, 182
Husserl, Edmund, 52

imago Dei, 72–73, 90, 261–62, 269–70, 272
immanence
    biblical basis, 261–63
    Bowne's position on, 264–67
    early belief in, 263–64
    and transcendence, 135–36, 271–77
    trends contributing to belief in, 258–60
immutability, 70, 122–23, 149
    arguments against, 102–13
    basis of the doctrine, 96–100
impassibility, 16, 149
    Creel's position on, 155–60
    of emotions, 151–55
    synthetic position on, 160–64
    of will, 149–51
    See also God, and outside influences
incarnation, the, 180, 245, 276
    Hick's concept of, 42–43
    and the openness of God, 78
incombatibilism, 82, 89
indexical references, 190–91
interpretation, biblical, 237
    by free will theists, 85–87
"inverted theology," 282
Islam, 24

James, William, 37, 150
Jaspers, Karl, 40
Judaism, 24

Kant, Immanuel, 19–20, 37, 41, 52, 263
Kenny, Anthony, 117, 127–28, 182
Kierkegaard, Søren, 82–83, 269

Kitamora, Kazoh, 152–53
Kneale, William, 126
Kretzmann, Norman, 22, 108–9, 118, 190–
    91, 198, 228–29
Kvanvig, Jonathan, 184–85, 196–97

Lampe, Geoffrey, 43
leadership, 27
Leftow, Brian, 118, 123
Leibniz, Gottfried, 37
Lewis, Gordon, 154
liberal theology, 266
liberation theology, 154, 261
libertarianism, 89, 249–50, 252
lifestyle, and theology, 17–18
Ling, Trevor, 42
Locke, John, 37
logical positivism, 20, 21
love
    God as, 76–77
    unconditional, 185, 291
Luther, Martin, 88, 148, 155

Mackie, J. L., 175, 176, 179
Mann, William, 214–15, 219–28
Marcion, 111, 230
Marsh, John, 131
Marxism, 152
Mascall, E. L., 118, 119, 121–22, 123–24
Mavrodes, George, 22, 172
Mayo, Bernard, 179
McGrath, Alister, 88, 148, 154–55
metaphysics, 20, 21
    process, 49–55, 60–61
    semiprocess, 84
middle knowledge, 200, 207n
modalistic controversy, 145–46
Modalistic Monarchianism. *See* modalistic
    controversy
Molina, Luis de, 199–200
Molinism, 89, 199–200
Moltmann, Jürgen, 152, 155
morality, 229
Morris, Thomas, 22, 88, 121, 134, 150–51,
    174–75, 177–79, 194, 205, 213, 218–
    19, 224–27, 240, 242, 247–48, 249–
    51
Mozley, J. K., 146, 148
multiculturalism, 258

nacham, 87, 106
Nash, Ronald, 65, 88, 134, 175, 176, 177,
    191, 210, 216

naturalism, 264
Nazism, 274
New Age religion, 24, 259
Noetus, 145
nominalism, 215–16

Ockhamism, 198–99
Olson, Roger, 256
omnipotence, 22, 73–74
    and the ability to cause the past, 180–83
    and the ability to do the contradictory,
        174–76
    and the ability to sin, 177–79
    biblical basis of, 166–70
    and the paradox of creating uncontrol-
        lable beings, 179–80
    and the paradox of the stone, 171–74
omnipresence, 63, 140, 189
omniscience, 74, 189, 291
    biblical/theological support for, 185–89
    and emotion, 156, 159–60
    and foreknowledge, 108–9
    and the future, 194–209
    and immutability, 190–93
    importance of the doctrine, 184–85
    limited, 200–203
    and moral perfection, 193–94
    and personality, 192–93
    See also foreknowledge
omnitemporality, 139–40
Openness of God, The, 67, 68–69, 204
"openness of God" school. *See* free will the-
    ism
Orr, James, 13
Owen, H. P., 142, 149–50

Packer, J. I., 79
Padgett, Alan, 132–34
Pain of God, The, 152
pantheisim, 23, 24
pantokrator, 169
Parmenides, 217
passibility, 15, 151–55
passio, 146, 147
pastoral care, 26
Patripassianism, 146
"perfect being" theology, 70, 158, 165, 193–
    94, 239, 248
personal idealism. *See* personalism
personalism, 264–67
phenomenology, 52
Phillips, D. Z., 32
Phillips, J. B., 16–17

physics
    Einsteinian, 54, 137–38. *See also* rela-
        tivity, theory of
    Newtonian, 54, 61, 121, 137
    revolution in, 259
Pike, Nelson, 22, 116–17, 121, 125–26, 149,
    249, 252–53
Pinnock, Clark, 16, 67, 79–80, 89, 90, 142,
    201
Plantinga, Alvin, 22, 110, 216–17, 218, 222
Plato, 52, 97–98, 118, 137, 144, 145, 215,
    241
Platonism, 226–27
Plotinus, 118
pluralism, 24–25, 261
    evaluation of, 45–48
    and the nature of religion, 32–40
    and the person of Christ, 42–43
    religious, 258
    and revelation, 42
    and salvation, 43
    understanding of God, 40–42
    and world religions, 44–45
    See also Hick, John
positive thinking movement, 258
positivism, 133
postmodernism, 49–50
pragmatism, 20–21
praiseworthiness, problem of, 247–51
prayer, 180–83, 185, 283–86
    free will theism and, 80–81
principle of indeterminancy, 55
Prior, Arthur, 127
process metaphysics. *See* process thought
process thought, 261
    doctrine of God in, 55–60, 153
    God as creative-responsive love, 57–58
    God as dipolar, 58–59
    evaluation of, 60–66
    and experience, 51–52
    and "freedom," 54–55
    and modern science, 52–54
    and the necessity of metaphysics, 49–
        50
    and the restoration of meaning, 50–51
promises, fulfillment of, 292
prophecy, 127–28, 189, 201
    and the openness of God, 75
providence, 189, 257
    and the openness of God, 74–75
Purtill, Richard, 136

rationalism, 37

Reichenbach, Bruce, 208
realism, 215
relativity, theory of, 132, 134, 136–40
repentance passages, 77, 87, 102–8
Republic, 97–99
revelation, 14, 45, 270
   Hick's definition of, 42
Rice, Richard, 67, 71–78, 84, 85–87, 90,
   103–8, 150, 151
Ritschl, Albrecht, 20
Robinson, Bishop, 116

Sabellianism. *See* modalistic controversy
salvation, 257
   Hick's definition of, 43
sanctification, 257
Sanders, John, 67, 68, 79, 88–89, 148
Sartre, Jean-Paul, 83
Savage, C. Wade, 172
Sayers, Dorothy, 72
Schleiermacher, Friedrich, 20, 125, 263
Schreiner, Thomas R., 209
Scripture, doctrine of, 257
Semantics for Biblical Language, 130
"seeing-as," 33–40
semiprocess metaphysic, 84
sentence/proposition distinction, 191–93
simultaneity, 119–20, 128
social action, 290
social classes, leveling of, 260
Society of Christian Philosophers, 21
"soft determinism." *See* compatibilism
sovereignty, 214
space, 271–74
spacelessness, 120
"specific sovereignty," 80, 83, 284
Spinoza, Baruch, 37
Stoicism, 145, 146, 157
stone, paradox of, 171–74
Stump, Eleanor, 22, 118, 198, 228–29
suffering, 158–59
supernaturalism, 264
supervenience, 225
supratemporality, 140
Swinburne, Richard, 22, 109, 110–11, 119–
   20, 133, 172, 174, 176, 201–3, 241–
   42

"technoministry," 27
temps vécu, 121

Tertullian, 146
theism, classical, 23, 69–71, 87–89, 288–89
   process thought's rejection of, 56–57
   See also impassibility
theodicy, 143
theologia crucis, 148
theologia gloria, 148
theology
   definition, 14
   organic character, 14–16, 14n
   philosophical, 21–22
   "relational," 161–62
Thirty-Nine Articles, 154
Thomism, 56, 65
Tillich, Paul, 79, 212–13
time, 274–77
   A-theory of, 134
   B-theory of, 134
timelessness. *See* God, and eternity
transcendence, 119
   biblical basis, 267–68
   and immanence, 135–36, 271–77
   traditional spatial model, 268–71
   trends contributing to belief in, 260–61
Trinity, 230
truth, standard of, 283

universalism, 164
universals controversy, 215
Urban, Linwood, 180

van Inwagen, Peter, 22
verification principle, 21

Walton, Douglas, 180
Ward, Keith, 22, 99
Ware, Bruce, 209
Westminster Confession, 154
White, Douglas, 142
Whitehead, Alfred North, 51–53, 56, 58,
   116
will
   of God, 236, 286–88
   human. *See* freedom, human
William of Ockham, 215–16, 231, 242, 245
Wittgenstein, Ludwig, 33, 36
Wolterstorff, Nicholas, 22, 117, 126–27
worship, 26

Your God Is Too Small, 16–17

Millard J. Erickson is Distinguished Professor of Theology at Baylor University's Truett Seminary and at Western Seminary, Portland. He is a leading evangelical spokesman with numerous volumes to his credit, including *Introducing Christian Doctrine, God in Three Persons, The Word Became Flesh, The Evangelical Heart and Mind,* and *Where Is Theology Going?*